African American Life
in St. Louis,

African American Lives in St. Louis, 1763–1865

Slavery, Freedom and the West

DALE EDWYNA SMITH

McFarland & Company, Inc., Publishers
Jefferson, North Carolina

All images are from the Missouri History Museum, St. Louis.

LIBRARY OF CONGRESS CATALOGUING-IN-PUBLICATION DATA

Names: Smith, Dale Edwyna, author.
Title: African American lives in St. Louis, 1763–1865 : slavery, freedom and the West / Dale Edwyna Smith.
Other titles: Slavery, freedom and the West
Description: Jefferson, North Carolina : McFarland & Company, Inc., Publishers, 2017 | Includes bibliographical references and index.
Identifiers: LCCN 2016057891 | ISBN 9781476666839 (softcover : alk. paper) ∞
Subjects: LCSH: African Americans—Missouri—Saint Louis—History—19th century. | African Americans—Missouri—Saint Louis—History—18th century. | Slavery—Missouri—Saint Louis—History. | Saint Louis (Mo.)—History—19th century. | Saint Louis (Mo.)—History—18th century. | Freedmen—Missouri—Saint Louis. | Slaves—Legal status, laws, etc.—Missouri—History. | African American pioneers—West (U.S.)—History. | African Americans—Missouri—Saint Louis—Social conditions—18th century. | Saint Louis (Mo.)—Race relations—History.
Classification: LCC F474.S29 S75 2017 | DDC 305.896/07307786609033—dc23
LC record available at https://lccn.loc.gov/2016057891

BRITISH LIBRARY CATALOGUING DATA ARE AVAILABLE

ISBN (print) 978-1-4766-6683-9
ISBN (ebook) 978-1-4766-2757-1

Front cover image: "Our City" (St. Louis, Missouri) / lithograph by A. Janicke & Co., St. Louis, published by Hagen & Pfau at the Anzeiger des Westens, 1859 (Library of Congress)

Printed in the United States of America

McFarland & Company, Inc., Publishers
Box 611, Jefferson, North Carolina 28640
www.mcfarlandpub.com

For my parents,
Joyce Ella and James Irving Smith, Jr.,

and

in memory of
Seitu James Irving Smith, III,
my beloved brother,
1952–2014

Table of Contents

Acknowledgments

The study of history requires access to a wealth of documents and historical evidence. I am very grateful to the Missouri History Museum and Archive in St. Louis. The archive staff members were uniformly and consistently efficient, patient, and accommodating in the years of my work there. Ms. Jaime Bourassa, Associate Archivist, Digitization, of the Missouri History Museum Library and Research Center in St. Louis provided invaluable and very patient assistance by facilitating permissions for images and making them available as digitized images very quickly.

Over the years, I have been abundantly blessed with the presence of a resilient and constant spiritual community that fed me body and spirit and without them I do not think I could have completed this book. I began research for this book in 2001, and over the course of more than a decade and a half of research and writing, a number of people provided consistent and essential intellectual, emotional, and material support. I will be grateful to them all of my life and would like to offer this small thanks for their devotion.

Stephan Thernstrom interviewed me when I applied for admission to the doctoral program in History of American Civilization (now American Studies) at Harvard University in the summer of 1988. After my admission, I asked Steve to be my dissertation advisor and he graciously agreed. He has been a staunch and enthusiastic supporter of my work all these years. Steve has never wavered. I will always be grateful to him and to his wife Abby (who relayed countless phone messages over the years, usually transcribed while Steve was out for his morning jog) for their care of me.

Early in my research, I read the work on Missouri slaves published by Harriet Frazier. I wrote her a fan letter, and when she answered, I asked her to read early drafts of chapters of my book in progress. Ms. Frazier read them avidly but with a historian's critical eye and suggested that I contact her publisher, McFarland. I am very grateful for her kindness and encouragement.

In fair weather and foul, a number of friends on the journey have supported me spiritually, mentally, and materially. Elisabeth Drake took me into her home during a particularly challenging time and has continued to support me in every way that she can over the course of many years. Lis' humble example of kindness, generosity, and cheerful good humor have sustained me through many a rough patch. Judith Gorman kept me, and my two dear felines, afloat for a period of years; she has taught me the value of laughing at circumstance and believing in "on we go!" A number of other friends have also provided a stitch in time: Marcia Behrendt, Grove Harris, Jesseca Ferguson, James Davis and his brother Paul, and Elena Vitug. I will always be grateful to them for their kindness and generosity. They define for me the meaning of "true blue" and "friend."

Members of my family have provided essential emotional nourishment for the journey, as well as frequent practical help. In 2007, my sister, Karen, and her husband, Dr. Eric Pitts, gave me their used Toyota Camry. I was unemployed at the time and used the car to drive to the Missouri History Archive every weekday; because of their gift, conducting research every day for this book became my job. That car, and my sister's family's invitations to concerts at the Muny Opera or the symphony, made the sometimes grinding methodology of history research more bearable and even fun.

Long, rambling conversations with my brothers Guy and Boyce about family, music and sports, television, teaching, food and recipes, and St. Louis heat make me wonder where the time goes. I am grateful to them for their sweet dispositions; they are, as my mother likes to say, "easy" and easy to love.

My parents were very young when I was born; they are old now. Through the years, they have provided me and my siblings with the essentials for building self-respect, discovering and setting our sights on a dream, believing we possess what we need to accomplish it, and always trusting in the loving sanctuary of home. My mother took me to the library every week and when, at four years old, my reading requirements cut into the limits each person could take out of the library, she taught me how to write my name so that I could get my own library card. The rest, as they say, is history. Daddy read the first writings I attempted at the age of 12, when he took a break from grading his students' papers at the dining room table to provide encouragement. I know it is a grace and blessing that they are my parents. I thank them for their constant love and support through this project.

My brother Seitu James Irving Smith, III, died on October 22, 2014. He was two years and nine months younger than me, and he was my first, and best, friend. We grew up in a St. Louis of halcyon days that we recalled in shades of rose as he lay dying. Gym was possessed of charm, great humor, and a fearless imagination that is mirrored in the bold colors of the paintings he left to posterity; he stood his ground to stare death in the face and challenge its terrible inevitability with stoicism and grace. He knew I was working on a book about black people in St. Louis and he was pleased about it. On days I considered difficult, I shared it with him, and he told me to "hang tough!" and so I did. I wish he had lived to read the final draft. I will hold him in my heart until the moment I leave the planet.

God has provided me with patient, kind, and focused religious spiritual advisors in the late Monsignor Joseph Pins of the St. Louis Cathedral Basilica and Father Robert VerEecke, formerly of St. Ignatius Church at Boston College. They are first and foremost priests and faithful shepherds, whose companionship on the way reminded me always of the nature of this pilgrimage. They will always be in prayers of thanksgiving.

Preface

When I was growing up in St. Louis in the 1950s and 1960s, nearly every St. Louis school child knew about Dred Scott, at least nearly every black school child did. What we did not know then was that in the period before the Civil War, like Scott, thousands of African Americans had lived, worked, and created free and slave families and communities in Missouri. Right there in St. Louis. Or that hundreds of slaves had escaped to freedom in the West, purchased their freedom, or sued for their freedom in St. Louis Circuit Court. A significant number of the lawsuits were based on slaves' residence in the free territories of the West. Indeed, the palpable presence of the frontier from St. Louis exerted a powerful magnetic pull to freedom, a constantly westward moving state of mind that, over time, made and remade "American" identities and with them the roles of blacks in the region.

For children of the 1950s, "the West" had been television or comic book cowboys and Indians—the Lone Ranger and Tonto, Dale Evans and Roy Rogers, Jeffrey Chandler daubed with Max Factor bronze make-up to conjure a believable "Indian" Cochise (before they were "native Americans"), the weekly dramas of *Rawhide* and *Wagon Train* depicted the courage of whites who carved out a "new" world from the "wilderness," *Gunsmoke* (think of it! *Smoking guns!*) and *The Big Valley* and mini-empires like the "Ponderosa" provided contemporary myths of how the West was made safe for civilization.... We children paid homage to and mimicked The [White] Cowboy, oblivious of the place or significance of The Indian, and, as historian Patricia Limerick has memorably noted, dared not "play" at "masters and slaves."[1] Or note the glaring absence of slaves or free blacks in the accounts of how the West was won. Yet St. Louis was a clearly defined

1

place that in the taking and settlement of the West emerged from an as clearly defined history with just as clearly defined values; everything was hammered out in black and white. There were no shades of grey.

History books written in those guileless days before the Sixties revolution also neglected to include the salient fact that St. Louis had been host to a thriving and diverse free community of color, some of whose members sacrificed their own freedom to wrest slaves free from the institution of slavery, the politics, and the trade; some of whom owned slaves themselves and labored equally to detain them unfree; and still others who vigorously opposed slavery and donated both service and money to activities such as the then fledgling Republican Party (founded as an antislavery party in 1854). Nor was it much mentioned aloud or memorialized in print, even if we suspected, that some of those "people of color"—perhaps the children or grandchildren of whites—took advantage when the ivory pallor of their skin dazzled authorities, to pass blithely across the color line to live as whites.

Dred Scott had not even been the first St. Louis slave to sue for freedom in the courts. In fact, by the time Scott, who had been born a slave and was then middle-aged, sued for his freedom in a 19th century St. Louis, Missouri, courtroom, more than 200 slaves had already done so. Their efforts represented a legal resistance to slavery as peculiar as the peculiar institution itself. Even so, black slaves seeking freedom in courts of law was only one of a variety of methods people of color in the region used to create free identity. Their experiences fill in those jarring lacunae in the historical record, which suggest by their omission that blacks in the early days of St. Louis were few, enslaved, and insignificant. My study thus provides a searchlight to illuminate that small, but determined minority of free people of color—some of whom won their freedom in the courts and others who purchased themselves, were manumitted, or escaped to freedom, alone or with their families or fellows. They were free people of color who, in the midst of the slave regime, persistently contributed to the evolution of distinctive American identities against the backdrop of westward expansion, a parallel extension of slavery and the business of the slave trade, and the construction of specific identities informed by the western frontier and the proximity of St. Louis to it.

In those early days, St. Louis was a true cultural cosmopolis and a microcosm of those thousands attracted by the boundless possibilities presumed inherent in the American experiment; St. Louis was, literally, the "gateway to the West." The village that began as a trading post to buy furs from Indians in exchange for household goods had grown quickly, and within only a few decades was populated by diverse clusters of communities, including free people of color who occupied nearly every social niche, whether preacher or entrepreneur, slave owner or land owner, cook or artisan, hero or scoundrel. Indeed, by the time of the Civil War, a struggle local Missourians often referred to as "the war of the rebellion," St. Louis was among the nation's largest cities.

Today, from the steps of the Old Courthouse in St. Louis, facing the Mississippi River and, beyond, the Illinois shore cluttered with modern industrial construction, one can still sense the urgency of life as it was lived by people of color in this same place during the 19th century. Over 200 years ago, notices had been posted on the massive double doors of the court building to announce the sales of slaves. Many of those slaves were auctioned on the steps under the same east portico, but free people of color also came to the Court on various errands central to their existence and livelihood as free people.

As legal cases and as living history, the freedom suits, in concert with other primary documents, speak to contemporary readers in unique ways, providing the sound, tone, and texture of an era whose legacies remain with us to this day. Through the instrument of the freedom suits, and the thousands of other legal papers concerning slaves and free people of color in the region, their voices speak with a clarity and urgency that the rote boilerplate of antebellum legalese is powerless to mute. The outlines of the narratives revealed in these writings are flushed out by details gleaned from analysis of court records and legal documents, correspondence, census records, photographs and illustrations, the four newspapers that operated in the antebellum era, pamphlets and broadsides, as well as a wide variety of secondary sources.

In addition to those slaves who sued to be free, there were many free and slave, black and white, whose day-to-day lives laid a path and provided a powerful context for this singular story of freedom identity painstakingly and often at great risk conceived and realized in those days when the West itself was still in the process of taking shape. What remains of these struggles are hundreds of documents, literally thousands of pages buried in steel till drawers in dim courthouse storerooms for over 200 years. Coal dust, black and velvety on the fingertips, collected in the folds and creases of many of the documents. The papers as fragile and resilient as papyrus, some a still strikingly vibrant "Lincoln" blue, and covered with words written in the swooping, curling letters of a bygone era in ink now the color of rust. It is through such documents that the slaves and free people of color of antebellum Missouri recount their histories.

Introduction

The American push west across the continent accelerated during the 19th century and quickened a firebell of alarm then resonating over whether slavery and freedom could continue to co-exist in the nation. African Americans, including slaves, played a discernible role in the drive west. In fact, African Americans, slave and free, were active participants in the settlement of the frontier, bringing both an "American" and a diverse "African American" cultural influence. In addition, the presence of the advancing frontier contributed to blacks' pursuit of freedom and simultaneously spurred both individual and collective actions calculated to ensure as much autonomy for blacks as possible in the rapidly shifting political landscape.

The visible presence of African Americans, free and slave, in frontier settlements along an advancing U.S. western boundary contributed to the evolution of ideas about how American slavery and American freedom should be defined, to the possible practical benefit to the polity of westward expansion, and to American identities generally, including the idea of "the American West"—how it was defined, redefined, and memorialized in history, myth, and memory over time. In the 18th and 19th centuries, African Americans traveled back and forth from St. Louis to the unsettled west with French and American fur merchants and traders peddling an array of commodities, and thus contributed to the success of early explorations, entrepreneurship, and the transplanting of American civilization. Blacks worked as interpreters, trappers, and soldiers, and also cleared land, constructed housing, and performed a variety of domestic chores, including cooking, laundry, and the rearing of children.[1] While appropriate acknowledgment of French and Indian contributions to the establishment and growth of St. Louis and the trans–Mississippi West has been studied, the role of slave and free blacks in the region is less well known.[2]

Although the region was host to a diverse population of slaves from the early days of French settlement and Missouri eventually entered the Union as a slave state, early court records also provide evidence of the presence of free blacks who owned property (including land, business enterprises, or slaves) at the same time that some of the earliest newspapers in the region document sales of individuals and groups of black slaves, solicitations for the "hire" of "likely negroes," and consistent efforts by slave owners to find and reclaim slaves who ran away. For example, the *Missouri Gazette* published an 1809 advertisement placed by none other than famed *Corps of Discovery* explorer William Clark, who sought to sell "two likely Negro men for cash."[3] And as we shall see, the presence of the frontier acted as both lure and refuge for runaway slaves.

St. Louis, Missouri, was the jumping off place for thousands of Americans who journeyed west, the geographic location of the Missouri Territory that had been carved out of the Louisiana Purchase and that later became the State of Missouri and its splendid river highway the Mississippi were in large part its appeal and strategic value. The city that began as a trading post on the river attained significance as a crossroads of trade and bridge to westward expansion and in the process created a crossroads metropolis that provided a living illustration of the sharply intensifying debate about the role of slavery in American society and law.

At the same time, it contributed to the evolution of ideas about and construction of a particular idea of "the American West." From its beginnings, St. Louis was a "gateway." The city straddled shifting boundaries between slavery and freedom and the fundamental disagreement about them within the national consciousness: should the territory be a political, economic, and cultural outpost for slave or free interests? This question ultimately erupted into civil war.

Both free and slave people of color contributed to the founding and establishment of St. Louis. In the American era, a steady flow of African Americans west became part of a historical pattern of black, as well as American, migrations with a direct impact on the continuing evolution of African American identities, and on American identities generally. The historical record documents the numbers and variety: French-speaking free black men who arrived in 1763, as part of the founding party; people of color who traveled west from St. Louis, Missouri, as slaves on errands of exploration or trade for their owners; free or slave scouts for both private and military missions (perhaps most famously York, who traveled with

Lewis and Clark and the *Corps of Discovery*); free and slave blacks (primarily men) who played a role in the war with Mexico; runaways; and slaves offered for sale or trade (to whites moving west or to Indians), among numerous others.

People of color—both slave and free—were a visible presence in St. Louis from its inception. A free community of color co-existed with a slave population continuously enlarged by a vigorous trade in black (and, in the founding era, Indian) slaves. Slaves seeking freedom took advantage of the city's geographic location at the edge of the western frontier; using the Mississippi River, they created an effective network of like-minded slaves, as well as sympathetic free people of color, to facilitate escape north and west, or to hide in plain sight in a variety of occupations on the river. Both slaves and free blacks worked on levees and steamboats, often making use of the mobility such work provided to disseminate information—about who might be trusted among free blacks, slaves, or whites; individuals well-disposed to engaged in profitable trade in labor or crops; and rumors of political discord among the whites—to people of color living along the river route. For some blacks, the river itself became a symbol of freedom, while the rapidly growing city of St. Louis was an environment in which free colored identities had room to thrive. An interesting (and fortuitous) legal loophole allowed slaves to sue for their freedom when their circumstances could be legally considered "false imprisonment." In addition, a slave's race or color (whites and Indians could not legally be enslaved), prior residence in a free territory or state, or if an individual or group had been legally free but stolen and enslaved were all grounds to sue for freedom. Such conditions contributed to the tension defining free and slave status that began at the founding and continued through the Civil War. Indeed, a significant percentage of freedom suits filed by slaves in Missouri courts in the antebellum period were based on the experiences of slaves who had moved west to St. Louis or who based their claims to freedom on prior residence in territories west of the Mississippi River.[4]

It has been suggested that frontier settlement towns were the advance column of westward expansion.[5] Generations of Americans initiated and continued a pattern of migrations that transcended race and class, reshaped the mainland, and constantly revised the relationship between Americans and the West they pursued so tenaciously.[6] Although a cornerstone of American historical scholarship rests on the conclusion that the westward expansion of American "democratic" institutions improved the frontier as the result of a unique or even "exceptional" individualism, it may be that in some cases blacks raced westward ahead of such settlement because they understood implementation of the institutions of American civilization carried with them a distinct—and in many cases, legal—narrowing or limiting of possibilities for them.[7]

The Mississippi River was the first major marker of American progress westward with St. Louis, Missouri, a likely capital.[8] Indeed, Americans understood that acquiring and maintaining control of the Mississippi River and the port of New Orleans, as well as the trading post at St. Louis, through the Louisiana Purchase provided a crucial internal lynchpin to western trade along with an international transportation network.[9]

The tentacles of slavery connected all levels of St. Louis society, culture, economy, and politics. In antebellum Missouri, as in the rest of the slave South, specific laws prescribed the narrow space within which people of color were required to live their lives. These laws provided the context of behavior for people of African descent. In fact, the laws addressed not only the required behavior for slaves, but also what was acceptable, which is to say, *legal* behavior for all people of color—slave or free. (In most cases, these laws also proscribed behaviors of individuals with a white parent or grandparent, if that person was a slave.) Certainly, the proximity of the trading center to free territories attracted free blacks, as well as slaves seeking freedom, and provided the basis for numerous slave freedom suits at the same time that it inspired pro-slavery and anti-abolitionist activities. The implications of the possibility of choices and possession of sufficient stores of a kind of autonomy engendered by the mere proximity of the west affected all who entered its gravitational pull, including blacks, including slaves.[10] Indeed, the westward movement of blacks through the region conflates predominant themes in U.S. and African American history; that is, the significance of the west and westward expansion, and migration.[11] Thus, the presence of the "west," as literal frontier and as figurative ideal of liberty, was writ large in the evolving identities of blacks in the region.

Americans were among the first "westerners" in the region, arriving in great numbers with the transfer of control of the trading center at St. Louis to the United States. At the time of the transfer, whites became aware of a "dangerous fermentation" among slaves in the region, who seemed to expect the coming of the Americans would make them free, too.[12] Soon enough, the black slaves of French and Spanish settlers were joined by American blacks, which resulted in an exchange of cultural ideas, practices, or rituals. The question of how those blacks would figure in the national and local polity was inextricably linked to whether they would be slave or free, and that question was tied to the role slavery would play in any "American" West. Certainly, the prohibition against slavery contained in the Northwest Ordinance of 1787 was known and would have drawn slaves seeking freedom to that region, perhaps through the gateway established at St. Louis.

In the modern era, few physical landmarks remain to mark the origins of colored St. Louis or to chart its evolution through the period of the Civil War, but early St. Louisans of color used a variety of methods to create their own particular identities, culture, and community. In his narrative describing the founding of St. Louis, city co-founder Auguste Chouteau noted the presence of free men of color in the New Orleans company captained by he and his mentor, Pierre Laclède. Chouteau omitted the names of the men; perhaps he did not remember their names, if he had ever known them. But for some reason, Chouteau mentioned their presence in the original founding company. These men and their descendants became progenitors of what became "black" St. Louis. The majority of black St. Louisans from 1763 through the end of the Civil War were slaves, but a significant minority were free. The written record of their lives and thoughts is scant, but thousands of legal documents recorded the activities of countless people of color in antebellum St. Louis, and thus provide the outlines, and in some cases, significant details, of the lives of blacks along the 19th century western frontier.

In part, the relative "freedom" enjoyed by black slaves in early and antebellum St. Louis was due to an urban environment that nurtured bustling commerce, a continuous stream of merchants and adventurers of diverse background, and the presence of a small but relatively stable population of free people of color. Historians continue to debate whether the geographic ambivalence inherent in border states' physical location and that provided elements of both northern and southern attitudes toward the institution of slavery might also have resulted in a "milder" form of slavery in border states. However, westward expansion and the advancing frontier perhaps also produced an environment in which black slaves enjoyed a degree of autonomy not present in parts of the United States that had enjoyed longer, more consistent periods of settlement. In addition, a reciprocal relationship between the frontier and the cosmopolitan center at St. Louis—as investors and tradesmen funneled cash and supplies westward and profits from such ventures returned—certainly played a role in ways people of color in the region defined themselves (and were defined by others). Not least among the factors influencing those definitions were the hundreds of freedom lawsuits filed in the region as well as the fact that the move west attracted Americans intent on creating and protecting a western brand of southern slavery and thus further invigorated the

internal trade in slaves. Resistance to slavery by the slaves themselves mirrored and exacerbated the slow but sure political fracturing of the Union
provoked in some ways by the existence of slavery.

One of the most striking and significant demonstrations of the intent
and tenacity of free people of color to shape their own destinies is found
in the records of the St. Louis Circuit Court. Between 1805 and 1865,
African American slaves, singly and in groups, used the legal system to
thwart the laws that enslaved them. African American slaves filed approximately 300 petitions for freedom in Missouri courts of law. Considered
collectively, the cases may represent a resistance to slavery as peculiar as
the peculiar institution itself. The cases provide significant insights into
the origins and nature of individual and community identities among slave
and free African Americans in antebellum Missouri. For not only was it
true that slaves sought legal representation—in spite of laws that prohibited teaching slaves to read and write or, for that matter, to have much
unsupervised association with whites who were not their owners, and who
might be instructing them in the ways of freedom—but it was also true
that free people of color at great risk to their own lives and those of their
families continuously involved themselves in assisting slaves who challenged the legal boundaries of slavery. The complex components that
made up African American identities, and which overlapped free and slave
status, may be difficult, if not impossible to ferret out or understand, and
the significance of the frontier and black participation in its settlement
may provide useful insights to understanding them, even if only superfi-
cially.

Slaves outnumbered free blacks in the city between two and three to
one, and so it should not be surprising that African American identity often
straddled the occasionally blurred boundary between slave and free status.
In addition, there exist numerous unambiguous examples of slaves and
free persons of color joining forces to challenge slavery. The court cases
also provide vivid illustration of those associations. One signal example
is the 1850 case of two free black men named Phillip Harris and Benjamin
Savage charged in the St. Louis Criminal Court with allegedly "enticing
slaves out of state," which means helping slaves to run away, or, in legal
parlance, "stealing" them. Juries found both men guilty. Harris was sentenced to serve five years in the then new state penitentiary, built of local
stone and granite to be escape-proof. Savage was sentenced to ten years.
It seems likely that Phillip Harris and Benjamin Savage sacrificed their
own freedom to help slaves get free. Perhaps they were part of organized
"underground railroad" activity, but the records are silent on that point.

All we can know for sure is that these free black men went to prison and black slaves went free.[13]

The debate over whether slavery would continue, or indeed, expand westward, coalesced in the debate over Missouri statehood. The geographic location of the Missouri Territory carved out of the Louisiana Territory and that later became the State of Missouri was a large part of its appeal and strategic value. At the height of the debate, the region occupied the eye of the storm. Congressional debate over whether slavery should be permitted to flow westward with the expanding nation to the new state of Missouri reached such a fever pitch of anger and potential disunion that former President Thomas Jefferson feared it signaled a *"firebell in the night"* of irreconcilable differences between North and South that might fracture the young nation in two. Although Jefferson may have constructed the phrase with deliberate calculation to bully northerners into relinquishing the battle against the expansion of slavery, his statement nevertheless provided a dramatically prescient assessment.[14]

By the time of the Civil War, Missouri was already a crossroads of fevered activity among free people of color and slaves. Perhaps because it was a border state, a civil war in microcosm had engaged within the state. Early battles erupted during the Kansas-Nebraska guerrilla warfare, a state of affairs that illustrated the presence of the "free" west produced violence as well as litigation. The proximity at the Kansas-Missouri line, therefore, may have created a "bulls eye" of antagonism over slavery—and of the place of blacks in the region, as well as the proverbial "gateway." During the war, black slaves fleeing the Deep South were often confined in camps of "contraband" runaway slaves defined as "war materiel" by the Union and held in the hope of hampering the Confederate war effort supervised by Union troops, while St. Louis's "old guard" free people of color worried over the impact and what they perceived as a decidedly negative influence the ragged refugees and their "slavery ways" would have on their own hard-won free identity. The varieties of black identity diverged sharply along lines cleaved by status: Missouri blacks fought in the War of the Rebellion on the side of the Union, and served as slave laborers for the Confederacy.

Argument or disagreement about the place of blacks in the region not only arose in political, economic, and legal venues. The impending war at times borrowed or claimed inspiration from religious doctrine and thus the question of whether religious faith, ideas, or strategies played a role in slave or free African American agency that has long been debated came to the fore. In antebellum St. Louis, people of color participated in a variety of religious institutions and in a variety of ways. St. Louis began as a Catholic outpost, but of the five independent black churches in the city, none was Catholic. Nevertheless, the impact of Catholic thought, ritual, and perspectives on slaves and slaveholders may have been significant. The Catholic presence exemplified a particular frontier experience, that of clearing and settling the non–Christian wilds. Although church doctrine did not oppose slavery as an institution and both Catholic churches and priests owned slaves, free blacks gradually made a place for themselves within the Catholic churches and schools of the Missouri frontier.

In the early to mid–1800s, free black girls were enrolled as students in a school operated by the Society of the Sacred Heart. In addition to reading, writing, and arithmetic, the girls (a number of whom were Protestant) were also given a Catholic religious education. During those years in which the Second Great Awakening exerted a significant impact on so-called "democratization" of the structure of churches, it is logical to consider the possible ramifications of racially integrated education of free black Protestant girls. But if one Catholic order seemed to believe in education for all, there may have been division within the ranks. The Catholic university later incorporated as St. Louis University may have been involved in the education of blacks, or not, but the university was also party to a lawsuit in which the university's slaves were at issue.[15]

The role of "gender" also informed the construction and evolution of identity among free and slave African Americans along the St. Louis frontier. Specific understanding of definitions of "masculinity" and "femininity" as they related to people of color affected how blacks lived and worked in the region in the period. Women, slave and free, emerge in the record as unique individuals often bent on delineating their own identities or personalities as much as making possible or protecting the existence of family and community. In fact, a black woman named Celeste filed the first slave freedom suit in the Missouri court in 1805. Another black woman, Judy Logan, sued the powerful free black minister John Berry Meachum repeatedly over a period of years in a demonstration which put the lie to the legend that Meachum's only or at least principal motivation for buying slaves in the first place was to teach them to read and write *in order to set them free*. And then there was the former slave Ester Clamorgan, who refused to be merely the discarded concubine of a colonial adventurer, but instead became a progenitor of St. Louis' colored elite and, through the lawsuits she originated, instigated generations of lawsuits to accumulate one of the larger land holdings in the city.[16]

In the west, as elsewhere in the republic, land provided the imprimatur of economic, if not of social or political power, and the record amply demonstrates that a number of African Americans understood that and wielded land-owning strategies occasionally with breathtaking skill and precision. As we shall see, their land acquisition maneuvers both reiterated and at times posed alternatives to those of the white male majority, and this was true even when, as in the case of Ester Clamorgan, among others, black women wrested control of land away from white men to establish clear title to the security or power land conveyed. Taken together, such women also contributed to the clarification of specific attitudes toward land in the West and their role in the construction and evolution of American and African American identities. Where gender is added to the mix of race, slave or free status, and power or individual autonomy, it makes for a fascinating range of possibilities, indeed.

My study of free and slave African Americans in St. Louis, their reciprocal relationship with the western frontier and evolving definitions of "the West," and the evolution of black identities, activities, and agency in the period from the founding of St. Louis through the end of the Civil War analyzes census records, church minutes, newspapers, correspondence, maps, broadsides, slave narratives, court records (freedom suits, petitions, depositions, wills, deeds), and records of the Freedmen's Bureau and military records.

The notion that 19th century blacks—perhaps especially black slaves— might have used the law, or a litigious strategy, to obtain or to maintain their own personal, individual freedom might seem astonishing or perplexing, even in the face of such irrefutable evidence as the petitions for freedom themselves, but during the half-century leading to the Civil War, slaves in Missouri (many, if not most, born in places as far away as Virginia, Delaware, South Carolina, Kentucky, Canada, even Africa, and who had moved or been brought west) filed hundreds of cases in civil courts, and free people of color filed at least as many in criminal, chancery and land courts, as well as in a division that focused on mechanics' liens.

Some of the cases reveal a stunning diversity of experience among people of color in antebellum Missouri, as well as provide evidence of connections between free blacks and slaves (between whites and slaves, and between whites and free people of color). In other words, the legal record proves these connections existed. The majority of slaves who filed freedom petitions were illiterate, but the legal record permits them to name themselves and memorialize certain details of their experiences and so contribute to an individual as well as collective narrative of the lives of Missouri slaves (as well as of the illiterate free persons of color who battled to establish and maintain their freedom in St. Louis courts). In addition to the petitions for freedom filed by slaves in St. Louis Circuit Court, hundreds of petitions either initiated by persons of color or in which persons of color were involved in some way in the Chancery, Criminal, and Land Courts gradually bring to light a nuanced portrait of black life in St. Louis and on the western frontier. The tentacles of slavery ultimately connected all levels of St. Louis society in a network of legal cases of which the slave freedom suits were only an admittedly significant part. And when all was said and done, the record of a variety of litigations indeed tolled like *"a firebell in the night,"* which reached the Supreme Court of the land, and forewarned of civil war.

Prologue

It was about the river.

The Mississippi River became the key and a significant boundary of the advancing American western frontier; described as the "great water" by many Indian nations, the river proved a source of both bounty and threat.[1] The blacks who accompanied the French Creole founders of the fort at St. Louis understood the multiple possibilities of the river, and their identities, culture, and lives were also deeply connected to its central importance.[2] This initial arrival of blacks by waterway obviously provided them with knowledge of geography, as well as perhaps insights into relations among Indian tribes and how Indians interacted with Europeans. This familiarity with and reliance on the river as a critical component of African American culture and identity continued through the war years.

In 1699, Frenchmen from Canada traveled south on the Mississippi to found the colony of Louisiana, which some historians referred to as "Africanized" because of its black slave majority population.[3] Almost from the moment they founded Louisiana, the French began discussing importation of African slaves and considered the idea and feasibility of exchanging Indians for Africans already enslaved in the Caribbean; one idea was to trade two Indians for one African because of the French perception that Africans were stronger and worked harder.[4] But the trade in slaves from Africa to Louisiana began in earnest in 1719, and ended in 1731 (although a slaver brought Africans from the Caribbean to Louisiana in 1743); by 1746, approximately a generation before the Creoles traveled north on the river to break ground at St. Louis, 4,730 blacks shared the Louisiana colony with 3,200 whites.[5] Because a minority of individual slave owners each owned hundreds of slaves, the density of African population and its majority status ironically protected and preserved certain aspects of African cultures.[6] This black majority contributed to the creation and persistence of a language that melded French vocabulary with African grammar and syntax and was widely spoken by both blacks and whites.[7]

The majority of Africans purchased for sale or trade as slaves in the colony were natives of Senegambia, and thus shared an understanding of certain cultural values, although the significance of this sustained forced migration of Africans into the colony depended also on conditions within the host colony itself.[8] Although the majority of recent African arrivals likely continued to practice a variety of African religions, significant numbers of these Africans practiced the Muslim religion and were literate in Arabic, a language whose alphabet they used to record in their own African languages their thoughts and history.[9] The Senegambians' agricultural tradition going back thousands of years included cultivation of rice, along with corn, tobacco, indigo, and cotton; they had also produced meat from domesticated cattle, goats, sheep, and fowl.[10] In the first years of the slave trade, preferences for both Africans skilled in rice cultivation as well as rice seedlings imported to begin Louisiana fields were stipulated in colonial trade reports; colonists expressed their preference for Africans between the ages of eight and 30 years old, because of their superior physical strength and stamina in day to day tasks, but nursing infants and young children were also among those brought to Louisiana for sale as slaves.[11] About one-third of Africans sold as slaves in colonial Louisiana were natives of Benin or the Congo.[12]

In the 1750s, the colony purchased slaves from British colonists trading in Jamaica, which suggests some African slaves in Louisiana at that time might have understood or spoken English. However, French was the language most widely spoken by all; it was only after settlement and transfer of the territory to the United States, when American blacks entered St. Louis and exchanged cultural traits with the French Creole and Spanish blacks who had helped to settle the region that English became the dominant tongue.[13] Thus, the founding "black" population at St. Louis was far from monolithic.

In St. Louis, this "diversity" of "black" cultures continued, although Creole French settlers tried a variety of strategies to drive a wedge between blacks, slave and free, and Indians, with varying degrees of success. Race and status were not automatically joined from the beginning of the Louisiana colony, and free colored landowners were listed in censuses as early as 1722.[14] Free people of color included African, mulatto (African and European) and *grif* (or *griffe*) (African and Indian) slaves freed for a variety of services to their slave owners or to the community.[15]

* * *

St. Louis, Missouri, was in fact the gateway to the frontier, but it was a gateway because of the river. The clearing hacked out of the forest by the Creoles was isolated in the midst of Indian nations, and for at least a generation, the river was the only reliable road in or out. In mild weather, settlers used boats to travel on the river or to cross it, and in winter, the river often froze solidly enough to permit walking on foot, pulling wagons, or even galloping on horseback across the ice to the other side, while skating or sledding was enjoyed as a form of recreation.

Because the river was a superhighway for the movement of trade goods, including slaves, it provided the lifeblood of the slave regime by channeling thousands of slaves for sale from the upper south and border states to Deep South plantations. But because it was also so obviously a throughway south to north, the Mississippi exercised a powerful pull on the minds and imaginations of slaves seeking freedom. People bent on escape from slavery recognized the river as a means to obtain freedom. The river also provided work; both slaves and free blacks worked in a variety of occupations on steamboats and levees; the majority of workers on the river were male, although about two percent were slave or free black women (and a smaller percentage of whites), who worked as chambermaids on steamboats. This benefited slave owners, who hired out slaves, at the same time that it encouraged the creation and expansion of relationships between slave and free blacks, two groups the law persistently sought to keep separate. At least as important was the dissemination of information among people of color that the ceaseless traffic on the river facilitated. In essence, the river was a portrait of the place.[16]

CHAPTER 1

Gateway to the West

Geographic location was key to the importance the United States saw in the region first known as "Louisiana." The Mississippi River bisected the mainland creating a major north-south highway that provided transportation for exploration, trade, settlers, and the military. The land east and west of the river nearly doubled the land mass of the young country and brought with it the prospect of a vast as yet unexplored treasury of resources which could be harvested or developed to enrich and support the nation. Furs, timber, precious metals, and land for settlement and agricultural development seemed there for the taking. Little thought beyond logistical strategy—meaning how to move or manage them—was given to the natives already living there, although some of the Indians were initially enslaved. Indeed, the location of the future state of Missouri somewhat soothed Thomas Jefferson's trepidation about the danger inherent in attempting to successfully manage a country with what he saw as the competing interests of slavery versus "freedom." In fact, the new acquisition provided Jefferson's rationale that the region could prove "a safety valve" to "diffuse" the burgeoning surplus black slave population of the older, settled east.[1]

Settlement of the newly acquired Louisiana Territory proceeded along the River. Moving northward from New Orleans and westward from Illinois, French Creoles, Africans, and Americans converged at a place on the river that would become the village of St. Louis, which its settlers first envisioned as a commercial, profit-making venture. In July 1763, the firm of Maxent, Laclède and Company was formed in New Orleans and granted an "exclusive" right to trade in the region by Louisiana territorial governor Jean-Jacques Blaise d'Abbadie, even though in a secret bargain not made official until 1764, France had already ceded Louisiana to Spain as part of negotiations to finally end hostilities of the Seven Years (or French and Indian) War. Because international as well as internal travel was unreliable and inconsistent at best, news did not reach Louisiana until 1765, when the village on the Mississippi was already well underway.[2]

The frontier village of St. Louis quickly attained the cosmopolitan diversity that was sometimes a byproduct of centers engaged in trade within the United States and Europe. The ultimate goal of settlement was to marshal sufficient men and supplies to mount a muscular thrust westward in trade and appropriation of land. Free and slave blacks took an active role in both. On any given day, a stroll through the village would bring encounters with French Creoles, Canadian fur trappers, Indians of various nations, black slaves, and free blacks.[3] Initial black settlers in St. Louis were drawn from a New Orleans population that, between 1719 (when African importations began) and 1791, had grown from statistical 0 to slightly over 17 percent.[4] Still, during the earliest years of settlement, Indian slaves of various nations were more numerous than black slaves.[5] In 1769, while the territory was under the control of Spain, enslavement of Indians was declared illegal, and indeed, numerous slave freedom suits were filed based on the plaintiff's claim of Indian blood.[6] And after passage of the Northwest Ordinance of 1787, created a kind of slavery-free zone in the Upper West, French settlers on the east bank of the Mississippi River moved with their slaves to the St. Louis side of the river; by the 1790s, this resulted in a slave population of 30 percent of the region known as Upper Louisiana.[7]

Until well into the 19th century, St. Louis was deliberately French in character, culture, and language.[8] African, African American, and Native American cultural elements blended to produce a unique frontier cultural milieu with Francophone overtones.[9] Like the Creole French they accompanied, the first blacks were French speakers, and this phenomenon continued into the antebellum era.[10] Founding village families and leading characters in the drama of settlement and growth included the Chouteaus, in particular Auguste and Pierre, and the redoubtable matriarch, Marie Thérèse (or simply *"Madame"*), the companion of city founder Pierre Laclède. To accommodate the precise Catholic doctrine on marriage predominant in old New Orleans, Madame never divorced her lawful husband Rene Chouteau, Sr. (father of her son, Auguste). However, Madame Chouteau ignored any complementary requirements (of law or Church) regarding offspring: her children fathered by her companion Pierre Laclède went by the name of her husband ("Chouteau"). This melding of families ultimately came to exemplify the region's fierce individualism.[11]

Pierre Laclède and his paramour's son, then 14-year-old Auguste Chouteau, made the grueling 700-mile journey upriver from New Orleans to what would become St. Louis. Governor of the Louisiana Territory d'Abbadie had envisioned the possibility of a successful trading post on the Mississippi River and the scouting party led by Laclède traveled north with the task of determining the feasibility of such a project. The governor's goal was to cement a profitable trading relationship, principally in furs, with the River Indian tribes, including the Little Osages and Missouris. The site chosen by Laclède had access to three rivers: the Mississippi, Missouri, and Illinois. The treaty ending the French and Indian War ceded French control of territory east of the Mississippi to England and Louisiana to Spain, but Laclède selected a site on the west bank of the Mississippi River, making landfall in November 1763. Some of the men who made the journey upriver in the Laclède party were free men of color, who had perhaps arrived in New Orleans by way of Santo Domingo, and so the first families of St. Louis included black and brown men, as well as the red men who were there when they arrived. The pioneers from New Orleans hacked a clearing out of the wilderness and settled in.[12]

A group of approximately 150 Missouri Indians arrived shortly after the men from Louisiana began erecting cabins. The Indians may simply have been curious about the newcomers and their intentions. They may have come to trade, or they have may have been part of large groups of Indians shuffled about or displaced by the turmoil of the Seven Years War and seeking new alliances or simply seeking refuge. Chouteau wrote in his *Narrative* that the Indians stole tools and provisions, and that Laclède sent them on their way. Choureau's recollection was that Laclède threatened the natives by telling them that if they did not leave the French settlers alone, their Indian enemies would "massacre" them, their "wives and children [would be] torn to pieces and their limbs thrown to dogs and birds of prey," and any survivors would be sold as slaves. In his recollection, Chouteau characterized this as being "a good Father [*sic*]" to the Indians. However, Laclède had leavened his threats with a bribe, giving the Indians corn, cloth, gunpowder, and knives, and finally, after several days, the Indians returned to their own village upriver.[13]

As the Indians departed, in one of the first mass migrations west to the village, whites from the east side of the river converged on the place that would be St. Louis. The arrival of the French-speaking settlers from New Orleans on the west bank and cession of the east bank to England inspired this "mass exodus of French-speaking inhabitants" from the Illinois side of the water, who, like the Indians, had often been uprooted by the recent war.[14] Some of these newcomers were free blacks, but there were also numbers of black or Indian slaves in the Illinois group, as well as mixed-blood individuals, couples, and children. A census taken in 1770 identified some individuals by race and marital status, as well as whether they were free or owned land: for example, an individual described as "Panis Noire (Black)"; a free black named Neptune and a free couple of color named Gregoire and "Janette," who was also a landowner (see below); and Marie Scypion, who filed one of the earliest freedom suits. All of these individuals named in the census arrived with the group who came to the "French" side of the river after cession of the east bank to England. Thus, involuntary westward relocations of black slaves began immediately with the settlement of St. Louis.[15]

Documents show that as part of the grant of a trade monopoly in the region, the early French settlers had been authorized to sell Africans to the Indians or exchange them for furs and other commodities. In 1765, correspondence between the Commerce Minister at Versailles and French settlers in Upper Louisiana suggest the Crown's only objection to such trade was the assumption by local Louisiana traders that they possessed the authority to grant or approve "exclusive" trade rights to others, which the Minister reminded them was the province of the Crown, presumably because the Crown expected profits from the trade.[16]

The physical plan for the settlement at St. Louis was based on a geometric strategy reminiscent of the street plan used to build New Orleans. Whether because they were homesick for New Orleans or simply thought the physical organization of New Orleans the most logical or superior, Pierre Laclède laid out a town with a "grid" street plan mimicking that of New Orleans and cities of continental Europe. Laclède's vision included plans for a public plaza and a commercial main street to run parallel to the river.[17]

The village of St. Louis remained clustered at the river's edge for decades, a clearing extending west no more than a mile (half a dozen present-day city blocks) before diminishing suddenly to frontier. No map had yet been drawn to identify precise boundaries or landmarks in the region beyond the area of densely intersecting roads on the river. Main Street (also called "First" Street) was the broad main thoroughfare that ran parallel to the river. By the time Laclède and his scouting party arrived that first September, a few rude shops had already been established and were ready for occupancy. Their first order of business was to erect a stone building to serve as "company headquarters," and, after that, a log house church. These first dwellings were constructed on platforms six or seven feet off the ground "to protect themselves from wild beasts." Slaves often lived in the same houses with slave owners, although some slaves may have lived in houses separate from their owners. The first village lots were organized in a contiguous pattern to facilitate the speedy construction of a stockade in the event of attack by Indians, and common fields set aside for farming by village residents extended two miles beginning at Fourth Street (to present-day Jefferson). The western boundary of the original village site was two or three miles west from the river (now, Grand). Later that September, the rest of Laclède's family Madame Marie Thérèse Chouteau and the couple's young children arrived. At a gathering on the river shortly after the streets were laid out, Laclède announced the trading post village would be named after the patron saint of King Louis XV of France: Saint Louis.[18]

In 1767, a contingent of Spanish soldiers and workers finally arrived as a result of the secret Treaty of Fontainbleau, by which Napoleon had ceded much of Louisiana to Spain in 1762, in an effort to prevent England from gaining the lands at the end of the French and Indian War.[19] Under the command of Captain Francisco Ríu, an expedition of several dozen composed primarily of soldiers, but also laborers ("a carpenter, a brick-layer, a stonecutter"), some of whom were Africans, set out for St. Louis in April 1767.[20] Ríu's apparent inability to maintain discipline and order among his men resulted in a number of desertions; a black stonemason named Joseph Balboa, who had been working near the confluence of the Missouri and Mississippi Rivers, complained of mistreatment and appealed for help to leave the region. Of Spanish descent, Balboa wanted to go to Cuba, but his plans were discovered and he was arrested and held instead, despite the Governor Ulloa of Louisiana's order that Balboa be sent back to New Orleans immediately. Balboa remained jailed for nearly eight months.[21]

In 1769, the Spanish governor Alejandro O'Reilly arrived in St. Louis to take over, and brought with him 80 members of a Spanish-speaking black militia. The city's African American population mixed French, Spanish, and Indian languages and traditions, but the majority population continued to use French in speaking and writing for social interaction and business transactions and the French Creole culture predominated.[22] That same year, while the territory was under its control, Spain declared enslavement of Indians illegal, although the decree of December 17, 1769, specifically outlawed the *trade* in Indian slaves, rather than actual possession of Indian slaves.[23] Despite this caveat, a thriving trade in Indian slaves was part of St. Louis commerce through the 1770s, and numerous slave freedom suits were filed in St. Louis Circuit Court well into the antebellum era based on plaintiffs' claims of Indian blood.[24]

An initial village census of 1770 recorded a population of about 500, including 69 slaves, although because people of color who were free were not always or necessarily differentiated from slaves in the record, some of that number might actually have been free. Seventeen percent of the population was Indian slaves, most of whom were female, in keeping with the typical profile of slaves in the region in the period.[25]

Some of the available biographical information also implies that free blacks sometimes actively participated in the western trade with Indians for furs. The life of free black landowner Jeanette Forchet, a recipient of an original land grant in the territory, is one example. Forchet may have been a slave manumitted about 1763, who moved from Cahokia to St. Louis by 1766.[26] By 1767, Forchet recorded possession of a town lot in St. Louis.[27] She married the free black Valentin in 1773. (Valentin was Forchet's second husband; Jeanette and Gregoire baptized their son in the Catholic Church [see below] in 1767; her first husband, Gregoire, died in 1770.) Valentin was a scout and gunsmith, who probably traded furs with the Indians, and who was with the Osages in their village when he died in 1789. (Forchet, who did not marry for a third time, died in St. Louis in 1803.) The Valentin household also contained the adults Marie Louisa, Lusana, Alex and Baptista Chebrouil.[28] The next count (1794–95) listed a total of 604 slaves in the Upper Louisiana Territory and 63 free people of color. In 1800, the number of slaves had increased to 1,191; 77 free people of color; and 5,643 whites.[29]

In spite of fear of Indians and the unknown, and of the likelihood of death to disease or other mishaps associated with the settlement of the frontier, the population of the village grew quickly. This swift expansion and settlement by whites, and some Africans, was not welcomed by the native Indians, who tried at least once to wipe the settlement off the face of the earth.

In 1780, a group of over 1,000 men representing a loose confederation of several Indian tribes and a contingent of the British attacked the outpost at St. Louis in what might be described as one of the last battles of the American Revolution. Technically, St. Louis was a Spanish colony and an American ally, and that made it a target of the British. The Creoles successfully defended themselves against the attack from what was referred to by the locals as "Fort San Carlos," but what was in actuality a single stone tower that stood at what is now Fourth and Walnut streets in downtown St. Louis. It was intended as the westernmost of four planned towers of a fort then still under construction for defense of the village. The Spanish military officer Fernando de Leyba captained the tower. Nearly two dozen St. Louisans were killed outright in the initial onslaught (another two dozen were taken prisoner by the Indians and killed later), crops in the field were burned, and livestock was slaughtered. Rumors that a large force of Indians and British soldiers was moving toward St. Louis had come weeks before, but villagers had continued to work in their fields as usual and were farming when the attack began. A slave named Louis was among those surprised by the attackers and unable to reach the safety of the fort. Louis' description of his escape from the Indians who pursued him may have been dramatically enhanced, but continued to entertain St. Louisans for generations after the attack.[30]

The tower was positioned at the southwest end of the village overlooking the common fields and mill pond so as to defend the village against attack from the west since villagers felt the river would provide them sufficient protection from the east. De Leyba had expected that by that time stone towers would stand at "the four corners of this village" to protect it, but at the time of the attack only the west tower had been completed, which left the settlement vulnerable to the "barbarians." According to De Leyba, he had even given money out of his own pocket to speed up construction of the west tower and to begin construction of a second tower at the north. DeLeyba sent for help from the settlers at Ste. Genevieve, and 60 armed men of that town's militia arrived in St. Louis in mid–May. Meanwhile, de Leyba and men from St. Louis hurried to complete as much work as they could on the towers even as the army of Indians and British soldiers approached. Black slaves who had been working in the fields defended themselves with farm tools and weapons, and a few of the women also took up arms against Indians and British soldiers. In his journal, De Leyba described in vivid terms settlers racing the clock, digging trenches as fast as they could at the south and north entrances to the village, and hurriedly mounting five cannons on the tower walls.[31]

By the time the "terrible cries and a terrible firing" of the Indians and Englishmen commenced, many women and children of St. Louis were hiding in the Governor's Mansion, which had an armed guard surrounding it. De Leyba's makeshift army apparently put up an admirable defense because after a while the attackers retreated. Villagers, including black slaves, caught outside the town limits working in *maiz* fields, were killed, along with stray livestock, as the Indians and British moved out. De Leyba and his men watched helplessly as a number of villagers were taken prisoner in the retreat, and they were horrified by the sight of "corpses cut into pieces, entrails, limbs, heads, arms and legs scattered all over the field." His report listed the loss of 14 whites and seven slaves killed and an additional 12 whites and 13 slaves taken captive. Without their vigorous defense and the blessing of "Divine Providence," de Leyba believed they would have witnessed "the last day of St. Louis." They had sustained great losses (de Leyba contracted with "merchant Cerré" to feed the soldiers due to the loss of crops in the fields), but they had survived. Within the next two years, American victors of their revolution against England began to exert a strong cultural presence just east of St. Louis, and after the transfer of St. Louis to the Americans, the fort tower was used as a jail until a proper jail was built in 1819.[32]

After passage of the Northwest Ordinance in 1787 created a kind of slavery-free zone in the Upper West, French settlers on the east bank of the Mississippi River moved with their slaves to the St. Louis side of the river; by the 1790s, this resulted in a slave population of 30 percent in the region known as Upper Louisiana.[33] As has been stated, slaves who claimed Indian antecedents increasingly protested their enslavement in courts of law, as well as their blithe inclusion in the record with "mulattoes" or "pardos" (the term the Spanish used to describe offspring with any perceived mixture of Indian and black).[34] Already two distinct understandings of the western frontier were emerging: for slave owners, it was a place to claim and maintain slave property; for some people of color, it was becoming a place to define, claim, and, if necessary, litigate for control over free status.

At least one consequence of the informal traverse of a "frontier" border creeping ever westward was the visible presence of a mixed race population at the margins of St. Louis society. A case in point involved the mixed race slaves of St. Louis merchant Gabriel Cerré. By 1791, Cerré owned more slaves (43) than any other slaveholder in St. Louis. (Two of those slaves were killed at the battle of San Carlos in 1780, and one had been injured there.) Cerré owned a teenaged slave named Victoire, whose parents were Joseph (an Indian) and a black slave mother.

In 1796, Joseph attempted to purchase Victoire, who was described in the record as a "mulatto," to set her free. But Cerré demanded $1,000 "in hard cash," not furs, and further, suggested to the court that Joseph's effort to purchase his daughter had been "suggested to him by people whose only motive for making such a sacrifice is one of debauchery," while Cerré's motive was "attachment both on [his] part and on the part of [his] wife." Joseph took the case to court and suggested a price of 600 piastres in furs or 500 piastres in cash, but a governing panel set the new price at $800.[35]

The Spanish had prohibited enslaving Indians, however, this case demonstrates early attention to how individuals of color should be defined in the law, especially if the individual(s) in question were suspected of having any black blood (or perhaps if it was advantageous to a slave owner that an individual claimed as a slave could be found to have a black antecedent).[36] The 1796 census included 34 free mulattos and eight free blacks (seven of whom were female); and an inverse proportion of mulatto versus black slaves (197 black slaves, 85 mulatto slaves), although there was an almost identical number of black and mulatto slave *children* (43 mulatto, 44 black).[37] We will see the continuing evolution of laws with respect not only to slavery, but also to race and color, throughout the antebellum era.

The potential to get rich quick in the west was certainly one of the main attractions that drew settlers to the region despite the dangers of living there. Auguste Chouteau's early account books document a rapid profit margin based on the post's trade for furs with the Indians. In 1793, a single entry recorded hundreds of bear, deer, raccoon, beaver, fox, and buffalo skins received in trade, as well as dozens of big cat and wolf skins with bear cub furs listed separately.[38] Among the items settlers offered for barter with the Indians were guns and bullets, and Pierre Ignace, a free black man (second husband of Jeanette), was one of the village gunsmiths and responsible for building and repairing guns.[39]

That same year, adventurer Jacques Clamorgan joined with a group of merchants to form the Missouri Company.[40] Despite the evidence of free blacks and slaves engaged in the fur trade with Indians, white settlers made an unambiguous effort to preserve the trade for themselves. For example, the Missouri Company's founding charter proposed "encouraging employment of white people in preference to Negroes, half-breeds, or savages, free or slave." The preference was apparently as much a security and economic strategy as a statement of racial bias, as it went on to say that this was to "encourage the labor of white men ... and to avoid the information and bad counsel they might give the nations." Trading regulations also levied fines for any trader who carried "intoxicating beverages ... into the Missouri ... for the purpose of trading, exchanging or giving to any person whatever, free or slave."[41] Despite the prohibition, in 1792, among the licenses issued to trade with the Indians was one to "Antonio Chouteau," who was identified as "meztiso" and the employer of five people.[42]

The so-called "transportation revolution" is typically dated from the early 1800s, but necessity is the mother of invention and no doubt spurred by the need to transport huge quantities of furs from the west to markets in St. Louis, in the 1790s, American James Piggott instituted regular ferry service across the Mississippi River.[43] Piggott died in 1797, and after several attempts by different people to continue the service, in 1815, John McKnight and Thomas Brady finally managed to establish a ferry service from Missouri based on an agreement with Piggott's heirs; in 1819, Samuel Wiggins started a ferry from the Illinois side of the Mississippi, and in 1820, Wiggins secured a monopoly of the Mississippi crossing by buying out his Missouri competitors.[44] In December 1804, the American John Boly received a three-year license to operate his ferry with the prescribed rates of 25 cents for a man or a horse, 62½ cents for a man and horse together, and $1.50 for a cart and horse.[45]

An almost immediate consideration of legal policing of slave property in the region was voiced in connection with this question of who should be permitted to cross the river and for what purposes. In 1795, Zenon Trudeau wrote a letter to Carondelet inquiring about "making arrangements for the slaves who cross as fugitives to their bank," stating that although Indians who committed murder would not be pursued across the river, "fugitive negroes at all times and in all cases will be pursued, and returned to the owners without need of convention."[46]

By the time the first American governor arrived in 1804, to take charge in St. Louis, a population of 9,373—7,876 whites and 1,497 blacks— was waiting for him, although because Creole men fathered children by both Indians and blacks and legal definitions of "race" and "color" were continually evolving, the numbers for those respective groups must be considered inexact.[47] However, slavery as an institution was well entrenched in Missouri by the time of the American takeover.[48] The move to protect slavery from the Creoles, and the conciliatory response by Americans, suggests a connection between westward expansion of American ideals in tandem with black slavery as part of their "vision of democracy in the West."[49] Nevertheless, crowds of French-speaking blacks gathered to watch the transfer of the village to the Americans because they believed the coming of the Americans meant they would soon be free. (Part of this was due to the initial plan to combine administrative oversight of the new territory with that of the Indiana Territory, which, as part of the Old Northwest, meant slavery would be outlawed.[50])

Creole merchants in St. Louis feared that such perceptions on the part of slaves could erupt in violent resistance and asked the new United States government for guarantees that their land grants and their rights to slave property would be respected. Fur trade companies operating out of St. Louis were similarly concerned about maintaining their business interests along the Upper Missouri.[51] A meeting of "French traders and farmers, expatriated Americans, and a few holdout Spanish officials" met in St. Louis in late 1804 to discuss concerns that U.S. rule meant the end of slavery based on Congressional restrictions on slavery in the Louisiana Purchase territory.[52] In an effort to gain firm guarantees from the Americans and to ameliorate some of their fears, members of St. Louis' Creole elite petitioned for immediate implementation of a strict "Black Code" to ensure "tranquility" as in times past.[53]

Capt. Amos Stoddard presided over the official transfer of the territory of Louisiana to the United States, although he did not personally understand either French or Spanish, and territorial governor Carlos Delassus spoke no English.[54] Marie Leduc (who was related to the founding Chouteau family by marriage as well as an early participant in land transfers in the region) probably stood in as their translator.[55] Business, cultural, and social changes followed swiftly in the colony in the wake of consolidation with the Americans. In 1808, Manuel Lisa entered the expanding fur trade with his St. Louis Fur Company, which within the decade was renamed the Missouri Fur Company. In 1809, the village was officially incorporated as a town with boundaries as of 1811 near Roy's Windmill and including six miles of development along the river. The windmill was a town landmark that had been built by Antoine Roy near the riverfront north of town in 1797 to grind grain for bread, among the commodities settlers planned to trade to local Indians. Limestone ledges along the river's edge provided a natural levee that separated the town from the Mississippi River, as well as a source of stone to build houses, about one-quarter of which were constructed of stone. The town's dirt roads possessed a high clay and sand content, which became slippery in the rainy season. Pedestrians slipped and slid along the sides of the roads because there were no sidewalks. The town commons, where townsfolk grazed livestock, extended south from the edge of the village for a distance of about seven miles. An inland lake south and west of the main settlement dubbed "Chouteau's Pond" provided fresh water for the town and livestock as well as water for washing. A fence was erected and maintained along the boundary of the commons both to keep wild things out and to keep domesticated creatures in. Town livestock, including cows and hogs as well as horses, could often be seen meandering along town streets. As a health and safety measure, the Town Board decreed that owners remove dead animals from the town streets immediately.[56]

The relative "freedom" enjoyed by black slaves in St. Louis was due in part to its urban environment. However, in the early years, westward expansion and the advancing frontier perhaps also produced an environment in which black slaves enjoyed a degree of autonomy not possible in more settled areas where a system of laws had been constructed or codified, especially laws prescribing or restricting the movement or activities of blacks free or slave. In addition, a reciprocal relationship between the frontier and the cosmopolitan center at St. Louis certainly played a role in the variety of ways in which people of color in the region defined themselves (and were defined by others). As investors and tradesmen funneled cash and supplies west, profits reaped in speculative ventures (trade with Indians, silver and gold mining, *the slave trade*) were channeled back again to support the burgeoning expansion of St. Louis and settlement of surrounding areas on both sides of the Mississippi River, and, beginning with the Lewis and Clark expeditions, ignited an almost constant parade of travelers west.

Between the War of 1812 and 1815, a veritable "flood" of migrants from Tennessee and Kentucky inundated Missouri; the new residents included blacks (maintaining a 10 percent ratio of the population even with the increase), as well as whites, and contributed to a gradual "Americanization" of the region from its previous French dominance.[57] This trend of westward movement to St. Louis from older, settled regions of the South continued to increase the black slave population. For example, in 1820, the census recorded 10,000 slaves in the state (15 percent of the population) and in 1830, 25,000 slaves (18 percent of the population), most of whom had come west from Kentucky, Tennessee, Virginia, and North Carolina.[58]

Courts of law eventually became centers of activity involving people of color, but for the first several decades, St. Louis had no permanent court building. Legal matters were heard, considered, or hashed out in a variety of locations, including a log cabin at Third and Plum streets, a Baptist church, and even "Mr. Yosti's tavern." As early as December 1804, Americans established a "prison" in a house rented from Jacques Clamorgan by the city court for $15 a month; the building required an additional $133.40 to get it into shape to serve as the city's jail.[59] In 1817, construction of a new jail began at Chestnut and 6th streets, but because the town didn't have enough money to complete it right away, completion was delayed until 1820.[60] Eventually, Auguste Chouteau donated a parcel of land to become the courthouse square, and in 1828, a two-story brick building with pillars supporting a roof and cupola was completed. A whipping post had stood alone in the square before the courthouse was completed.[61]

Within a decade, the needs of the city overwhelmed the original courthouse and a new one was planned. In 1843, the copper-sheathed dome of the new, larger courthouse was raised. The limestone floor of its rotunda was laid in 1844, and the building opened on Washington's Birthday in 1845. The building created its intended impression of the power and authority of the law with brick sidewalks, a wrought iron fence, and a border of locust trees, but nevertheless, it was still somewhat primitive: water had to be brought into the building from pumps or a well and its public privies were only swept out once a day, except on Sunday.[62] The courthouses served as centers for public meetings on subjects of local and national interest, including U.S. expansion west, war with Mexico, the California gold rush, construction of the transcontinental railroad, and race and slavery.[63]

The first town Board of Trustees included William C. Carr (a lawyer who had a role in several court cases involving free people of color and slaves suing to be free) and was headed by town father, Auguste Chouteau. Territorial governor William Henry Harrison appointed Chouteau, Jacques Clamorgan, and Charles Gratiot to serve on the Court of Common Pleas, even though none had legal background or experience.[64] One of the first orders of business for the new board was the issue of slave control. An armed patrol was speedily established on which "each male inhabitant over 18" was required to serve with the exception of "invalids, paupers, and preachers." According to local newspaper accounts, members served "willingly, even proudly."[65]

Thus, slavery came with the territory. A century before *Dred Scott*, black slaves labored in the lead mines of what was then still referred to as Upper Louisiana. In fact, more than one-third of the late 1700s population in the region was reported to be of African ancestry. The earliest Africans probably arrived as the slaves of Jesuit missionaries, such as *Père* Marquette. In the early 1770s, there had also been a small population of Indian slaves (69 in all, including 41 females and 28 males). And there was a growing population of free people of color involved in trapping and trading, scouting, mining, and the crafts. Some of these were people who had once been slaves, while others had come from different parts of the country as free scouts or settlers, or were of mixed blood (either part Indian or part white, or both). Many if not most of these free people of color were probably indistinguishable from other Creoles, or even of Indians, in terms of cultural outlook. As laws drew an increasingly firm line around anyone who wasn't white, this gradually changed. But regardless of cultural affiliation, in the settlement period, the majority of people of color in the village, including Indians, were slaves. Even free people of color walked a fine line between personal autonomy and enslavement: as early as 1804, the law provided that free blacks who failed to pay their taxes could be hired out to raise the money to pay them.[66] On the other hand, slaves might be able to flout the restrictions to keep the Sabbath by hiring themselves out to work and earn money on a Sunday, as several St. Louis slaves did in 1812, when they constructed a wooden building.[67]

By 1820, the total population of St. Louis was 66,000, with a colored slave population of 10,000, and a free black population of 375. In 1840, the free population of color had risen to 531, and in 1850, that population had increased still more to 1,398, out of a total population of nearly 80,000. The slave population rose apace, with a population of 1,500 in 1840, and 2,600 by 1850. In the city of St. Louis, the combined total population of color was more concentrated and remained steady at about 20 percent.[68] Keeping track of native Indians in the census was more difficult, most likely because many led a nomadic lifestyle, but contemporaneous accounts often mention the presence of Indians in the town. By the time of Statehood, most Indians had moved well outside the settled areas and only came to town to trade. German emigrant Gottfried Duden, who came to the United States to find land for a German immigrant settlement, wrote that he had seen Indians in St. Louis frequently, including Osage, Kansas, Fox, and Sioux. (Duden also mentioned that Choctaw Indians on the Illinois side of the river had adopted the "European way of life," including ownership of slaves, despite frequent mention of black slaves from St. Louis going across the river to Illinois to establish residence in a free territory.) Early on, the city was diverse and cosmopolitan.

The establishment of churches and the expansion of commerce in and around St. Louis ran a parallel course. Some Indian tribes kept Indian slaves, and traded or sold Indian slaves, or at least slaves with Indian blood, to whites and blacks in the St. Louis village. The Spanish governor's 1769 ban against Indian slavery outlawed the trade in the practice, rather than the practice itself, which continued. In the same way that black slave families were permitted to exist (or denied the right to exist) at the whim of their owners, Indian slavery also produced young children or adolescents who were sold away from their parents.[69]

After headquarters for village business and trading interests were completed, the settlers set about building churches. Free and slave blacks threw themselves into the building of the churches, and then attended as members. St. Louis was a Catholic settlement and organization of everything—trade and commerce, schools, racial definitions, and slavery—was affected by Catholic doctrine. For example, the free blacks who arrived in 1763, were likely familiar with the "Edict Concerning the Negro Slaves in

Louisiana" promulgated in 1724, and that required the Catholic conversion of all slaves to the faith. Known as the *Code Noir*, this document defined as "rebels" any slaves who resisted conversion or claimed faith in other gods. Obviously, the focus of the *Code Noir* was primarily to control the behavior or activities of slaves, but free blacks also fell under its aegis, as did non–Catholic "overseers," who were punished by having their slaves confiscated.[70]

Once commercial and legal buildings had been erected, the question of a place for Catholic worship was settled. Creole men descended from the founding families or those who had gained an early lead in prominent entrepreneurial circles (including the Chouteaus, Marie Leduc, Manuel Lisa, and Antoine Soulard) joined with Anglo- and Irish-American businessmen to build a stone cathedral for Catholic worshippers. The cathedral replaced the log church on the riverfront. Priests were supported by a tithe on church members, often paid in trade goods such as furs or whatever village inhabitants could cultivate in their gardens or fields, including vegetables or tobacco. The first Mass was celebrated Christmas Day, 1819. In this period (under Bishop Louis William Valetine DuBourg), sermons in English were added to supplement sermons in French in order to accommodate increasing numbers of English-speaking Catholics.[71] DuBourg also lobbied town fathers for a Catholic university, which officially opened in 1818.[72] In 1827, Joseph Rosati, who was sued at least once by St. Louis slaves seeking their freedom, became the first bishop of St. Louis. St. Louis remained predominantly Catholic, but Baptist churches were organized in 1807 and 1818, Methodist in 1821, and Presbyterian between 1816 and 1817.[73]

Under the French regime, black slaves were required by law to convert to Catholicism. Although because slaves were defined in the law as "chattel" (or "property"), civil law did not recognize marriage between slaves as a legal contract entered into by consenting adults, slave marriages were nevertheless "recognized" by the church and often presided over by priests. Despite the tangle of ironies precipitated by such competing definitions or requirements, religious rituals fostered an interracial network that supported the creation and growth of black families. In fact, the church was known to sanction slave owners who failed to ensure that their slaves were "properly" married in the church.[74]

When free blacks or slaves were baptized, the selection or assignment of godparents illustrated a variety of family connections. Whites (Jean Baptiste Provenches and Mariane Marie Michel) stood as godparents when the previously mentioned free black couple Jeanette and Gregoire baptized their son, Paul. It is also possible that white slave owners engaged other whites from among their own social circle to act as "godparents" for slave infants in an arrangement seemed more concerned with the protection of slave property or preparation for a transfer of ownership of slave property in the event that something "happened" to a slave owner, rather than interest in a slave's spiritual wellbeing. Thus, it seems unlikely that slaves of the so-called "widow Dodier" Francoise and Jacques selected the widow's relatives Francois Dodier and Mariaine Helen Michel to be godparents to their son, Pierre. Slaves also sometimes selected other slaves to be their children's godparents, and in the early years of the territory before law rigorously separated slave and free blacks, slaves also sometimes selected free blacks for that important role. For example, a slave named Marie Jeanne chose the slaves Jean Baptiste (owner Madame Dodier) and Mariane Ursule (M. Lami) to be godparent to her son, Jean Baptiste. The free black Joseph Neptune and the slave Melanie (Fr. Bernard) shared the duties of godparents for Marie, a slave of Sylvester Labadie, who was married to Pompei by Fr. Bernard of the village church.[75]

Blacks often worshipped in segregated pews of white churches, but also established separate, black churches. However, there is rarely mention of Indians joining church congregations in St. Louis or establishing Christian churches of their own. The expansion of organized religious institutions included the arrival of missionaries bent on "Anglicizing" Indians to "save their souls." Presbyterians seem to have been especially interested in this, but the response by Indians was lukewarm at best. One Osage chief responding to a white preacher's sermon about Jonah and the Whale said, "white people talk and lie..., but that is the biggest lie we have ever heard."[76]

Free blacks in St. Louis established Protestant churches in the region. By the 1840s, the Reverend John Berry Meachum, a free black, headed the congregation of the city's African Baptist Church at Third and Almond streets, which he asserted had 500 members. Five black churches had been established in St. Louis by 1850 (three Baptist, two Methodist; four of which were referred to as "African" churches and the last as Ebenezer Methodist). Because St. Louis was clearly a Catholic outpost, it is reasonable to consider whether Catholic slaves—or Catholic free people of color for that matter—experienced life in ways different from those who were Protestant or "unchurched," or if the ways in which they constructed identity was substantially affected by their Catholicism.[77]

Local lore has created a legend of John Berry Meachum as a man who taught slaves to read in the middle of the night on board his own steamboat while it lay anchored at mid-river, and who purchased slaves for the express purpose of setting them free. That he was known as a Biblical orator and preacher respected by blacks, and perhaps by whites as well, is clear from a number of references to Meachum in surviving journals, correspondence, and newspaper articles. For example, in 1837, James Essex, who was white, wrote in his journal that he had arranged for Meachum to preach the funeral of his slave, Betsey, and that "a number of Blacks attended." Meachum was a prosperous citizen of the town. Receipts show that he shopped for necessaries at the American Fur Company owned by the Chouteaus, paying for his purchases in cash or signing for credit in his own hand. It is clear that he was successful in commercial circles. However, it is not as clear that Meachum deliberately added to the numbers of the free population of color in antebellum St. Louis, especially in light of the fact that over a period of years, several slaves sued Meachum for their own freedom.[78]

John Berry Meachum arrived in St. Louis in 1815, after having purchased his own freedom in Virginia, and making his way west by moving first to Kentucky. He operated an apparently successful barrel-making business and by mid-century was the owner of two brick buildings in St. Louis and real estate across the river in Illinois Town. His holdings were valued at $8,000, which made him one of the three largest black landowners in the state.[79]

It has been suggested that the Rev. John Berry Meachum combined religious writ and democratic political ideals to construct a philosophy for the education of black children in St. Louis aimed at preparing them to succeed, as Meachum had, within traditional capitalist guidelines. In 1846, Meachum's speech before the National Negro Convention emphasized the importance of both education and hard work to economic success. In fact, Meachum's public profile existed despite a campaign by Missouri elected officials, including Governor John C. Edwards's approval of 1847 legislation, which sought not only to prohibit the education of black or mulatto children, slave or free, but sought to severely constrain the activities of black preachers. The legislation prohibited religious "meetings or assemblages" by negroes or "mulattoes" without a white official (sheriff, constable, marshall, or justice of the peace) present.

Meachum was no stranger to the courts. As early as 1823, he brought suit against David Massey, charging that Massey had "ejected" him from his properties in St. Louis between 2nd (Church) and 3rd streets and North E and F streets, which included a stable, coach house, outhouse, and town lot.[80] Meachum claimed injuries and sought $1,000 in damages.[81] A court summons required Massey to appear to answer the charges.[82]

Massey told the Court Meachum's survey of the land he claimed to own was inaccurate and further declared he wasn't guilty of the charges of trespass and ejectment.[83] A survey commissioned by the Court showed Meachum's property adjacent to that owned by Pierre Chouteau, Jr., and near that of William Clark. What is referred to in the documents as "Massey's Hotel" is at one end of a lot between 2nd and 3rd streets fronting North E Street, while Meachum's is at the other. From the survey, Massey's Hotel appears to overlap onto property claimed by Meachum.[84]

In 1840, Meachum sued again, this time charging that William Smith had taken his white cow with the missing right horn, and her red and white calf. But it is not as clear whether Meachum deliberately added to the numbers of the free population of color of antebellum St. Louis, especially in light of the fact that John Berry Meachum owned slaves himself, and several sued him for their freedom.[85]

In 1836, a slave woman named Judy sued Meachum for her freedom. Judy claimed Benjamin Duncan brought her west to Indiana from Kentucky. She said she worked for Duncan in Indiana for "about one month" and then returned to Kentucky briefly before being sold to Meachum in Missouri. Judy stated that Meachum permitted her to hire out her own time, for which she paid him $12 per month. Judy said that she hired her time in Galena, Illinois, with Meachum's knowledge and consent for about one month.[86]

Judy's former owner's son, Benjamin Duncan, was deposed, and stated that Judy had been owned by his father, also Benjamin Duncan, who sold her to James Newton about 1822 or 1823. Duncan described Judy as 30 or 35 years old and "bright yellow" in complexion. When asked whether he could attest to Judy actually being in Indiana, Duncan the younger stated that he could not; he said he had heard "reports or rumors" of Judy being in Indiana, but did not know for a certainty that she had been.[87]

Lewis, a man of color, was "admitted to testify" for Judy and told the Court Judy had been hired to Edmund Jennings of Indiana by Benjamin Duncan of Kentucky. Lewis recalled that Judy worked for Jennings in Indiana for about "four weeks," after which Duncan sold Judy to James Newton, who sold her to Berry Meachum. Based on evidence submitted in the depositions, the Court ruled that Judy was "entitled" to her freedom and damages of $1. Meachum immediately petitioned for a new trial, which was denied. Meachum then asked that his exceptions be appended to the Court's ruling, and they were.[88]

Part of Meachum's objection included his statement that because James Newton, the man who sold Judy to him, was white, and had pledged to "defend the said Meachum in the quiet and peaceable possession of said Judy," Lewis, a man of color, should not have been permitted to testify.[89] However, the Court found Lewis "competent" to testify and did not have discretionary authority to exclude competent testimony.[90]

Having been declared free, Judy sued Meachum for the freedom of her son, Green Berry Logan, based on the law that the status of offspring was based on the legal status of the mother. In this second suit, Judy stated that her son was born in Indiana "long after" she was entitled to her freedom.[91]

* * *

Religious inspiration sometimes resulted in the establishment of schools in St. Louis. In 1818, Baptist minister John Mason Peck co-founded (with James Welch) a church school for blacks, and the following year, a church school for whites.[92] Both schools instructed students in literacy as a means of facilitating instruction in the gospels.[93] In 1827, the Society of the Sacred Heart became the first private or public school in the city, when it opened a convent and began instruction programs specifically for girls. Sister Rose Philippine Duchesne and four nuns had arrived in St. Louis from New Orleans on the steamboat *Franklin* in 1818 to join the order.[94] Lessons in reading, writing, spelling, arithmetic, and religion were offered both to paid boarders and day students, who paid fees apparently calculated on a "sliding scale"; in fact, some students' parents paid in goods or supplies. The order's vocation emphasized outreach to the poor, and the convent established the first orphanage in the city and provided free instruction "in manual labor" to white orphans, who were also required to work at the convent. The convent also provided instruction for free black girls on Sundays, even though the institution owned black slaves. The School of the Sacred Heart was apparently both Catholic as well as catholic in its approach: although in the first years, most students were French-speakers, by 1840, the vast majority of students were English speakers, and by then, the school also enrolled Protestants. After its first year, the Sacred Heart School enrolled more than 100 girls in its various programs; by 1839, 200 of the city's 1,000 white students were enrolled at the Convent of the Sacred Heart. Secular, public schools were established somewhat later in 1838, and free public schools in 1847, the same year that Missouri officially made it illegal to teach blacks.[95]

In April 1839, the Sisters of St. Joseph expanded their Institute for the Deaf located at Carondelet to include courses in English and French for girls between the ages of six and 18.[96] Based on the success evidenced by increased enrollment and contributions, in 1845, the convent established a school in St. Louis for colored children. The curriculum for these free black girls included "French and ornamental needlework," and on weekends, slave girls were instructed in the Catholic catechism for purposes of Confirmation.[97] Although classes for black girls were well-received among blacks, increasing threats from whites forced the school administration to stop the classes within a year to keep from closing down entirely. Instruction in the catechism went on as usual.[98]

Journalists and newspapers were important to the construction of iconic ideas and images of the gateway to the west and to the frontier. They encouraged and recorded successive migrations west. In July 1808, the *Missouri Gazette and Louisiana Advertiser* (later *Louisiana Gazette*) became the first U.S. newspaper west of the Mississippi. Editor Joseph Charless, an Irish immigrant, arrived in the territory with William Clark, who, with his friend Meriwether Lewis, provided Charless financing to start the newspaper.

In its early days of publication, the newspaper masthead referred to St. Louis as "St. Louis, Louisiana." In addition to news of Indian activity, the paper reprinted articles from newspapers east of the Mississippi, including the *Boston Mirror* and *Virginia Patriot*. Typically, with good weather and uneventful travel, it took about five weeks for the eastern newspapers to arrive in St. Louis, although it could take up to three months. In the run-up to a decision about Missouri statehood and debates over whether Missouri would become a free or slave state, Charless' *Gazette* supported admission as a free state, while his competitor at the *Enquirer* took a firm pro-slavery stance.[99] Front page news announced when and where the local militia would muster (on occasion called upon to help find and return an errant slave), names of residents or locations where settlers might find lost horses, husbands who would not be responsible for the debts of straying wives, and sales of household articles, including slaves. The paper also provided prominent placement to advertisements seeking the return of runaway slaves and posted rewards.[100] In September of 1820, after years of criticism against him and his editorial policies, Charless sold the *Gazette* to James C. Cummins, and on March 20, 1822, the *Gazette* became the *Missouri Republican*.[101]

Despite the popularity of the newspapers, in the first decades of settlement, few among the city's population could read or write. A petition to build a school in the city was signed by nearly half of the signers with an "X." A variety of private elementary schools for whites were established in the late 1700s and early 1800s, and some of these classes were held in private homes. Private lending libraries eventually took hold, including one established by Auguste Chouteau, built around books he had inherited from Pierre Laclède. Boarding academies and colleges also opened, including St. Louis College, a Catholic institution organized by Bishop Louis DuBourge in 1818, and which also figured in slave freedom suits as one of the institutions that owned and was sued by slaves.[102]

Regardless of who brought the lawsuits, Missouri court records demonstrate a tendency toward litigiousness by early residents. Lawyers flocked to the new Territory of Missouri and 12 had already settled there during the first year after the Louisiana Purchase. Among the settlers in the Territory attempting to utilize the courts to obtain justice for their causes were black slaves, who, as has been mentioned, had somehow concluded that the arrival of Americans to the formerly Spanish and French territories meant their imminent, and collective, freedom. The handwriting was on the wall by the time free white settlers clamoring for statehood stood within sight of that goal: attorney Hamilton R. Gamble represented 13 of the 14 slaves who filed petitions for freedom (of the 163 total filed) in the court semester 1818–19, although in one case Gamble represented the slave's owner.[103]

By 1860, St. Louis was one of only five Southern cities with a population of more than 50,000. (The other cities were New Orleans, Louisiana; Baltimore, Maryland; Louisville, Kentucky; and Washington, D. C.) Poised on the Mississippi River, Missouri's location as the nation's dividing line between slave and free states made it a natural place for a decades-long struggle by black slaves for freedom in the courts. Black slaves experienced a growing awareness that free territory lay on the other side of the river and, if not permanent escape, at least the basis for suing for freedom based on prior residence in free territory. For some, the river itself became a symbol of freedom, while the rapidly growing city of St. Louis was an environment in which free identity had room to thrive.[104]

Chapter 2

The Color of Law

Commerce came first, then the law.

Once the trading post at St. Louis was firmly established, the writing of laws began. An examination of legal documents and writings provides a certain picture of life among people of color in early St. Louis and of how the establishment and evolution of laws in the region affected them, even though almost no legal papers were actually composed or crafted by people of color themselves. For example, activities described in the record as "crimes of anonymity" may point to barely discernible intentions of people of color over time as the French, Spanish, and finally the Americans reacted to the colored presence in the region with the creation of ever more restrictive laws. Such "anonymous" crimes included both unproved acts of resistance by slaves or situations in which slaves and free people might have collaborated to benefit them both.[1] But the laws seem written to precisely define people of color—black or Indian, slave or free—as different from whites, and not at all equal. As we shall see, the economic, political, and cultural relationship of the city to the west—perhaps especially as proximity to the advancing frontier affected perceptions, experiences, or legal definitions of freedom—played a significant role in the creation of those laws. However, it is first important to consider the origins of those laws.

The Spanish arrived in the Louisiana Territory in 1769, disseminating their cultural influence through their lawmaking, which included regulations regarding the "immigration" of slaves from French or English territories, curfews, "recreation" (for example, separate dances for people of color), and even "dress codes" to distinguish colored women from Creoles.[2] A transient population of frontiersmen, boatmen, and traders included free blacks and mixed race Indians, who plied the river, foraged and traded for furs in the western frontier, and frequented French taverns on the river.[3]

Spain prohibited the enslavement of Indians in the territory, and under their administration, a black slave had the legal right to buy her or his freedom by paying a price set by the slave owner and the court.[4] With the evolution of slavery as a racial category, it is likely that increasing numbers of slaves were designated descendants of Africans, or even "mulatto" (descendants of Africans and whites) to block slaves filing suits for freedom based on a claim of Indian blood and thus free status under Spanish law.[5] The French *Code Noir* had prohibited the separate sale of members of a slave family, a nicety the Spanish did not recognize.[6] Under the Spanish, African slaves benefited from the right to own property, and, perhaps the logical next step, the right to buy themselves free.[7] And it was the Spanish who permitted slaves to sue for their freedom if they thought their owners had mistreated them.

In 1824, this law was incorporated into the laws of the State of Missouri, permitting "any person held in slavery to petition the circuit court." Like the earlier law of 1804, the Missouri state law also provided for the assignment of legal counsel and adequate time for the slave suing for freedom to meet with counsel. The form of the suit also continued to be "trespass, assault and battery, and false imprisonment" with the petitioner stating that at the time this "assault" occurred, she or he had been and still was a free person.[8]

The arrival of the Americans heralded the implementation of the laws of the United States, which would thereafter prevail. This included the Northwest Ordinance of 1787, which set forth in Article VI, that slavery would be prohibited in the territory, although, in keeping with the peculiar ironies or seeming contradictions of the law, the Ordinance also provided that fugitive slaves would be "reclaimed and conveyed" to their owners.[9] Missouri's proximity to the Northwest Territory certainly influenced laws whose primary concern was to protect slave owners' property in slaves. For example, in 1785, Marie Thérèse Chouteau, companion of the city's founder, sued for financial compensation when her slave, Baptiste, was killed after joining a search to capture a group of runaway Indian slaves. Chouteau's son-in-law, Joseph Marie Papin, had organized the search, and Chouteau felt he should be held accountable for "act[ing] inconsiderately … failing to recognize that he was risking the slave's life." The territorial governor (of what was then Upper Louisiana) found otherwise, however, and concluded the owner of the runaway slaves should bear the burden of repaying Madame Chouteau for her loss of property. The record fails to indicate whether Baptiste had a "wife" or children, and if so, who might recompense them for their loss. A surgeon's certificate merely stated that a "dead negro" had been found "on the ground in front of the door" of the Widow Chouteau's barn. He had been shot in the chest. The man, Madame Chouteau's slave Baptiste, was not identified either by name or physical description.[10]

The enterprise in which Baptiste lost his life—helping to locate and bring a runaway slave back to his owner (a "right" guaranteed by the afore-mentioned Northwest Ordinance—was part of the strategy for policing slaves. Maintaining the proper order for slaves' behavior was part of pro-tecting monetary investments in slaves, even if this fact was sometimes artfully concealed within the vocabulary of the debate.

> Sir
> The Committee of the Town of St. Lewis [sic] at the Special Request of the Inhab-itants have the honor to observe that unruly and alarmed at the conduct of their Slaves, this Some time past; they Believe to embrace the views of Government, which are without Doubt to maintain ... peaceable in possession of their property, and to preserve the New Territory of the United States from the horrours [sic] which different American colonies have lately experienced. By giving you notice that there exist amongst the Blacks a fermentation which may Become dangerous and which seems to be increased by the reports spread by some whites, that they will be free before long—
> In all Countries where Slavery exists, there is a Code that establishes in a positively [sic] manner the Rights of the Masters, and the Duties of slaves. There is also a ... policy, which prevents their Nocturnal Assemblies, that Subject to their Labour [sic], provides for their Subsistence, and prevents as much as possible their Communication with the whites.
> In the Name of the People, we Solicit your honor to take these objects in consid-eration....
> Under the old French Government and Spanish, the Black Code was our Guide. Be so kind Sir as to have it put in force, Keep the Slaves in their Duty according to their Class; in the Respect they owe generally to all whites, and more especially their masters; put them again under the Subordination which they where [sic] heretofore, and by this Ensure the Tranquility of a people who depends [sic] entirely on your vigilency [sic]
> Amos Stoddard[11]

A second letter written to Auguste Chouteau, then president of the Committee, considering how slaves might be controlled in St. Louis, expressed a similar sentiment.

> St. Louis 6 Aug.t. [sic] 1804
> Sir, ... It would give me great pleasure if the Committee would suggest such rules and regulations as appear necessary to restrain the licentiousness of Slaves, and to keep them more steadily to their duty; and you may rest assured that I will add my sanction to whatever may contribute to the peace and security of the respectable town of St. Louis. This assistance of the Committee would be the more acceptable to me, as I am unacquainted with the usual policy adopted in Slave Countries. Those whites, who have propagated among the slaves the hope of a speedy emancipation, could not have done themselves, their neighbors, or the public, a greater injury.[12]

Despite the best efforts to maintain a stern and objective legal code to define slaves' lives and behavior, the strict letter of the law was complicated by the human connections between slaves and slave owners. For example, when Madame Chouteau died in 1814, she freed her slave Theresa, whom she described as an "Indian," and who had cared for Chouteau in her last days; St. Louisans remembered the women's relationship and "considered the two women a formidable combination."[13] Although Indian slavery had long been illegal, Theresa had been a gift from Pierre Laclede when she was a teenager, and apparently there were few in the city willing to challenge Madame Chouteau.[14] Jacques Clamorgan died in 1814, too, having freed his four children by three different black slave women in 1809.[15] While the record proves there were slave owners whose emotional connection inspired them to free their slaves, or at least to ameliorate their condition as chattel, probably more often, that was not the case. In September 1818, Thomas Hempstead sold slaves Hagga and Stephen for $1,250, at which point Hagga and Stephen were taken out of state; in 1819, slaves George and Lucy expressed a desire or expectation of freedom to Hempstead and in response he sold them south.[16] In April of 1819, when William Clark prepared to sell his slave Scipio south, Scipio killed himself by shooting himself in the head.[17] These and many other events occurred as debates over whether Missouri should enter the Union as a slave or free state, and thus expand slavery westward, intensified.

Despite the relatively small numbers, slave laws also provided the context of behavior for all people of African descent. In fact, the laws addressed not only the required behavior for slaves, but also what was acceptable, legal behavior for all people of color, slave or free. The laws were administered by the Court of Common Pleas, which oversaw resolution of civil cases, and justices of the peace appointed to the general quarter session to rule on criminal cases, consider public expenditures and taxes. There was also provision for a probate court.[18] As we shall see, both slaves and free people of color figured in cases before the courts, as property or as free people seeking to protect their rights to property.

The French *Code Noir* (Black Code) remained the inspiration and foundation of slave law in St. Louis. In 1804, on the heels of rumors of black slave insurrection in the town, the territorial government at St. Louis affirmed its reliance upon the Black Code as the founding principle for the absolute autonomy and discretion of "masters" to govern slaves. The rumor purportedly set in motion by some whites that the slaves would soon be free because of the arrival of the Americans was considered by the slave holding elite to have perhaps done those whites and "the public, a great injury." Therefore, "the rights of the masters and the duties of the slaves" was reiterated. Among the clauses emphasized was prohibition of "noctural assemblies," requirement of their (slaves') labor, provision of "subsistence," and "preven[tion] as much as possible [slaves'] communication with the whites."[19]

In 1821, after Missouri entered the Union as a slave state, its voters approved a constitution that authorized its general assembly to bar free blacks and mulattoes from entering the state, a clause that caused approval of the constitution to stall in Congress.[20] After months of debate, the constitution was finally approved after the Missouri Legislature promised never to invoke that section of its constitution.[21]

Slaves, like any other property or livestock, could be seized and sold to pay a debt. Thus, in 1831, Sheriff John Walker served a writ on the wife of John Jones in the presence of a witness to "attach the lands, tenements, goods, chattels, monies, rights, credits or effects" to pay what he owed John Carman. While he was there, Sheriff Walker also took from Mrs. Jones' possession "three Negro children ... Mary Ann, Thaddeus and John."[22]

As property, slaves represented security for their owners and were offered as such in a variety of ways. In 1827, Abner and Sarah Wood provided their son, William, with his "inheritance" while they were still alive in the hopes that William would support them in their old age. William received

> one cart and oxen, all his present farming utensils, one mare and yearling colt, three cows, two yearling steers, one calf, one year old heifer, six hogs, one gun and apparatus, one large trunk, one bed and bed covering, all title and interest in and to a certain Negro girl named Catharine and a Negro man named Daniel, and also one hundred bushels of corn.[23]

Even so, slaves had legal right to file petitions based on what was referred to as "false imprisonment," consult legal counsel, and rely on the court's protection against being removed from the court's jurisdiction. Thus, Missouri laws on race and slavery were a hodgepodge of cultural legacies, although the consequences of these laws could not have been anticipated, especially in the constantly shifting environment of a frontier settlement.

Ultimately, slave law reinforced the rights, power, and authority of slave owners and precisely defined the duties of slaves in a way that rendered the power of slave owners absolute. Even so, sufficient legal loopholes permitted hundreds of slaves to challenge the institution of slavery in Missouri courts. Slave law also directly contributed to evolving definitions of race, especially distinctions as to who was and who was not considered "white" or "black." Such definitions refined the parameters of enslavement while *simultaneously* delineating specific constructions of "whiteness" and "blackness." Indians and individuals of "mixed race" ancestry also figured in slave law; although, under the law, neither Indians nor whites could be held as slaves, Indians continued to be enslaved in the early antebellum period and a number of freedom suits were brought by slaves who claimed freedom based on their Indian or white blood.

The French *Code Noir* (Black Code) that provided the basic foundation of slave law in the region was a tangle of religious and legal notions meant to hobble black efforts at independent thought and action. For example, as we have seen, the *Code* required Catholic baptism of slaves and there is evidence that individual slave owners acceded to that requirement. In addition, the record also provides evidence of early adherence to this statute by the Church:

> October 20, 1767
> I the undersigned missionary priest ... baptized with all the prescribed ceremonies for adults six slaves. First, Pierre, black, age about thirteen years, belonging to Mr. Pierre-Francois de Volsey Lieutenant of a detached company of the French marine, resident of the Illinois at St. Louis. His godfather was Mr. Louis de St. Ange commandant of the Illinois Country and godmother Dame Elisabeth de Villiers, wife of Volsey, who signed with me.
> S.L. Meurin[24]

The same priest, S. L. Meurin, apparently made regular and frequent circuits of the territory during which he baptized numerous slaves, including the son of free black landowner Jeanette Forchet and her husband Gregoire (see chapter 1).[25]

Despite at least the suggestion of inclusion of blacks (including slaves) within the town social fabric according to religious requirement, the civil status of children of slave women and free men was dependent on the race or color of the father. And as we shall see, the leeway given to free *black* men provided a potent impact on black male identity and ideas of masculinity. For example, a free black man might claim his wife and children through marriage and in so doing free them as well, *or* he had the power to maintain them all as slaves, straddle the line separating the races, and create a precarious economic bridge for himself alone built on the backs of his wife and children. Thus, black men shared a narrow space for the construction of economic autonomy with white men of the era.[26]

For people of color, the next best thing to owning oneself might be to own or acquire property. A significant minority of Missouri slaves earned enough money or property through their labors eventually to purchase their own freedom. It was not a widespread practice, but some slave owners "hired out" slaves to farmers, explorers, or commercial enterprises and allowed the slave hired out to keep a small percentage of what she or he earned. But what did the laws say about this? In fact, the *Code Noir* went on at some length about the right of slaves to own or acquire property. Slaves' ability to earn *extra* money or goods meant they would have to work at a time when their owners either didn't require their labor or gave their consent. (It also meant that the slave's already limited leisure time would be further constrained; however, the possibility of earning enough money to buy one's freedom, or the freedom of a spouse, children, or parents, made the sacrifice more than worthwhile.) The letter of the *Code* further limited when such *spare* time might be because it declared that no one, slave or free, was permitted to work on "Sundays and holy days." In addition, explicit permission from an owner was required for a slave to sell anything to anybody—even plants cultivated for food that slaves produced in gardens set aside for that purpose, since technically, everything a slave produced on land owned by an owner belonged to the owner.[27] Obviously, hiring out slaves was inspired by and had the potential to profit the slave owner, but because of the parallel potential to contribute to slaves' sense of autonomy or to make it possible for slaves to cross the boundary between slavery and freedom, questions about the practice of "hiring out" slaves affected the creation of laws.

In 1827, a St. Louis Grand Jury issued a statement to certain slave owners based on its consideration of the situation of slaves hiring themselves out *and receiving wages*, which it concluded to be a widespread practice.[28] The Grand Jurors noted that the slaves hiring out their own time paid a prescribed sum to a person in town selected by their owner, but that the slaves were otherwise pretty much on their own, a situation the Grand Jurors found created a "public nuisance" because they believed more slaves made money "by stealing or gambling than by honest labour [*sic*]."[29] (As we'll see below, the St. Louis Criminal Court meticulously tracked the activities of people of color, slave or free, who might have engaged in activities either clearly against the law or tinged with any hint of ambiguity.)

Again in 1829, the Grand Jury expressed alarm that the practice of slaves hiring themselves out had increased with a "pernicious" effect on the community, as well as endangering the "moral condition" of slaves.[30] Specific examples of such endangerment were listed by name in the Grand Jury's finding; slaves and their owners were cited by name.[31] Although the Grand Jury noted its "general disinclination to interfere in the private concerns of others," it urged slave owners to rein in "these half-emancipated slaves."[32] It is possible that certain slave owners, understanding the proximity of free lands in the west and north might entice slaves to free territory, decided in favor of extending a longer rein of almost freedom rather than impose stricter controls on slave and free black activities.[33] However, the Grand Jury deliberations likely led to an 1840 ordinance prohibiting further entrance of free blacks to the State of Missouri and requiring free blacks who were already residents as of 1840, to register for a license indicating their legal permission to remain.[34]

To the fear of slaves behaving like free people was added the specter of the possibility that slaves might align their interests with free blacks, or vice versa. In fact, an 1834 Grand Jury addressed this specific concern when it found that free blacks were the "cause of disorders, insubordination and crime among the slave population" and that free black interactions with slaves made slaves difficult to control.[35] The Grand Jurors suggested statutes prohibiting *the entrance of free blacks into the state* and that slave owners "control their slaves and ... not treat them as free persons." We shall see the difficulty, and in some cases the impossibility, of doing this for slave owners who might have had deep emotional commitments to their slaves and which, on occasion, led them to free those slaves. The members of this 1834 Grand Jury also reminded slave owners to act without cruelty and to keep slaves out of saloons.[36]

From the 1830s through the Civil War, numerous blacks and whites were charged in St. Louis Criminal Court with a variety of offenses involving "stealing" or "enticing" slaves or transporting free blacks into the state against the statute.[37] For example, in 1846, a free woman of color named Polly was acquitted of the charge of "abducting slaves"; James Atkinson (also Atkins or Adkins) was sentenced to two years in the penitentiary for "enticing a slave away from owner"; John Johnson was sentenced to two years in the penitentiary for "decoying a slave" from its owner; and Eliza Sly was found guilty and sentenced to five years in the penitentiary for "enticing a slave out of state."[38]

Punishment of slaves was meant to fit the crime. Because of the sanctity of property to slave owners, a slave who stole herself or himself committed one of the most egregious crimes. A slave who ran away and stayed for a full month was branded with the French king's symbol the *fleur de lis*; if the same slave ran away and was captured a second time, he was "hamstrung" and branded a second time with the *fleur de lis*. But finding runaways was often difficult and a schedule for a formal patrol to monitor slave movements was organized as early as 1764.[39] Slave owners often avoided branding a slave because it made the slave less saleable by drawing attention to the fact that she or he was a discipline problem.[40] But punishments of slaves were often grotesque—hacking off ears or limbs, branding, and beating, and owners often ordered slaves to impose the punishments on other slaves. To discourage free blacks from helping slaves who ran away, the *Code Noir* prescribed fines or enslavement of free blacks to reimburse an aggrieved slave owner the amount of the fine. But persistent proof of connections between slaves and free blacks suggests a commonality of slave and free black perceptions of and actions to support black freedom.[41]

What slaves discussed among themselves could only be wondered at, but the assumption by whites was that slaves who congregated together meant whites no good. The *Code* prescribed the death penalty for slaves who flouted the law prohibiting assemblies.[42] Likewise, the *Code* required putting to death a slave who hit his owner or his owner's spouse or child and drew blood, or for that matter, a slave who "abused" *any* free person.[43] (It is not clear from the record, however, whether this law also applied to a slave striking a free *black* person.) A runaway slave caught after a third attempt to run away was also to be put to death.[44] When the Spanish arrived in the 1760s, they inserted a provision that slaves found guilty of insurrection be put to death.[45] The Americans likewise imposed a punishment of death on anyone found guilty of insurrection, conspiracy to commit insurrection, slaves' administering of medicines, selling a free person into slavery, or stealing a slave.[46] Arson was punishable by death, and in 1805, Pierre Chouteau wrote a letter to an acquaintance describing the destruction of significant property because of a fire set by a slave woman he owned; Chouteau's letter infers, although does not clearly state, that the woman, whose name he did not mention, was executed for the crime.[47] In 1790, the Americans mandated death by hanging and permitted a judge's authorization of dissection of slaves executed for murder.[48]

Although it was rare for whites to be arrested, tried, found guilty, and punished for crimes against blacks, slave or free, regardless of the circumstances, in November 1813, Joseph Leblond was arrested after a free black woman named Sylvia was found dead in his St. Louis home.[49] Sylvia had died of gangrene caused when Leblond chained her in his house, but the court set his punishment at a fine of $500 and two months in jail. In 1854, a slave named John Anderson was convicted of killing a white prostitute named Rebecca Ann Hewett and sentenced to castration, the punishment mandated when a black man raped a white woman. Perhaps the fact that Anderson had paid Hewett 50 cents for her services was extenuating circumstance enough, or perhaps it was the fact that some of St.

Louis' finest protested, but the Missouri Supreme Court extended executive clemency.[50]

Missouri state law regarding race and slavery also echoed significant elements of the French Code Noir, which defined slaves as property. In some ways subtle and not so subtle, law and religion were interwoven to create a seamless perception and common law where slaves were concerned. St. Louis was above all a Catholic place—the *Code Noir*, influenced by Catholic doctrine and sentiment, was a case in point, but it should be clear that slavery was the context within which Catholicism flourished, and not the other way around. The distinction between slave and free was so important, even from the earliest days, that anyone discovered to have "stolen" or sold a free person as a slave, "knowing the said person so sold to be free," was sentenced to death "without benefit of clergy." And it was equally important to know who was, and who was not, "black."[51] Already by 1804, the law defined "mulatto" as any person with one black grandparent, even if the other three grandparents were white.[52] The law attempted to further widen the gap dividing people of color by making associating with slaves (a population that, in time, would be predominantly "black") by whites, free negroes, or mulattoes punishable by a cash fine or "twenty lashes well laid on his or her bare back."[53]

Despite the suggestion of nuance or complexity in the laws, this often vanished in an instant where race seemed the primary or governing consideration. The following is a case in point. In 1841, a spectacular crime committed by three free black men and a slave resulted in the murder of two white men and a widely advertised and witnessed execution of the blacks. The crime was directly tied to geography, the critical role of the Mississippi River in commerce and communication between east and west, the employment of blacks in work along and on the river, and the ease with which slaves and free blacks in the region struck up friendships or alliances.

The men had robbed a bank, and when they were discovered during the course of the robbery by two white bank employees, the men killed the employees and burned the bank down to destroy evidence of their crimes. Edward Ennis, a free black barber, revealed the names of the men involved in response to a reward posted for $5,000. Free men of color named Charles Brown, Amos Alfred Warrick, and James Seward, and a slave named Madison were quickly rounded up from as far away as Ohio, and jailed in St. Louis. Some of the most well-known and experienced lawyers in St. Louis represented them, including Hamilton Gamble and John Darby, along with Joseph Spalding and Wilson Primm. Found guilty by an all-white jury, the men were sentenced to death by hanging. Thousands witnessed the

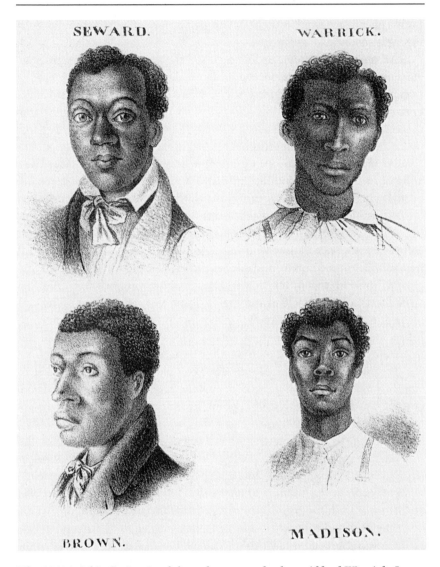

SEWARD.

WARRICK.

BROWN.

MADISON.

The 1841 trial in St. Louis of three free men of color—Alfred Warrick, James Seward, and Charles Brown—and a slave named Madison Henderson demonstrated how people of color interacted despite free or slave status.

hanging on July 9, 1841, and many arrived at the execution on Duncan's Island aboard the steamboat *Eagle*, which charged $1.50 for the round-trip execution excursion. The heads of the executed men were displayed in the window of a St. Louis pharmacy, where they remained a curiosity for passersby and a warning to slaves and all people of color.[54]

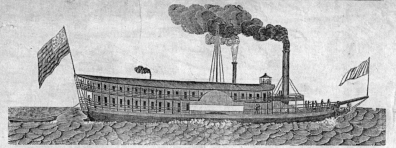

1841

FOR SAINT LOUIS!

The Regular Steam Packet
EAGLE!

THE undersigned, having chartered the above Steam-boat, for the purpose of accommodating all the citizens of **ALTON**, and the vicinity, who may wish to see the

Four Negroes Executed,

At St. Louis, on *FRIDAY NEXT*, would inform the public that the Boat will leave this place at **SEVEN** o'clock, A. M., and St. Louis at about **FOUR**, P. M., so as to reach home the same evening.

The Boat will be repaired and fitted up for the occasion; and every attention will be paid to the comfort of Passengers.

FARE FOR THE TRIP TO ST. LOUIS & BACK
ONLY $1 50 !!!

The Negroes are to be hung on the point of *Duncan's Island*, just below St. Louis. The Boat will drop alongside, so that **ALL CAN SEE WITHOUT DIFFICULTY.**

For Passage, apply to

W. A. Wentworth,
P. M. Pinckard.

ALTON, JULY 7, 1841

The steamship *Eagle* provided transportation to the executions of Madison Henderson, Alfred Warrick, James Seward, and Charles Brown on July 9, 1841.

Such acts of shocking violence—met with furious retribution—were blessedly rare, and Missouri law continued to permit slaves to sue for their freedom. The foundation upon which slave petitions for freedom ultimately rested, however, was an 1807 law titled simply "Freedom." The purpose of this act was to "enable persons held in slavery to sue for their freedom." Under this law, the court described the action of holding the slave who brought suit as "assault and battery and false imprisonment." This was a legal, rather than a factual description, although on occasion, it was both.[55]

The law had early on anticipated possibility of the growth of a free black population in Missouri and made efforts to slow, if not halt that development. In the wake of Missouri statehood, voters had ratified a constitution that barred free blacks and mulattoes from entering the state.[56] A case brought against free blacks (and blacks who may have had one Indian parent) the year before the ratification illustrates the level of surveillance of the activities of free blacks. The case apparently began when white men were observed socializing with free blacks and slaves at a house in St. Louis "kept by a slave named John Jordan," who did not appear to have permission from an owner to be at large or to hire himself out. The white men were identified as Phineas Bartlett and Dennis Doland, Jr., and Sr. The free blacks were Charlotte, John Faljoux, Dinah, and two women described as "half" or "part" Indian, Angelique and Pelage. The petition noted that neither of the Dolans seemed to be "employed in any honest calling." A slave named Ireland also frequented the house and hired himself out without written permission from his owner, "Mrs. Benton." The Court ordered the individuals named in the petition "apprehended" to answer charges of frequenting a "disorderly house."[57] The summons described the Dolans as suspected of "associating with slaves at an unlawfull [sic] meeting" and "breaches of the peace" for being with "disorderly persons." The Sheriff was ordered to jail them until the next term of court.[58] (A petition filed in October 1824, charged Dennis Dolan, Jr., with the assault of Dennis Dolan, Sr., at the "home of a slave."[59])

Although religion and law occasionally conspired to "protect" certain configurations of "family" among free or slave blacks, neither was necessarily reliable in that respect. In 1829, Nicholas Jones, a free man of color from Prince George County, Maryland, filed suit in St. Louis Circuit Court charging he'd been seized and held against his will. Jones did not claim that he had never been a slave, only that his former owner, Truman Tyler, had manumitted him many years before he arrived in Missouri.[60] Jones' whereabouts and activities were traced through a series of court depositions. The first was by William Henry Peace, who swore he'd thrown a shell and hit the 12-year-old Nicholas Jones on the ear due to a dispute between them in about 1816 or 1817.[61] Richard Jones swore that in 1821, he had provided $5 to a free man of color named Aaron Jones to "defray expenses" for his 14- or 15-year-old son Nicholas, who worked as a laborer on a ship running between Annapolis and New Orleans; Richard Jones stated in his deposition that he understood Nicholas Jones "was entitled to his freedom."[62] Grace Tyler swore in her deposition that in about 1806, Truman Tyler handed over a three-month-old infant named Nicholas to his father, a free man of color, after the infant's mother, who had been Tyler's slave, died. Tyler stated that she did not know if the baby had been manumitted, but knew that once the baby had been turned over to his father, he had not ever been in Truman Tyler's possession again.[63]

In 1832, a "free negro man" named Elijah Chester was placed in the custody of the sheriff in St. Louis for being in violation of the 1825 law prohibiting black settlement in Missouri. Chester was sentenced to receive ten lashes on "his bare back" and thereafter to immediately leave the state.[64] On the same day, Solomon James was sentenced to ten lashes on his bare back for the identical offense of being in the state "contrary to the act concerning negroes and mullatoes."[65]

By 1843, growing sentiment in the country against slavery precipitated publication of a prospectus for *The African, An Anti-Abolition Monthly* in St. Louis. The prospectus declared opposition to anti-slavery activities, targeted "the errors of Abolitionism" by "exhibiting truth," and proposed the publication of articles important to the health and vigor of the slave states.[66]

In 1845 and 1847, new laws illustrated the hardening of Missouri's attitudes toward the presence of free blacks in the state by prohibiting free blacks and mulattoes from creating independent churches or schools. The laws specifically prohibited anyone from teaching "negroes or mulattoes" to read or write. In addition, "negroes" and "mulattoes" were forbidden to gather in assemblies for religious purposes unless a "sheriff, constable, marshal, police officer, or justice of the peace" was present. Such meetings were to be considered "unlawful" and were to be suppressed.

1. No persons shall keep or teach any school for the instruction of negroes or mulattoes, in reading or writing in this State.

2. No meeting or assemblage of negroes or mulattoes, for the purpose of religious worship, or preaching, shall be held or permitted where the services are performed or conducted by negroes or mulattoes,

SAINT LOUIS, MO., SEPT. 16TH, 1843.

DEAR SIR—

    Accompanying this, is a prospectus of a periodical, for which I desire you to act as agent in your county. It certainly is important that the doctrines of the abolitionists should be opposed particularly and strongly. The African will do it.

    It is true, I have no personal acquaintance with you, on which to found my hope of your exertions, to obtain subscribers for this monthly; yet, I believe, your interest in the institutions of the slave states, is a sufficient guarantee that you'll do all in your power. I have thought, your official station, leading to much intercourse with the citizens of your county, will enable you to see them all with the loss of very little time. Your deputies also can assist.

    To pay yourself for all trouble and expense, to which this may lead you, retain, of the amount you receive, a satisfactory percentage; and forward the balance to me. In sending the names of subscribers, be careful in giving the post-office and county.

    Your best endeavors in this matter, will confer a special favor on your ob't. servt.,

J. W. HEDENBERG.

P. S.   Tear this letter from the prospectus before circulating it.

PROSPECTUS

OF

THE AFRICAN,

AN

ANTI-ABOLITION MONTHLY,

PUBLISHED BY J. W. HEDENBERG.

The African will withstand the errors of Abolitionism. These are spreading themselves farther than many suppose. The Abolitionists have a great number of periodicals, by which they promulgate their pernicious doctrines, and no set of teachers, the inculcators of no dogmas, are more partisan, enthusiastic, and disregardless of consequences than these Abolitionists.

This pamphlet, in opposing these errors,—this blind enthusiasm, and this lawlessness, will be mild, plain, pointed and uncompromising. It will compound with no system which it esteems erroneous; but will exhibit truth, however bitter and piercing it may be to abolitionists.

One great inducement for persons to subscribe for this periodical, is, that it will contain articles written particularly for it, by planters and other gentlemen of the highest talent and standing. These, being in the slave states, have every possible opportunity of studying the institution of slavery in all its ramifications; and will treat it in the most intelligent and philosophical manner.

It will advocate principles just such as every slaveholder should approve with all his heart, and sustain with all his influence. His interest—his true interest—is connected with, and will be strenuously maintained by it. He should then most certainly give it his earnest support.

The first number has been issued; and the second will be, soon. It is printed monthly in St. Louis, Mo.; and contains thirty-two closely printed octavo pages. The price is $2., per annum, paid in advance. If gentlemen will form themselves into clubs, THREE copies will be sent for $5.; SEVEN copies, for $10. This is no more than the price of another pamphlet published in St. Louis; and which, at the same time, only contains about half as much matter as The African. Though now cheap enough, it will be made cheaper; for as its subscription list increases, it will be increased in size, and improved in appearance; and without any increase in its price!

SUBSCRIBERS | ADDRESSES.

In 1843, a prospectus circulated for an anti-abolitionist periodical to be published in St. Louis reflected increasing concerns over opposition to the westward extension of slavery and slave resistance to slavery.

unless some sheriff, constable, marshal, police officer, or justice of the peace, shall be present during all the time of such meeting or assemblage, in order to prevent all seditious speeches, and disorderly and unlawful conduct of every kind.

3. All meetings of negroes or mulattoes, for the purposes mentioned ... shall be considered unlawful assemblages, and shall be suppressed by sheriffs, constables, and other public officers.[67]

By 1847, free persons of color were prohibited from emigrating to Missouri for any reason whatever at the risk of a prison sentence of no less than ten years. However, the entry or "return" of slaves to the state was another matter. As late as 1860, with the prospect of Civil War imminent, St. Louisan Peter Camden lamented the loss of his slaves, Fayette and Madison, whom he strongly suspected had run away to Chicago, Illinois, where they were prospering as a drayman and a clerk in a carpet store. Camden went so far as to travel to Chicago to try to convince them to return to St. Louis to be with "their father, mother and other relatives and friends." He wrote to his friend Dr. George Case from Chicago that

> notwithstanding their bad conduct in running away, and avoiding me when I sought them—I am willing to sell them their time and give them free papers, if they will return here and behave in such manner as not to prejudice others and cause dissatisfaction amongst the colored servants here. Or, if they prefer staying in Chicago, I will give them free papers upon their paying a reasonable, fair price for the same.... I am determined to take some final steps ... for I feel that I am remiss and have come short of my duties ... in suffering their cases to remain so long quiet.[68]

Despite increasing restrictions, it was still not impossible for a slave to purchase herself free, as was the case of "Lizzie" Keckley, who worked as a seamstress until she had earned enough to buy freedom for both herself and her son.

> ... for and in consideration of twelve hundred dollars, ... I hereby emancipate my Negro woman, Lizzie and her son Georg—the said Lizzie is known in St. Louis, as the wife of James, ... by trade a dressmaker, and called.... *Garland's Lizzi*—the said boy George ... is about Sixteen years of age, and is almost white, and called ... *Garland's George.*
>
> Ann P. Garland[69]

As a free person, Elizabeth Keckley later moved to Washington, D.C., became dressmaker to Mary Todd Lincoln, and wrote her memoir. And as a free person, Keckley's son, George, joined the Union Army as "white," and was killed in the Civil War.

Under the laws of the state of Missouri, Indians and whites could not be held as slaves. Thus, it should not be surprising that slaves occasionally sued for freedom based on claims to be white or Indian, which meant they

Know all men by these presents, that I, Anne P. Garland
of the County and City of St. Louis, State of Missouri, for and
in Consideration of the sum of twelve hundred dollars, to me
in hand paid this day in cash, hereby emancipate my
negro woman Lizzie and her son George — the said
Lizzie is known in St. Louis, as the wife of James, who
is called James Keckelly, is of light complexion, about
thirty seven years of age, by trade a dress-maker, and
Called by those who know her, Garland's Lizzie — the
said boy George, is the only child of Lizzie, is about
sixteen years of age, and is almost white, and called
by those who know him, Garland's George.

Witness my hand and seal, this 13th day of
November A.D. 1855.

Witness   Anne P. Garland   {Seal}
John Wickham,
Willi L Williams

In County St. Louis Circuit Court October Term 1855

November 18th 1855
State of Missouri }
County of St. Louis } ss Be it Remembered that
on this fifteenth day of November Eighteen
hundred and fifty five In Open Court came
John Wickham & Willi L Williams the two subscribing
witnesses examined under Oath to that effect
Proved the execution and Acknowledgment
of said deed by Anne P Garland to Lizzie and
her son George, which said Proof of Acknow
-ledgment is entered on the record of the

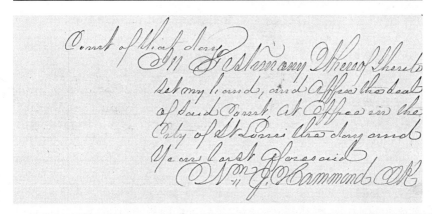

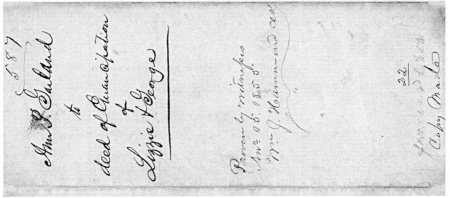

Opposite and above: **Elizabeth Keckley and her son, George, were set free in an era of increasing anxiety over slavery and restrictions on free people of color. Elizabeth Keckley later became dressmaker to Mary Todd Lincoln and her son, George, died during the Civil War fighting in the Union Army.**

were held as slaves illegally. In one such case, a professional slave trader or "negro dealer" played a significant role.

In 1844, a woman named Martha Drusella filed a petition for freedom in St. Louis Circuit Court claiming she was "so near white, she had not got one fourth of negro blood in her veins" and therefore could not legally be kept as a slave. Drusella stated she'd been born free in Alabama to a free woman named Malinda, and had been apprenticed from about the age of one year to a man named John Cotton. When Drusella was 11 years old, Cotton moved in with one of his married daughters, and, shortly after that, he died.

After Cotton's death, his son-in-law (Jefferson Isobel) "transferred" Drusella to his brother, William Isobel. William Isobel took Drusella to St.

Louis, where he either placed her in the custody of or sold her outright to Richmond J. Curle, a man well-known in town as an agent for buying and selling slaves, in order to sell her. Drusella told the Court the Isobel brothers took her out of state expressly to sell her because they "would not dare to attempt to sell her in Alabama or Arkansas, where the fact of her being born free is well known." The urgency of Drusella's plea increased because she believed Curle meant to sell her south out of the jurisdiction of the St. Louis court.[70]

In an effort to keep Drusella in town long enough to get to the bottom of the story, Judge John Krum ordered writs of *habeas corpus* served on Richmond J. Curle and William Isobel. The orders demanded they produce Martha Drusella in the Judge's office at No. 49 Pine Street in St. Louis on Monday, November 4, 1844, by 9 a.m. Sheriff William Milburn served the writs on the parties. Curle and Isobel were also ordered to produce the certificate of "indenture of apprenticeship" of Drusella to (Thomas) Jefferson Isobel. Curle and Isobel stalled by filing a flurry of counter petitions and writs of their own, including a series of motions to dismiss the case, causing consistent delays.

In November 1846, Curle petitioned the court for another delay because William Isobel, a witness so crucial to the case Curle feared proceeding without Isobel present to testify, was traveling in Cuba. Curle asked that the case be delayed until the next term of court. In the meantime, witnesses on both sides were deposed under oath. A man identified as James Little stated in his deposition that he had first seen Drusella "with other negroes" in the custody of William Isobel. Little's memory might have been so sharp about the matter because he'd had a particular interest in Martha Drusella. He said he asked Isobel if he could buy Drusella, but Isobel told him she was not for sale.

A couple of weeks later, Little said Isobel approached him and asked him how much he would give for Drusella, probably because Little had purchased a slave from Isobel in the past. Isobel told Little he'd purchased Drusella from his brother and had a bill of sale to prove it. He suggested a purchase price for Drusella of $400 or $450. Little said he'd countered by saying he had heard that Drusella was free, that she'd been born free. Then, according to Little, anyway, Isobel admitted Drusella was still under an indenture for two or three years, but he was willing to sell the time remaining on her indenture for $150. Little said he went away to think about it. When he was asked to describe Martha Drusella for the record, Little said he thought she was probably about 16 years old, and he said that she was "a bright mulatto,—nearly white." When asked about his relationship with Curle, Little said Curle's "occupation is that of General Agent, for selling and leasing property, as well as the buying and selling of negroes."

After the case was filed, Little continued to ask Richmond Curle about Drusella, who told Little he was still willing to sell her.

Martha Drusella was awarded her freedom by the court.

* * *

The 1853 case of Thornton Kinney is equally intriguing. Kinney claimed he had been born free in Virginia to a free Indian mother. Well-educated and well-traveled, Kinney testified he'd apprenticed to a "tanner and shoemaker," obtained his certification of freedom at the age of 21, left Virginia for the West, where he worked a number of years on steamboats, and then lived in Monrovia, Liberia, on the African continent for about five years. When he returned to the United States, Kinney "resumed his business on Boats, as Steward, Cook, and other reputable employments" for a while before being incarcerated by James Gavin, a defendant in this case identified as the "agent" of John Hatcher. The second defendant, Charles Bridges, was also identified as an "agent" of Hatcher.[71]

Thornton Kinney stated that he was about 40 years old when he brought suit for his freedom in St. Louis court. Kinney claimed his free papers were "so worn out" that about 1831 or 1832, while traveling in Liberia, he "threw them away" because he assumed he would remain on the "Continent of Africa." He claimed his acquaintanceship with the Reverend Robert Finney of the American Colonization Society prompted his move to Africa with other "free persons of color in the ship Monrovia."[72]

Five years later, Kinney decided to return to the U.S., and landed at Salem, Massachusetts, before gaining employment as a ship's steward. In that employment, Kinney traveled first to Cuba, then to New Orleans. He carried a passport issued in Sierra Leone which he assumed would be useful to "prove" his freedom, but the document attracted the attention of a steamboat captain when Kinney applied for a job. Kinney was taken to what he referred to as the "jail of a negro trader," and put up for sale. After about three months, he managed to escape.

Again, Kinney found work on steamboats and married a black woman who had purchased her own freedom. By working on steamboats, Kinney helped his wife purchase her youngest child and they were in the process of attempting to buy her other children. His deposition also noted that Kinney had two free brothers, John, a cooper in Cincinnati, and one in Ohio (name not legible on document). Kinney described himself as "sober, industrious, peaceable."

In the midst of his new life as a married man, Thornton Kinney was again taken into custody; this time as a "runaway." Charles Bridge, the "agent," had recognized Kinney and petitioned for his arrest on behalf of John Hatcher, who at that point claimed to have a bill of sale for Kinney. Held in Bernard Lynch's infamous "negro jail," Kinney was afraid he would be hurried out of the court's jurisdiction and sold, and pleaded for permission to sue for his freedom and kept in the jurisdiction of the St. Louis court until witnesses who could attest to his free status could be brought before the court.

Witnesses were deposed to support that Kinney was free, while others swore in depositions that he was a runaway slave. Charles Bridges declared the entire story of Thornton Kinney was false. The sheriff's written remarks described "Fountain" Kinney "alias Williamson" as a black man about five feet, ten inches tall, of slender build, and about 35 years old who had been arrested as a runaway, but who claimed to be a free man born of a free mother. The record is unclear as to the disposition in this case.

*　*　*

The preoccupation with restricting activities of free people of color was consistent, and as late as May 27, 1861, with the Civil War just under-way, formal protest against licensing free people of color was heard. The Court refused to officially enter the protest in the record, but did place the petition in the city file.

> In the Matter of Granting license to free negroes and mulattoes, at the last term of the Board of County Commissioners, begun and held, on the third Monday in April 1861, in the City of St. Louis State of Missouri—free negroes and mulattoes crowded the room for several days with applications to obtain license to remain within this State. I then raised objections to the granting of license in several cases, and being overruled by the Board, notice was given that I would, at some future day, enter my protest.
>
> I now desire to have my protest entered on the record in all cases in which licens [sic] were granted on affidavid [sic] of freedom, taken in states other than Missouri, for the reason that I do not believe, that an affidavid [sic] of a negroes [sic] freedom, is such a Certificate of Citizenship as is contemplated by the laws of Missouri. I will here cite one case, Negro woman born in Kentucky licensed on the 22nd April 1861—, no Certificate of Citizenship—
>
> I also protest against licensing of negroes and mulattoes bourn [sic] in states other than Missouri, and have never made this state their home—as in the Case of Mahoney, born in Pennsylvania, no proof that he had ever made this state his home also negroes or mulattoes not born in the United States, as in the case of Isaac Watkins born in Canida [sic] West, license granted May the 8th 1861—also free negroes or mulattoes born in states other than Missouri and producing from the state in which they were born a certificate of Citizenship for the reason that the Supreme Court has decided that a free negro or mulatto is not a Citizen of the United States as in the Dred Scot [sic] decision-now if the decisions of the Supreme Court of the United States is [sic] the law of the land then no free negro or mulatto can be recognized as a Citizen, the

certificate of any state to the contrary notwithstanding. I therefore protest against the license granted to all free negroes or mulattoes Except such as were born free in this state, or those who were here before the 2nd day of January 1840, and were residents at the time of there [*sic*] application, all those emancipated and set free in this state, the husband or wife of a slave lawfully brought into this state by the owner of such slave, the parties have been maried [*sic*] by the Consent of the owner of such slave before such slave was brought into this state-an [*sic*] to none others—

Tippett
May 27th 1861—[73]

* * *

The ambivalence of Missouri laws where people of color, free or slave, were concerned might have contributed to the number and variety of cases filed in all divisions of antebellum Missouri courts. For example, cases were brought by and against free people of color, by and against black slaves, and by and against white people, but which included some connection or allusion to free people of color or slaves. From its origins, slave law in the United States sought not only to restrict or limit the behavior of individual and groups of slaves with respect to their labor and the profits obtained from it, but to maintain order in communities by strictly defining relationships between or among slaves and perhaps especially to prevent egregious violations of laws regulating behavior between slaves and whites.

The Criminal Court record includes a number of cases involving the charge "Enticing Slaves Out of State." Similar activities are analyzed in detail in the chapter on slave resistance, but brief attention is appropriate here.

Some of those charged with this offense were white and some were people of color. One free person of color charged with "Enticing Slaves Out of State," and who may have been involved in Underground Railroad activity, was Mary Meachum,[74] the second wife of the Rev. John Berry Meachum, whom several slaves sued for their freedom. The existence of a particular strategy to remove slaves from Missouri to free territory may be suggested by the cases of Philip Harris and Benjamin Savage, both free men of color. Harris was sentenced to five years in the penitentiary for "Enticing Slaves out of State." Savage was sentenced to ten years in the penitentiary for the same charge. Thus, two free men of color forfeited their own freedom in order to assist slaves to gain freedom for themselves. It was not clear whether Harris and Savage were working together.[75]

After the attack on Fort Sumter in April 1861, and fear that matters could get out of hand in the city, the St. Louis Board of Police Commissioners issued the following orders, published in the *Missouri Republican* newspaper:

1. A notice that the "Sunday law," prohibiting all shows, exhibitions, games, plays, and liquor sales, would be strictly enforced.

2. A notice that "negroes" would no longer be granted permits by the chief of police for "parties or other assemblages. All saloons, or public hour of whatever character, kept or owned by negroes are forbidden and will be suppressed."

3. A notice that "crowds or assemblages of idlers, loafers, or others on the prominent thoroughfares of the city, interfering with the legitimate use of the public streets and sidewalks, and the safety and security of the good and orderly citizens, are positively prohibited; and the Chief of Police is strictly enjoined to see that the spirit of this order is enforced."

4. A notice that "churches of negroes, or churches wherein negroes or mulattoes officiate as preachers, will not be allowed to open unless an officer of the police is present and appointed to be there by the undersigned (the president of the Board, John Brownlee) or the Chief of Police."

5. A notice that "the requirements of law in regard to slaves hiring their own time, in violation of law, will be rigidly enforced."

6. A notice that "all free negroes" found within the city limits without a "license" would be dealt with according to the law. The chief of police was given the order to "arrest all free negroes, mulattoes, or slaves found selling liquor, or keeping any house where liquor of any kind is sold, and to disperse all unlawful assemblages of free negroes, slaves, and mulattoes." In addition, all persons "keeping public gambling-houses or rooms wherein gambling is allowed" would be arrested.[76]

The Republican noted, "all negroes found in the street after the hour of ten o'clock without a pass will be arrested and brought before the recorder."[77]

From the founding of St. Louis through the Civil War, laws increasingly restricted activities of people of color, whether Indian or African American. The focus was on preserving the absolute authority of the slave owner and severely limiting the autonomy of slaves. Laws also defined rigid racial categories and narrowed opportunities for free blacks. Two lacunae in this strategy for social control affected the lives of blacks in this period. One was the right of slaves to sue (if they were mistreated and for their freedom), and the other was the inexorably advancing western frontier, which inevitably reshaped black thought, actions, and identities through the period of the Civil War.

Chapter 3

To the Frontier

Free and slave men and women of color moved back and forth between St. Louis and the advancing western frontier almost continuously from the founding of St. Louis through the Civil War. During that period, how "the West" was defined, as well as the geographic space that term embraced, changed dramatically. Americans, and indeed Europeans generally, perceived the land mass from the Mississippi River to the Pacific as rich in abundant resources ripe for the taking; true, its mountains and plains were inhabited by "wild" Indians, but, if they noted that at all, Americans saw them as interlopers who could either be "civilized" or removed.

For African Americans, western exploration often combined resignation at being moved west involuntarily—as slaves—with the exhilaration and opportunity that accompanied establishing new settlements as representatives of American civilization.[1] In addition to helping shape a peculiarly "American" west, blacks continued to contribute to building St. Louis itself.[2] As African Americans from disparate backgrounds came together to construct a diverse cultural milieu along the frontier, they also took an active part in the presumptuous, but triumphant and celebratory march west that was part of their American inheritance and obligation.[3] Blacks also moved west to settle permanently and their presence, either as slaves or as free actors, doubtless affected the ongoing debate over which territories should be organized as slave or free states.[4]

The place of St. Louis in the history and mythology of the American West is clear and irrevocable: it was the indisputable "gateway" to the west. Although not the first Americans to venture so far west, the Lewis and Clark expedition (1803–06) provided a crash course in American civilization, albeit a perhaps misleadingly diverse one represented by the simultaneous arrival of white, black, and red envoys.[5] The black was the slave man, York, and the red, an Indian woman, who was most likely a slave and who more often than not went unnamed in the expedition journals, although she has attained mythical status as the interpreter and guide, Sacajawea.[6]

Perhaps one of the most significant, yet unknown African Americans of the frontier era was York, the slave of William Clark, who accompanied the *Corps of Discovery* from St. Louis to the Pacific and back again. A vaguely delineated figure in the journals of the expedition, York had likely first moved west from Kentucky to Missouri as the teenaged slave of William Clark.[7] York's autonomy on the trail west seems supported by the fact that he was armed, hunted during the expedition for game to feed the scouting party, and interacted well with the Indians, both on his own initiative and at the behest of Clark.[8] York also apparently possessed knowledge of folk medicine, which permitted him to "pick medicinal greens for his master" and nurse a sick member of the expedition (Charles Floyd, who died).[9] Clearly, York took actions based on his own initiative, rather than merely based on the commands of white owners.[10] Still, the journals reveal that York's life also consisted of varied physical labor, as well as personal duties performed for Clark.[11]

On the other hand, the Arikara Indians were respectful of York, whom they referred to as "the big medicine"—which Clark for some reason interpreted to mean the Indians found York "mysterious or unintelligible."[12] Indians seemed intrigued by York's skin color, the texture of his hair, and Indian women found York sexually attractive.[13] Both Mandan and Arikara warriors "believed that spiritual power is a constituent of sperm" and may have offered their wives to York in an effort to appropriate his spiritual "medicine" for themselves in the person of a child.[14] Shoshone, Nez Perces, and Mandan oral traditions boasted that the children of York were members of their tribes.[15] But whether the stories were true or not, York had his own slave family, which he had left behind when he set out with the *Corps of Discovery*.[16] In 1805, York sent a buffalo robe to his wife, who was a slave in Louisville.[17]

York reasonably expected his time and work in the West to make him a free man. Upon his return to St. Louis, he was outfitted in "tailor-made clothes and boots" and accompanied Clark on his travels through Kentucky (where York was able to visit briefly with his wife) and Virginia.[18] It has been suggested that York's petitions for freedom were based in part on his knowledge of rewards bestowed on white members of the *Corps of Discovery*: for example, the 1807 Congressional approval of land grants to the *Corps'* leaders, Lewis and Clark, as well as to the surviving white men of the expedition, all of whom received 320 acres each in the region west of the Mississippi.[19] Over the next couple of years, York persistently petitioned Clark for emancipation so that he could live in Kentucky with his wife; although Clark expressed a willingness to sell York to someone in Kentucky, he seemed mystified by York's insistence on living with his wife, a stance Clark thought ungrateful.[20] When it occurred to Clark that York might run away to be with his wife, Clark told his brother that if York continued to be intransigent, he would sell him to New Orleans.[21] Clark regretted the taste of freedom York had experienced during the western expedition, which he fretted meant the man would not "be of much service" to him again and reiterated his belief that York had done nothing "so great" to earn his freedom.[22] Clark was adamant about both punishing York for his "ingratitude" and realizing a financial profit from him by selling him South, but then Clark's friend and associate, Missouri Governor Meriwether Lewis, convinced him to hire York out in Kentucky—at least temporarily—so that he could be near his family.[23]

After spending several weeks in Kentucky, York returned to St. Louis in 1809, where Clark beat him for his failure immediately to "mend" his attitude and temporarily restrained him in "the calaboose."[24] When Clark permitted York to be hired out in Louisville again, reports filtered back that York was ill-clothed by his temporary owner there and that his wife was about to be forced to move south to Mississippi with her owner.[25] In later years, historians are unsure whether York ended his days as a free man in St. Louis, Tennessee, or the Indian Territory of Wyoming, where someone identified as York reportedly lived and died among the Crow Nation.[26]

York reached the Pacific Ocean as a slave working on an exploratory expedition of the United States government, but free blacks—many of whom were farmers from Missouri—also traveled to the Oregon Country to work the land as free men and women.[27] In 1845, Missourian George Bush migrated to Washington in search of a society more free of American race restrictions, and in 1851, George Washington, emancipated from slavery in Virginia, also moved to Washington hoping to escape the bondage that hobbled even free black efforts at autonomy.[28] Both men hoped to be able to accomplish that in Washington, even though Washington required blacks to obtain legislative exemption to settle there.[29] Missourian Nathan Ford and his family required even more energetic legal maneuverings to remain in Oregon as free people: the Fords were transported to the territory as slaves in 1844, and although they were later freed as promised by their owner Robin Holmes, they were forced to sue Holmes to gain the legal freedom of their children. The Court ruled that because slavery did not "legally exist" in Oregon, the children were free.[30] Thus, the presence of blacks willing to test the limits of legal freedom for people of color put the question on the record in a way that clearly defined the rights of free people of color.

Despite the difficulties endured by York and others in efforts to gain their freedom either to live in the West as free people or based on their temporary presence or residence there, it happened on occasion that slaves were freed after their service on the frontier. In 1832, Theodore Papin wrote to his brother Pierre, who was at that time trading among the Osages, to send ahead the "freedom papers of my Felix," whom Papin expected to arrive in St. Louis soon.[31] Theodore Papin wrote that he wanted to have the papers in hand, so that he could show Felix how much he owed Pierre Papin, as well as "dictate a little moral as to how he must conduct himself in the world."[32]

The relationship between blacks and the frontier was a reciprocal one in that it had an impact on a range of "black" identities, as well as on how "the West" was defined over time. However, regardless of any particular race or individual agenda blacks themselves might have possessed, their presence in the West was nevertheless part of the advancement of American culture in the region and blacks also often saw themselves, and were seen by others, as ambassadors or envoys of American civilization. The move west by blacks was often accomplished in stages: blacks moved first to Missouri from states in the east, sometimes settling there.[33] Although the western frontier was a decidedly male world, there are records of African American men and women living, working, and forming families at fur-trading forts as well as living among the Indians. Although most of the African American women noted in documents related to the frontier were slaves or servants who accompanied the wives of military officers to frontier forts, census records also indicate the presence of free blacks in the frontier West, as well as slaves working for American fur-trading companies.[34]

Despite clear advantages to life on the frontier, an often-repeated feature of life at the forts along the western frontier was isolation. Being so long distant from society often brought on an emotional desolation that contributed to high rates of desertion by engagés, alcoholism, rape of Indian women, gambling, depression, and a host of other anti-social behaviors becoming commonplace.[35] The forts could be isolated outposts in a hostile land where the danger of being killed and scalped by Indians (both those considered allies and those who were known enemies) was ever-present, and indeed, Indians had sometimes stated that their goal was to eradicate the American presence from what they referred to and understood to be Indian Country.[36] To alleviate some of their loneliness, American men—black and white—routinely took Indian wives, sometimes more than one at a time, and fathered countless "half-breed" children.[37] It is possible that some of the Indian "wives" were slaves, women either bartered or purchased as part of a fur trade transaction.[38] Certainly, loneliness was a critical motivator in obtaining a wife, however, some of the wives also likely represented a diplomatic strategy to cement relationships between Americans and Indians by family or tribal agreements symbolized in the wives.[39] Although most women in sexual relationships with American men—black and white—on the frontier were Indians, some were African Americans.[40] Thus, in some cases, emotional connections between men on the frontier and their wives may have been tenuous, a factor of necessity in which a range of strategies were used to maintain a semblance of domestic tranquility. Flogging was one typical method of keeping workers of all colors in line on the frontier.[41] This included "wives," who were apparently "whipped" frequently.[42] In fact, the beating of Indian women was common on military, as well as civilian, posts.[43]

The frontier fur-trading forts were anchored at each perimeter corner by barricades or blockhouses used to keep watch, but there was still frequent coming and going of Indians, whites, and blacks. Between the failure to maintain human hygiene and the unlikelihood that latrines or outhouses were widely used, as well as the presence of horses and other animals within the fort's walls (to protect them from being stolen by Indians, although it seems that as least as often the horses of Americans and Indians alike simply wandered away), a singular stench was present.[44] Garbage was left in piles outside fort walls, and Americans spoke of the habit of certain Indian tribes of leaving their dead unburied on the fort grounds.[45] The accumulation of trash and decaying corpses probably contributed to the thriving community of rats at the forts, which had initially arrived on board steamboats and which were trapped, killed, and, on occasion, eaten by fort inhabitants.[46] (It seems that rat skins were also exchanged among Indians for more elegant furs or sold in the legitimate trade.[47]) In an effort to beat back the flourishing population of vermin, the bourgeois requested and imported cats to live within the walls of the forts, but it was a running battle between the cats and the rats, and most felt the rats won.[48]

A number of blacks appear in the record as having traveled from St. Louis to Fort Union on the Upper Missouri. The fort has been described as home to a "diverse" and "mixed" community.[49] The population included transient and occasional residents of color; the status of such blacks was not necessarily clear, that is, whether the blacks in residence at frontier forts were free or slave.[50] In 1833, Joshua Pilcher wrote to Pierre Chouteau to complain about the habit of Chouteau relatives—in this instance, Peter Sarpy and "Mr. Cabanne"—permitting "Normand" to be a kind of "free man" at the upper Missouri forts and thereby setting a bad example to other workers, as well as being an "embarrassment to the person in charge of the post."[51] Pilcher stated that Normand performed duties "about the house as a kind of domestic—cook for the other men & etc.," and wanted his disagreement with that policy "as a general principal [sic]" on the record. Wrote Pilcher, it was more preferable—at least apparently, to those in charge—that workers be clearly distinguishable as "one thing or the other," free man or not.[52]

In 1823, Bartholomew Berthold wrote to Bernard Pratte in Philadelphia regarding investment and potential profits from the western fur trade, as well as supplies needed for camps moving west. Berthold wrote that he had sent one of the fur traders and "two negroes belonging to.... Monsieur Cadet [Pierre Chouteau]" to intercept their employees because icy weather had created dangerous conditions and they were stuck on a barge at Herculaneum. Berthold also mentioned that the man who had "shot and wounded" a mulatto named "Noel" had been "killed on the spot" in a later contretemps.[53]

The isolation endured on the fur-trading frontier likely contributed to an informality among races that was not common in more settled areas.[54] Most were involved in some way, although at times tangentially, in the fur trade which had its primary business offices at St. Louis. A few served as cooks or laborers, although John Brazo seems to have been hired to "flog men." Jim Hawkins was a cook at the fort, who had apparently hired out there with the permission of his owner in St. Louis. This arrangement gave Hawkins a semblance of freedom, as there was confusion among some at the fort as to whether Hawkins was a slave or free.[55] Such confusion did not exist in the case of Joseph Basile, who was listed as a resident at Fort Union as a slave of Kenneth Mackenzie.[56]

Perhaps the most well-known black western adventurer of the period was James Beckwith (also Beckwourth), initially presumed to be the son of a black slave woman owned by Pierre Chouteau, Sr.[57] It is difficult to imagine a more apt illustration than Beckwith of the rugged individualist historian Frederick Jackson Turner described as in the vanguard of clearing the way for the "superior" institutions that would be the foundation of American civilization. Clearly, Beckwith was a man who filled the bill as the "strong, motivated, self-reliant" pioneer the frontier required.[58] It is difficult to disagree with at least one historian's pointed assertion that Beckwith's race might have been the primary obstacle that denied Beckwith his due. Had he been white, Beckwith would be the history textbook "archetypal hero" who "defined the national character."[59] The American paradoxes continued since, as historian Margaret Washington concluded, it was the *absence* of "American democracy, institutions, and civilization" that made it possible for blacks to prosper, to the extent that they did, in the West.[60]

Before Beckwith's paternity was confirmed as Virginian Sir Jennings Beckwith, speculation about his parentage and who owned him included Chouteau as his presumed father and members of the Sublette family and O'Fallon (with whom Beckwith first journeyed west from St. Louis) as possible owners.[61] Beckwith's father apparently moved west from Virginia to the St. Charles–St. Louis region of the Louisiana Territory by 1809.[62] Beckwith's three siblings included "Winey" (Winifred), manumitted by their father before 1819, and who "later became a property owner, having purchased a lot lying in 'Julie C. Soulard's First addition to the City of St. Louis ... on the east side of Columbus Street.'"[63] It is also possible that their father freed their sister, Lurana (Louise).[64] Both women are described in court and census records as mulatto or "mulatrix."[65]

As was often the case in frontier settings, James Beckwith seems to have enjoyed many of the perquisites of freedom, including attainment of a superficial literacy by attending school in or near St. Louis.[66] How available educational opportunities were for blacks in and around St. Louis, and at what point such opportunities began, is open to debate. As in the case of Beckwith, educational opportunities for slaves were limited by the laws of the State, and depended to a large extent on the inclinations of owners and their relationships with specific slaves.[67] When he came of age and set out for the West, Jennings Beckwith signed a Deed of Emancipation to formally grant liberty to his son, James, "a mulatto boy."[68]

The presence of Indians in, around, and near St. Louis is mentioned often in memoirs of the founding and antebellum period. Beckwith also noted the persistent community fears of Indian attack. For example, he recalled in grim detail how an interlude playing with neighbor children near St. Charles was disrupted by their discovery of the bodies of members of a settlement family, including children his own age, who had apparently been killed and scalped by Indians.[69]

In 1822, Beckwith set out for Fever River—in 1826, renamed Galena— well-provisioned and with his father's blessing.[70] That year, he was listed among a group of 180 men who signed on to work for William Ashley and Andrew Henry as trappers at "the three forks of the Missouri."[71] A census taken in 1823, recorded 74 men, women, and children, black and white, and noted the presence of black slaves and of James Beckwith as part of the military contingent sent along to protect the civilian settlement party.[72] Beckwith remained at the settlement for a year and a half, during which time, he developed friendly relationships with Indians in the area; eventually, he set out for New Orleans, but his adventure was cut short when he contracted yellow fever and returned home to his father.[73]

In 1824, Beckwith accompanied an expedition led by General William Ashley to the Rocky Mountains.[74] A protégé of mountain men like Jedediah Smith, through the 1820s, it seems Beckwith traveled in Indian country to trade for furs and horses, sometimes in the employ of the Chouteaus.[75] Francis Chardon recorded Beckwith passing through Fort Clark during Chardon's time there as bourgeois; in fact, Chardon sent mail by Beckwith and his company addressed to Pierre Didier Papin in St. Louis, a common practice.[76] Beckwith is listed as an "engagé" with Chouteau's Upper Missouri Outfit (UMO) from 1833 to 1836; it is likely he was hired because of the esteem in which he was held by the Crows and which persuaded the Indians to trade with the UMO.[77] Beckwith likely took wives from among the Blackfeet and Crow nations; it has also been suggested that he was a chief among the Crows.[78]

Slaves accompanied white fur traders into the west from St. Louis and served in a variety of occupations, including as interpreters who facilitated trade with Indians. In 1837, a slave "boy" was sent from St. Louis to the Mandan Village (on the Upper Missouri) to train as an interpreter. As Indian agent, John Sandford submitted an invoice to the government for repayment of $37.50, which he stated was the fee to hire "a negro boy" to accompany him to "attend on Indians."[79] (Please note that the designation "boy" seems to reflect the racial tendency of the period to classify blacks in paternalistic terms, rather than an accurate description of Black Hawk's age or physical stature; based on the description of his exploits, Black Hawk was clearly not a child.)

> Mandan Village 27th June 1837—
>
> Dear John—
> Yours of the 17th April came to hand the 19th.... I received the two kegs of 5 galls each, and many thanks to you for the trouble you have taken for me. I will assure you that I will take your advise [sic], and make it last as long as possible—Also the negro Boy that you sent me (Black Hawk) suites [sic] me very well, he is just such a one as I wanted—all the Indians, men and squaws are in love with him, he is all day absent

at feasting, I am in hopes in one year he will be a first rate Interpreter, I have a first rate Buffaloe [*sic*] Horse, every evening I put Black Hawk upon him, and make him run the mile ... to exercise him to run Buffaloe [*sic*]....

... I am sorry to say I could procure no curiosities for you....

Your friend

F. A. Chardon[80]

It seems clear from most accounts that the frontier was host to diverse "communities" of whites, blacks, and Indians struggling for dominance, and that at times, whites intervened to promote friction if not outright hostility between blacks and Indians.[81] On January 13, 1838, Chardon dispatched his slave, Black Hawk to the Arikara village to remain there for a period.[82] Chardon recognized the importance to the fur-trading enterprise for Americans obtaining knowledge of the internal workings of Indian villages as much as possible, so Black Hawk's felicity with language and rapport with the Arikaras was invaluable.[83] Black Hawk returned to Fort Clark on March 17, 1838; Chardon noted that he had sent Black Hawk "to remain" with the Arikara and that Black Hawk "speaks the language tolerably well for the short time."[84] In the interim, a number of different Arikara tribesmen either traveled "up" to Fort Clark, or Chardon sent someone "down" to the camp to deliver furs and skins.[85] (Chardon also noted he'd sent one of his men down to the Arikara Camp "to be cured of the Venerial."[86]) Although the Upper Missouri was organized as free territory, Chardon continued to hold at least Black Hawk until Chardon's death in 1848.[87] Black Hawk was freed by Chardon's will.[88]

In 1838, it is estimated that over 17,000 Indians in the Upper Missouri region, including members of the Mandan tribe, died of smallpox, and that Indians understood whites' distribution of infected trade goods was the source of that epidemic.[89] (There had also been a smallpox epidemic at Fort Clark during the summer of 1837 [July and August], which Indians blamed on whites.[90])

In 1844, it was reported that Chardon, enraged that Blackfeet Indians had killed his slave, Reese, participated in the retaliatory killing and scalping of six Blackfeet. Not surprisingly, this act alienated the Blackfeet and interfered with the trade for some time.[91]

Despite evidence supporting a conclusion that slaves (at least slave men) enjoyed something akin to freedom when they worked on the fur-trading frontier, the example of William Clark's slave, York, who accompanied the *Corps of Discovery*, has been held up as a cautionary tale. Having proven his importance as a guide and hunter on the journey with the *Corps*, York harbored an expectation that he would be freed, so that he could return to his family in Louisville. But Clark disputed the value of

York's participation and denied his request. To enforce his decision, Clark recorded in his journal that he "trounced" York more than once. Although Clark threatened to sell York south, he ultimately set him free.[92] More to the point perhaps was the case of Clark's slave, Scipio, who was beaten to improve his attitude to work and also threatened with sale South. Scipio took Clark seriously at his threat and shot himself to death.[93]

The 1834 slave freedom suit of Lemmon Dutton provides yet another perspective on blacks' involvement in Americans' westward migrations, as well as the presence or role of women of color.[94] Dutton offered as evidence of her free status the formal manumission of her grandmother, Hannah, in 1787, and which included legal language including "all [Hannah's] children or children's children that might descend from said Hannah," who, even if born in slavery would be free on their 23rd birthday.[95] All the named slaves were "discharged from all claims of service and right of property" to one of the named parties (Dallam) or his "heirs, executors, or administrators" as of the dates specified.[96] Dutton was the daughter of Hannah's daughter, Grace, and thus fit the category of "children's children" specified in the manumission. In addition, Grace had given birth to Hannah after she passed her 23rd birthday and was therefore free when she gave birth to Hannah. But apparently, not every member of Dallam's family was on board with the manumission as Dallam's daughter brought Hannah with her to her marriage to John Paca, the defendant in this case.[97]

John Paca appealed the St. Louis Circuit Court's finding in favor of Lemmon Dutton, stating that the Maryland Court required signatures of two witnesses at the time his father-in-law registered the manumission order.[98] The Missouri Supreme Court reiterated the act of the Maryland colonial legislature, which, in 1752, permitted individuals who owned slaves "of a healthy constitution, sound in mind and body, capable of labor to procure to himself [sic] sufficient food and raiment with other requisite necessaries of life and not exceeding fifty years of age" to set them free by a deed of writing. The Maryland legislature required two witnesses "for manumitting [slaves] whose freedom is to commence immediately" but not for those "whose freedom is to commence in future," which was the situation of Lemmon's grandmother, Hannah.[99]

There is also occasional evidence of what might be termed "political" activism by people of color in St. Louis, which seemed influenced as much by proximity to the slave south as to the free west. The Reverend Moses Dickson had been born free in Cincinnati in 1824, apprenticed as a barber, and moved to St. Louis in 1846. (Free blacks in St. Louis were required to place a bond to guarantee their character and good conduct; 700 free men and women were registered from 1841 to 1859.[100]) Dickson organized the Knights of Liberty to supplement Underground Railroad activity to free Southern slaves after he witnessed the excesses in the system firsthand while traveling in the South. The Knights met at Green (Lucas) and Seventh streets. After fighting in the Civil War, Dickson joined forces with the Missouri Equal Rights League founded when the 1865 Missouri Constitution denied suffrage to blacks.[101]

From the early years of French, Spanish, and American settlement near St. Louis, free and slave African Americans were part of fur-trading and settlement parties into the West. These people of color filled a variety of roles that included explorer, trapper, interpreter, the physical labor of clearing land and establishing forts, soldiers, husbands, and wives. Some acclimated well to the frontier and became part of the civilizing force that set up cities such as San Francisco. However, others found it necessary to fight for their legal free status in courts of law and in doing so relied on the slavery-free zone in the west established in law (for example, the Northwest Ordinance). Although the iconic figure of the American West tends to be white and male, there were also women and girls of color who made a notable impact on the region in this period.

Chapter 4

"The dangerous class": Women of Color and the St. Louis Frontier[1]

Gender was not an irrevocable stumbling block to freedom or success for women of color in St. Louis and the surrounding region from 1763 through the end of the Civil War. And gender didn't necessarily uniquely or narrowly define status, experience, or opportunity for free or slave women. On the contrary, women of color were present from the early days of St. Louis as both slaves and free land owners, traveled to and worked at frontier fur trading and military forts, committed spectacular crimes, worked to earn sufficient funds to purchase themselves (and often their children), resisted slavery in a variety of ways and were successful runaways (again, often taking their children with them), endured years of tedious labor as slaves before dying slaves, and challenged the status quo through the Civil War years, making use of the advancing western boundary of the United States to define their own freedom.

Few historians dispute the precarious position female biology—as opposed to specific "gender" definitions or constraints—imposed on women of color during the slave regime. Gender predetermined and set out often non-negotiable parameters for all women, regardless of color and, to a certain extent, regardless of social class.[2]

History rarely notes the thoughts or acts of individual slave women, or for that matter of free women of color, without mention of their offspring. While deliberate "breeding" of slaves is difficult to prove, records strongly suggest a female slave's fertility or child-bearing "success" were important considerations in purchases or sales. For instance, in 1832,

Hyacinthe Papin bragged in a letter to his brother Pierre, that he'd acquired "a good mulatto" at an estate sale of one of his Chouteau uncles; he added he'd purchased a slave mother with three children ("one at breast") a few years before. Papin asked to be notified if his brother Pierre heard of other similar slave women for sale.[3] Even so, the record is clear the role of slave women was not merely a passive one.

* * *

The first woman of color in the region to sue for freedom was named Celeste. In 1805, Celeste sued in St. Louis court, "District of Louisiana." Her putative owner, Madame Chevalier, denied Celeste was being detained at all and stated, instead, that she was living with Madame Celeste "of her own free voluntary will, consent and accord, and without any kind of compulsion whatsoever." Madame Chevalier added that Celeste was "an Indian and free."[4]

As prescribed by the laws of Catholic St. Louis, Celeste had been baptized as an infant in 1776, and shortly after was given as a gift to her owner's daughter.[5] Celeste's suit arose during a property dispute over the ownership of herself and her mother, an Indian slave named Marie Jean Scypion, and Celeste's sister, Catiche.[6] The question of the legality of holding the girls as slaves was complicated by the strong suspicion that their father was black, although his identity was not proved in the record.[7] While plans to sell the young women were being considered, Celeste and her sister filed suit for their freedom.[8] The slaves' owner reported that Auguste Chouteau, who had apparently whipped his Indian slaves when they threatened to sue for freedom, urged Chevalier to prevent the pending suit from getting too much public attention.[9] The slaves' owners insisted the cases should be considered moot because the women were not Indians anyway; they were black.[10] For more than a generation (from 1806 to 1836), Celeste, her sister, and their children fought for freedom in the courts—first in St. Louis Circuit, then in Missouri Supreme Court, and, finally, the U.S. Supreme Court—before they won.[11] By that time, many of the litigants were long dead.

Because St. Louis was situated at the edge of the frontier, it provides an opportunity to observe experiences of free and slave women of color like these, as well as their presence and possible impact on American westward expansion. The varied roles inhabited and agency exhibited by women of color in antebellum Missouri suggest consideration of the "abandon[ment of] the victimization model in favor of an emphasis on the slaves' resiliency and autonomy."[12] Examples of such "resiliency and autonomy" abound in the record.

By 1791, Gabriel Cerré owned more slaves (43) than any other slaveholder in St. Louis. Two of those slaves were killed at the battle of San Carlos in 1780, and one had been injured there. Cerré owned a teenaged slave named Victoire, whose parents were Joseph (an Indian) and a black slave mother. In 1796, Joseph tried to purchase Victoire, described in the record as a "mulatto," to set her free. But Cerré demanded $1,000 "in hard cash," not furs, and further, suggested to the court that Joseph's effort to purchase his daughter had been "suggested to him by people whose only motive for making such a sacrifice is one of debauchery," while Cerré's motive was "attachment both on [his] part and on the part of [his] wife."[13] Joseph took the case to court and a governing panel set a new price of $800. The Spanish prohibited enslaving Indians, however, this case demonstrates early attention to how individuals of color should be defined in the law, especially if they possessed any black blood.[14] The issue of race or color was thus often more important than gender in resolving questions of law or commerce. Religion was also a consideration.

Under the French regime, black slaves were required by law to convert to Catholicism. Although as "chattel," marriage between slaves was not recognized in civil law, slave marriages were recognized by the church and were often presided over by priests. Religious rituals fostered an interracial network that supported the creation and growth of black families. Slave owners could be sanctioned in the church for failing to ensure that their slaves were married in the church.[15] When free blacks or slaves were baptized, selection or assignment of godparents illustrates a variety of family connections. Whites (Jean Baptiste Provenches and Mariane Marie Michel) stood as godparents when the previously mentioned free black couple Janette and Gregoire baptized their son, Paul. But, again, because slaves were "chattel" property, it is possible the motivation of white slave owners in persuading other whites from their social class to be "godparents" to slaves was to protect owners' right to slave property (or prepare for transfer of ownership title to slave property in the event that something "happened" to a slave owner)—rather than interest in the wellbeing of a slave's soul or body. Thus, it seems unlikely the slaves of the so-called "widow Dodier" Francoise and Jacques selected the widow's relatives Francois Dodier and Mariaine Helen Michel to be godparents to their son, Pierre. Slaves sometimes selected other slaves to be their children's godparents, but in the early years of the territory before law rigorously differentiated slave and free blacks, slaves sometimes selected free blacks for this important role. A slave named Marie Jeanne chose the slaves Jean Baptiste (owner Madame Dodier) and Mariane Ursule (M. Lami) to be godparents to her son, Jean Baptiste. The free black Joseph Neptune and the slave Mellannie (Fr. Bernard) shared the duties of godparents for Marie, a slave of Sylvester Labadie, who was married to Pompei by Fr. Bernard of the village church.[16]

Although the earliest extant Missouri freedom suit had been filed by the slave woman, Celeste, land-owning free women of color were among the earliest residents of the territory.[17] For blacks, freedom meant ownership of their selves, which provided the opportunity to marry. For example, free black landowner Jeanette Forchet actually married twice, to the free black Valentin in 1773, after her husband Gregoire died in 1770. Valentin was a gunsmith who probably traded furs with the Indians, and who was with the Osages in their village when he died in 1789. Forchet died in St. Louis in 1803.[18]

In the early days of the settlement, white society was cleaved by both ethnic origin and religious affiliations, and education followed that pattern. Gender identities and roles were likely shaped by Catholic education for white and girls of color. For example, white Catholic girls attended convent schools, such as that founded by Philippine Duchesne, and after 1833, Protestant girls attended academies such as Linden Wood, founded by Mary Sibley to provide a defense against the Jesuit evil. Despite the forebodings of Sibley and others, the sound of the French language nevertheless seemed to symbolize a certain *cachet*, and many parents sent their daughters to convent schools so that they could learn the language and perhaps be invited to enter the glittering world of the Creole elite.[19]

For French Creoles, status was all—money did not make a "peasant" a gentleman, and for those born black, even conversion to Catholicism could not eradicate one's inherent moral taint. Thus, the venerable Louis William Valentine du Bourg, a slave owner himself, helped organize separate convents for women of color. For those women of color professing a religious vocation, the bishop envisioned them working as missionaries among the "Negroes of Missouri and Louisiana," although most black women with Catholic affinities were assigned as domestic workers for white priests or nuns.[20]

One might reasonably wonder what, if any, practical impact the profession of "mainstream" religious belief had on the lives of African American women in antebellum Missouri. Black slave women quite literally fulfilled the dual purpose of completing whatever tasks they were assigned and also contributed to the reproduction of the workforce by producing children who were also slaves. Slave women thus experienced "abbreviated" or "unfinished" childhoods, in some cases giving birth as young as

11 years old to their own babies, and were most often tutored in the essential lessons of being slave and female by their mothers.[21]Religious inspiration, whether as a desire to proselytize or a selfless impulse to educate, sometimes resulted in the establishment of schools. In 1818, the Baptist minister John Mason Peck co-founded (with James Welch) a church school for blacks, and the following year, a church school for whites.[22] Both schools instructed students in literacy primarily to facilitate instruction in the gospels.[23]

Sister Rose Philippine Duchesne and four nuns arrived in St. Louis from New Orleans by the steamboat *Franklin* in 1818.[24] In 1827, the Society of the Sacred Heart became the first private or public school in the city, when it opened a convent and began instruction programs specifically for girls. Slave owner Bishop DuBourg envisioned "a kind of Third Order of the Sacred Heart for colored women, whom he wished the nuns to train for mission work ... among the Negroes of Missouri and Louisiana."[25] However, despite apparent recognition by a few black women of a calling to enter religious life, racism continued to dictate the place of blacks in the convent as servants to white nuns and priests, one of whom wrote that men of the order saw no reason to do their own household duties "in a land where there are negroes."[26] Lessons in reading, writing, spelling, arithmetic, and religion were offered both to paid boarders and day students, who paid fees apparently calculated on a "sliding scale"; in fact, some students' parents paid in goods or supplies. The order's vocation emphasized outreach to the poor, and the convent established the first orphanage in the city and provided free instruction "in manual labor" to white orphans, who were required to work at the convent. The convent also provided instruction for free black girls on Sundays, even though the institution owned black slaves.

The School of the Sacred Heart was apparently both Catholic and catholic in its approach: although in the first years, most students were French-speakers, by 1840, the vast majority of students were English speakers; the school also enrolled Protestants. After its first year, the Sacred Heart School enrolled over 100 girls in its various programs; by 1839, 200 of the city's 1,000 white students were enrolled at the Convent of the Sacred Heart. Secular, public schools were established somewhat later in 1838, and free public schools in 1847, the same year Missouri officially made it illegal to teach blacks.[27] Based on the number of freedom suits filed by black slaves in St. Louis Courts, such laws might have come too late.

* * *

Of the 270 petitions for freedom filed in civil, criminal, and chancery courts in 19th century Missouri, over half (154 or 57 percent) were filed by women. One striking aspect is the number of suits by women that included petitions for their minor children. The women were of various ages and born in different regions of the country and even different parts of the world (Virginia, Kentucky, Mississippi, Canada, and even Africa). The bases for their suits varied, but included residence or birth in free territory, allegations of prior emancipation or manumission, claim of self-purchase, permission to sue as a poor person, trespass for assault and battery and false imprisonment, birth to a free mother, or some racial basis (the plaintiff claimed to be white or, as in the case of Celeste, Indian).

When she brought suit for freedom in 1845, Jane McCray claimed she'd already purchased her own freedom. McCray claimed that on April 15, 1837, she bought herself from her then owner William H. Hopkins. She alleged that she had paid $600 to Hopkins and his heirs; McCray said she paid Hopkins $500 of her purchase price on April 15, 1837, that there were witnesses present, and she'd been given a receipt for the payment.

> St. Louis April 15 1837
>
> have this day sold my servant woman, Jane McCray to herself for the sum of Six Hundred Dollars—of which purchase money I have received five Hundred Dollars, and obligate myself on the payment of the balance, say One Hundred Dollars—to execute a bill of Sale to her making herself the sold proprietor of her person.
>
> W. H. Hopkins
> Witness Wm. R. Hopkins
> Witness, Bartholomew Brown
> Witness—J. D. G. Maury (?)

McCray said further that on January 1, 1838, she paid Hopkins the remaining balance she owed him of $100, and that Hopkins gave her the following paper.

> Whereas Jane McCray did on the fifteenth day of April one thousand eight hundred & thirty seven pay me the sum of Six Hundred Dollars, being the price of herself, and whereas I did obligate myself to manumit her, by an instrument of the same date; I do hereby authorize and permit her, the said Jane McCray to go and reside in any county in the State of Illinois, & there to do and act for herself. Witness my hand this first day of January, one thousand Eight hundred and thirty eight.
>
> W. H. Hopkins[28]

In the summer of 1838, William H. Hopkins died intestate. At the time of his death, he had not yet executed a deed of emancipation for Jane McCray, and Hopkins' heirs refused to execute such a deed.

To bolster her claim to her freedom, McCray crossed the Mississippi River and established residency in the free state of Illinois. Hopkins' heirs apparently knew of her plans to do this, and for some reason, although they continued to refuse to execute a deed of manumission in her name, they gave their "consent and approbation" to her move to Illinois. But the Court ultimately denied McCray's petition for freedom.

One of the clearest connections between the developing west and African American presence and identities in St. Louis is the fact that so many of the slave freedom suits were based on slaves' claims to freedom after their residence in the free state of Illinois or in the free Northwest Territory.[29]

In 1832, a woman of color named Mahala filed suit for freedom in St. Louis, claiming she'd been born free in Illinois in 1812, to a woman of color named Lydia, who had been manumitted by her former owner, Elisha Mitchell, in 1809.[30] According to Mahala's suit, she and her mother had been "regarded by all who knew them as free persons."[31] Having traveled to Missouri, Mahala was arrested as a runaway slave and jailed based on Martin Mitchell's statement that she was the property of Elisha Mitchell's estate.[32] Mitchell stated further that he intended to take Mahala to Kentucky, and part of Mahala's suit asked the Court to require Mitchell to post security and issue a writ of *habeas corpus* to ensure she would not be removed from St. Louis.[33] The Court assigned Gustavus Bird as Mahala's counsel and Mitchell was ordered not to remove her from the jurisdiction nor inflict any "severity" on her as punishment for filing the freedom suit.[34] A writ of *habeas corpus* was issued that required Mahala be presented in Court July 23, 1832, between 10 a.m. and 12 noon.[35]

Depositions followed. On November 28, 1832, Ichabod Badgley was deposed before St. Louis Justice of the Peace Patrick Walsh. Several other people of color suing for freedom against the Mitchell estate were joined to the case brought by Mahala. They included "Sam, an infant of color by his guardian *ad litem* against Alexander P. [illegible] and Elijah Mitchel [sic], also Marianne, a woman of color against Alexander P. Fields and Elijah Mitchel, also Anson, an infant of color against Henry G. Russel, ... also Matilda, a woman of color against Henry G. Russel impleaded with Henry G. Mitchel, also Michael an infant of color against Henry G. Russel impleaded with Henry G. Mitchel."[36]

In his deposition, Ichabod Badgley stated he "became acquainted" with Elisha Mitchell, who had recently arrived in Illinois, in February of 1808. Badgley stated the following May Mitchell asked him to witness an agreement regarding his rental of land for two years from a man named George Valentine. Badgley witnessed the agreement and then asked Mitchell if he was aware that Illinois law considered slaves free after they'd been resident in the state more than 60 days. Badgley said Mitchell thanked him, and added, "it was not his intention that they should be slaves, that he knew they would remain with him during his natural life, that it was not his intention that they should be slaves after his death, that the old wench had been a mother to his children in raising them and he knew she would not leave him—"[37]

Badgley stated that sometime later that year, Mitchell moved to Missouri, taking his slaves with him, and sometime after that, it was Badgley's understanding that Mitchell died. Badgley said that after Mitchell's death, his widow returned to Illinois with the "family of negroes." Badgley said he recalled the "old wench" "Lyd" had an unknown number of children and had sued Mitchell's widow or estate for her freedom. It was Badgley's recollection that after Mitchell's death, Lydia returned to Illinois from Missouri, where she remained for 20 years or so. He said he was aware she had children named Sam, "Duck," Mahala, Matilda, and Vina, and he thought she had other children but did not know their names. Badgley also stated he thought some of Lydia's children had been born in Illinois. He said he thought that during her time in Illinois, Lydia had been married to a man of color named Nuse Titus, and some of the children were his. Badgley also testified that, in addition to Lydia and her family, Mitchell had owned a slave man named Bob, whom he hired out to someone named John Byron.[38] The resolution of the case was not part of the existing record.

From the 1840s through 1860s, a variety of laws affected the freedom of women to move about the city of St. Louis. Most of the laws referred explicitly to "vagrants," although the term came to include women considered part of "the dangerous class"—for the most part, prostitutes viewed as exercising "sexual wiles" to "corrupt" men, a "crime" that undermined social order. Additionally, in some instances, certain women were targeted because they flouted racial conventions of the city, whose white citizens—despite the presence of a visible mixed race class—insisted they preferred the races rigidly segregated.[39]

Under the French, free women of color had the same rights to own property and to marry as white women (although under U.S. law, the right of women to own property was contingent on being unmarried because once married, the husband automatically assumed legal possession of a wife's property). The laws of 1835, required permits for free people of color and that free children from the age of seven be hired out.[40]

Certainly, there were slaves in law who lived a kind of quasi-freedom in that their owners permitted them to hire themselves out and to live on their own. Rachel Steele brought a suit in 1845. Charlotte Grimes certified she'd known Steele for 13 years as "an honest upright woman one that can be trusted [*sic*]." Grimes noted that Steele's owners, Mr. and Mrs. Taylor, had left the area but left Steele in St. Louis with the authority to hire herself out either on a steamboat or in the city. Grimes' husband was part of the crew of the steamboat *Uncle Toby*.[41] Steele based her suit on the fact that in 1831, as the slave of Samuel Gilbert, she'd hired out to Russell Farnham in Keokuk, Missouri, which was north of the 36° 30' line prescribed by the Missouri Compromise. Steele stated she had lived in Keokuk for more than nine months, until Gilbert died, but that according to the law, her nine-month residence rendered her free. Steele said that after Thomas Taylor married one of Gilbert's granddaughters and claimed that because she was his wife, she was entitled to her property, which he believed included Rachel Steele.[42]

Elizabeth Keckley "desired not a fugitive's freedom but the autonomy to become a free mother *and* to remain in urban St. Louis. Her commitment to self-purchase may be better understood as a calculated response to these deeper legal currents as western annexation began to reshape the geopolitics of slavery and freedom."[43] Clearly, Keckley managed to create an image of respectability and responsibility since when her owner Hugh Garland was persuaded (perhaps more by his own mounting debts than humanitarian concerns) to allow Keckley to buy her own freedom and that of her son, George, for $1,200, some of her clients loaned her the money she needed.[44]

The 1843 freedom suit filed by Mary Charlotte against Gabriel Chouteau is a seminal one; the case highlights the presence and role of women in the region. Over a period of decades, generations of slaves filed suits against generations of Chouteaus, the city's founding family, including an April 1821, case of Marie, "a free mulatto girl," against Auguste Chouteau; a July 1825, case of Marguerite, "free woman of color," against Pierre Chouteau, Sr.; the November 1827, case of Theotiste (also Catiche) against Pierre Chouteau, Sr.; and the July 1835, case of Sally, "an infant mulatto girl" (13 years old), against Henry Chouteau.[45] But the case of Mary Charlotte (and a parallel suit by her brother Pierre [also Peter]) against Gabriel Chouteau relied on, and challenged, intersecting legal bases for the right of people of color to sue for their freedom in Missouri courts.[46]

Mary Charlotte brought suit not only for herself, but also for her children, Antoine, Augusta, Victoire, and Euphasia. Mary Charlotte charged she was entitled to free status she claimed already be recognized because she was the daughter of "a negress named Rose," born in Montreal, Canada about 1791, and taken into the Northwest Territory of the United States. (Rose may also have had Indian blood, and this case also questioned the legality of enslaving Indians in Canada.[47]) From the Northwest Territory, Rose traveled to St. Louis as the slave of a Catholic priest named Father Didier, who a few years later sold Rose to Auguste Chouteau (Gabriel's father).[48]

When his parents died, Gabriel Chouteau inherited Mary Charlotte. She insisted the priest's purchase of her mother, Rose, was illegal because her mother had lived in territory where slavery was outlawed. Thus, this case also challenged the legality of slavery in Canada.

A witness named Paschal Cerre recalled in his deposition that he had seen blacks and mulattoes living in Canada, but could not say for sure if they were slaves. (This recollection was similar to those reported by whites regarding the uncertain status of blacks on the American western frontier.) This visitor to Canada said he and his father left their black slaves on the United States side of the border with Canada "for fear they would become free" if they entered Canada. (And of course, depending on where exactly blacks took up residence on the U.S. side of the border—for example, within the boundaries of the Northwest Ordinance—that, too, might have resulted in an arguable basis for freedom.) A Canadian named Auguste Dufresne swore he had not ever seen slaves in Canada in his 72 years residing there. He said he had seen only "2, 3, or 4" blacks in that country, and they "seemed to go where they pleased." The question of Mary Charlotte's mother Rose's status was also addressed.

Witness Michael Wash remembered Rose as a cook for a merchant in Prairie du Chien in free Northwest Territory. He said the memory of the woman stuck in his mind because one "did not see many blacks ... there." On the question of what he knew of Rose's freedom, Dufresne stated he knew Rose "about thirty-five years ago" as the slave of Auguste Chouteau, and that he recalled Rose's three children, Charlotte, Peter, and Louis (all of whom subsequently filed freedom suits against the Chouteaus). Dufresne said Mary Charlotte "was then, I suppose, 4 or 5 years of age."[49]

Both Mary Charlotte and her brother, Pierre (who initiated his suit for freedom against Thérèse Chouteau, mother of Gabriel, then brought a second suit against Gabriel after his mother's death), were denied their freedom, first by the Circuit Court of Missouri and, finally, by the Supreme Court of Missouri.

* * *

If the most famous (or infamous) tale of interracial love to be found in the annals of U.S. slavery is that of Sally Hemmings and Thomas Jefferson, it also seems clear by now that story is only the tip of the iceberg. Certainly, Missouri had its share of relationships between black women and white men (and likely those between black men and white women). The story of Maria Whitten is only one of them.[50]

Sometime in 1829, Maria Whitten sued for her freedom and for the freedom of her son, Patrick Henry.[51] By that time, Maria Whitten had traveled around quite a bit. The man she loved, and the father of her infant son, Patrick Henry, was a man named Jesse. And based on the record, it seems clear that Jesse loved Maria. Jesse was white.

Maria had been sold to Garland Rucker, perhaps in an attempt to separate Jesse from his family. (William Whitten, Jesse's father, stated at deposition that Maria was a "bright mulatto" and the baby was "nearly white.") The problem was Maria refused to stay sold.

She set out for Kentucky and managed to get back to Jesse with their child. Rucker clearly understood the nature of the relationship between Maria and Jesse Whitten because he went right to Kentucky to look for her. According to the record, Jesse "denied knowledge" of Maria's whereabouts and even "helped [Rucker] look for them." Then, when he thought the coast was clear, and not having much support for the relationship from his own family, Jesse ran away with Maria and Patrick Henry, bound for free territory. But along the way, Jesse fell ill and died. Maria's owner caught up with her in Illinois and made plans to move her to Missouri because folks told him if he dallied in Illinois, his slave could "get free."

Much has been made of the comparatively smaller numbers of successful female versus male slave runaways.[52] However, it should be noted that, especially in the early years of Missouri settlement and again in the initial phase of transition to the American political culture, large numbers of slaves—female and male—were part of an involuntary mass exodus west. Significant numbers may have been young girls sold apart from their families in the mid–Atlantic states; perusal of St. Louis newspapers and wills of the period identifies numerous classified ads and bequests transferring young black slave girls in the region.[53] Those who attempted to help slaves run away were defined as "criminals" under the law. Various forms of "help" to slaves included forging free papers or "enticing" slaves to freedom and which were defined as "slave-stealing" and were punished by imprisonment.[54] After statehood, removing slaves from the control of their owners, even one slave at a time, was interpreted as an effort to undermine the institution of slavery itself.[55] (In the territorial period, stealing a slave was punishable by death.[56]) In 1835, the Missouri General Assembly had defined the minimum appropriate sentence for slave-stealing as two years.[57] From

1837 to 1865, 42 people served time in the Missouri penitentiary for some form of slave-stealing.[58] In 1845, the Missouri statute was amended (expanded) to define numerous forms of slave-stealing, including "enticing, decoying, or carrying away" slaves "with the intent to procure or effect" their freedom; in addition, anyone who assisted persons involved in such activity could be sentenced to no less than seven years with "related offenses" potentially receiving sentences "not exceeding five years."[59] Five men of both races died in prison while serving sentences for some form of slave-stealing.[60]

In addition to suing for freedom and running away, African Americans also participated in individual or collective anti-slavery activities. Only two women were imprisoned in Missouri for "abolitionist" activity, one white and one black. The black woman was 21-year-old Eliza Sly, who began serving her five-year sentence in Jefferson City in 1857, but was pardoned after eight months.[61] Most likely, Sly was released because in the construction of the prison, no provision had been made for the incarceration of women.[62] At her release, Sly was instructed to "leave the state and do not return during [her] natural li[f]e."[63]

Virginia-born Elsa Hicks was given as a wedding gift to "S. Burrell" and James Mitchell. About 1834, Mitchell moved to the Wisconsin Territory, where slavery was prohibited, but continued to hold Hicks as a slave there for more than six years. In 1841, Mitchell arrived in St. Louis, Missouri, bringing Hicks with him. When he began to make plans to move again, Hicks took the opportunity provided by Missouri law and filed a suit for her freedom based on her prior residence in free territory. Judge John Krum ordered a writ of habeas corpus served on Mitchell to prevent him from taking Hicks beyond the court's jurisdiction. Krum authorized the hiring out of Hicks and ordered that Mitchell pay a $500 security bond for her.[64]

It is perhaps understatement to suggest that Burrell and Mitchell did not cooperate with the Court. The Sheriff reported that Mitchell was "secreting himself for the purpose of avoiding service" of the writ. In addition, Burrell tried to board a ship with Hicks to take her out of the court's jurisdiction. The fact that the captain of the boat refused to take Burrell and Hicks on board stopped her only momentarily. After being refused entry to the boat, Burrell allegedly attempted to hire someone to take Hicks out of the jurisdiction.

It is possible the Court dismissed this initial suit, but in any event, two years later, Elsa Hicks filed a second freedom suit in St. Louis Court. The defendant in Hicks' second suit for freedom was Patrick T.

McSherry.[65] However, James Mitchell and his family charged Patrick McSherry with acting in "collusion" with Elsa Hicks to enable her to create a legal basis to her claim to freedom. The Mitchells claimed that

3. Said McSherry never claimed said Plaintiff [Hicks] to be his slave, never set up any pretension of title to her, never withheld her liberty from her, but her residence with him was free and voluntary, and he has been selected as a sham defendant, in order that judgment of liberation might be obtained as against him, without any serious resistance.

4. Before, at and since the institution of said suit, said McSherry against the will of the owners of said Plaintiff has entertained and harbored her, has encouraged her in remaining as a fugitive, has at all times disclaimed any claim of title to or ownership of said plaintiff, and expressed his opinion that she was free and has recently sworn to the same thing and under such circumstances it would be a mockery to continue the suit, when the Defendant and Plaintiff are both eager and anxious that the same judgment may be rendered, the Defendant at the same time harboring no claim to or interest in the property.

...

7. ... McSherry has ... permitted her to remain freely and voluntarily at his own house, with her consent.

Sheriff of the St. Louis Jail, Sam Conway also filed a petition with the Court. According to Conway, a mulatto woman called Elsa Hicks (also known as Alice) and her infant child had been incarcerated in the city jail since February. Conway's memorandum stated that, although he'd been authorized to hire out Hicks to pay her costs at the jail, he had been unable to do so and doubted that he would be able to do so. The sheriff said that being confined in jail had "impaired" the health of Hicks and her child: Hicks had lost a great deal of weight and looked "badly"; the sheriff said he feared continued incarceration might even be "fatal to one or both of them."

Conway said he told Hicks he'd been unable to find her employment and it was unlikely he would be able to find her a position during the pendency of her suit against McSherry. He said Hicks denied she'd filed suit for freedom against McSherry or any knowledge of a suit against McSherry. Conway said that Hicks told him no one named McSherry had ever held her as a slave, but that she had intended to sue James Mitchell. The purpose of Conway's memorandum seems to have been to obtain reimbursement for Hicks' expenses; in fact, Conway asked to be released from his responsibility to Hicks unless the court paid him for his "trouble."

The attorneys for James Mitchell's minor children then filed a petition based on the sheriff's statement that Elsa Hicks had not filed a freedom suit against Patrick McSherry. In their new petition, the Mitchells charged that if Hicks was released from jail they believed she would be "taken & harbored & secreted by persons tinctured with abolitionism." The Mitchell attorney claimed a "Rev. Joseph Tabour," who was "strongly suspected of being an Abolitionist [*sic*]," had tried to hire someone to bring Hicks to him. The attorney said setting Hicks free would "expose the rights" of her owners to the "unfortunate influences" of abolitionism and Missouri's precarious location on the border of slave territory even made this likely.

Elsa Hicks' petition was denied.

*   *   *

The "firebell" of African American impatience—whether rung by slave or free—had not yet become insistent when a young Missouri slave girl named Celia killed her owner to stop him from raping her, again. In the early years of St. Louis settlement, the *Code Noir* prohibited rape of female slaves and selling children away from parents.[66] However, by the antebellum period, adherence to the law had waned, if in fact, it had ever held much credence with slave owners. One case demands attention as it illuminates the consequences of the routinization of sexual violence during the slave era.

If the period of Missouri slavery began with Celeste's legal writ, it is worth investigating the rare violent resistance to slavery in the years leading to civil war. A Missouri farmer named Robert Newsom purchased Celia in 1850, when she was 14 years old.[67] Newsom raped Celia almost immediately after he bought her, which began what became a pattern of sexual abuse, during which Celia gave birth to two children.[68] In 1855, after entering a romantic relationship with a slave named George and discovering that she was pregnant for the third time, Celia told Newsom to leave her alone; in part, this was due to George's insistence.[69] When Newsom approached Celia for sex after her ultimatum, she killed him.[70] Then Celia burned Newsom's body and asked his unknowing grandson to clean up and get rid of the ashes.[71] When Celia's lover, George, was questioned by Newsom's family, he apparently provided evidence that incriminated Celia.[72]

Although antebellum law of Missouri prohibited Celia from testifying in her own defense against whites, attorneys for her defense were appointed by the Court and quickly entered a plea of not guilty supported by the theory that the case was justifiable homicide because Celia had acted in self-defense against years of sexual abuse that began when she was very young.[73] Celia had told her attorneys she had not meant to kill Newsom, only to make him stop his attempted rape, but when he persisted, she fought back, and Newsom died; she said she had no help in killing Newsom or disposing of his body even though she was pregnant and sick at the time.[74] In ruling on the plea, the judge found that the master's rights over his property (including human property) made Celia's claim untenable.[75] The jury found Celia guilty and sentenced her to hang.[76]

The case became a *cause célèbre* and while the Supreme Court deliberated on appeal, supporters broke Celia out of jail, although she returned to jail voluntarily.[77] Her appeal was denied and Celia was executed December 21, 1855.[78]

CHAPTER 5

Sold West: The Slave Trade and the Advancing Frontier

St. Louis was geographically positioned to facilitate a muscular expansion of the slave trade into the west and simultaneously provide a bridge west for the migration of free people of color, slave blacks who worked in the territories, and runaway slaves. In many ways, viewed from the perspective of western settlement, St. Louis became the new eastern capital of the trade.[1] Indeed, for those seeking to realize a profit in the western trade, it seemed well-known that the "one speculation that still offered great advantages" was the "trade in [N]egroes."[2] For a time, St. Louis was both the western boundary of the settled United States and the eastern embarkation point for trade of slaves to the west. The trade in slaves in and through the St. Louis "gateway" was fed by a flourishing internal trade within St. Louis and the region in its immediate orbit, including private sales and public auctions, family and "gentlemen's" agreements; the internal trade within the United States from east to west (and sometimes from St. Louis to and from Deep South states); and a profitable trade overseen by slave sales "brokers" and professional traders. The opening of western lands to settlement provided countless opportunities for westward expansion of the trade in slaves.[3]

The case of William (Billy) Tarleton is just one illustration of this. In September 1813, claiming to be a free man, Tarleton filed suit in the St. Louis Court of Common Pleas (Territory of Missouri) against Jacob Horine, stating that he had been taken from Virginia to Kentucky and sold as a slave in St. Louis. The Court appointed "D. Barton Esquire" counsel for Tarleton and ordered Horine to permit Tarleton "reasonable" time to meet with his attorney at the same time that it prohibited Horine from removing

Tarleton from the court's jurisdiction. Horine was required to appear to answer the charges against him. Horine responded that it was his understanding that Tarleton had been "a slave from birth" and that he'd purchased Tarleton in Kentucky in 1810, when Tarleton was about 24 or 25 years old. Horine informed the Court that he had sent for a copy of the bill of sale from Tarleton's previous owner, Squire Brooke, but had not yet received it and felt that not having the document might compromise his case.[4] The ultimate decision of the court as to whether Tarleton would be free or remain a slave cannot be determined from the record.

Because the U.S. Constitution prohibited the international trade in slaves as of 1808, people of color claiming birth in or abduction from Africa was rare by the antebellum period. But in 1831, a slave named Jack claimed that he was born in Africa, sold into slavery in South Carolina, and then purchased and taken to Illinois, where he worked for one year, before being taken to Missouri.[5] The same year, a woman named Dunky also claimed to have been taken from Africa and sold in Charleston, South Carolina, "about twenty years ago."[6] Dunky claimed to have been working as an "indented servant" in Illinois from the time of her original sale until she was taken to Missouri shortly before filing her petition.[7] Although depositions described Dunky as bearing African tribal markings and being left to "hire her own time," as well as producing evidence to show she'd lived in Illinois as early as 1811, the focus here is not whether either of these individuals had the basis for a freedom suit, but to illustrate the clear westward trend of the slave trade.

The construction of a network of military, as well as fur-trading forts west from St. Louis also facilitated expansion of the slave trade; in fact, U.S. Army officers received an allowance that permitted them to purchase a servant and maintain the status appropriate to their rank.[8] Obviously, many forts where officers were stationed with their slaves were in free territory.[9] The sale in slaves west, as well as south, was brisk from the settlement of St. Louis through the end of the Civil War. This fact was well remarked by newspapers throughout the region, including the *Mobile Register* and the *New Orleans Crescent*. The *Register* quoted a St. Louis source, stating that "upwards of 400" slaves were shipped to the South for sale every week.[10] On occasion, slaves who had been resident in western territories where slavery was prohibited later brought successful suit for freedom in St. Louis courts.[11]

In 1833, Ralph, a man of color, appealed to the Missouri Supreme Court for a new trial after the St. Louis Circuit Court denied his freedom suit. Ralph brought his case based on his residence in the Northwest Ter-

Professional slave traders, such as Bernard Lynch's Slave Market, operated a brisk business in the sale of slaves and also provided a "slave jail" for the confinement of slaves awaiting sale.

ritory (the Ohio Saline and the Galena, Illinois, lead mines) from 1814 to 1819, during which time he hired out his time there. The Supreme Court found in Ralph's favor and reversed the lower court's refusal to approve a new trial based on the fact that he had worked in free territory and probably with his owner's permission.[12]

Professional slave traders also often facilitated the sales of slaves. Several slave traders established offices in St. Louis or traded regularly with private St. Louis buyers and sellers.[13] In fact, professionalization of the accumulation, evaluation, and purchase and sale of slaves received a boost from the 1803 Louisiana Purchase and anticipation of the 1808 ban on the Atlantic slave trade. In 1819, Milly, a black woman, brought suit against Mathias Rose for bringing her into the Northwest Territory from Kentucky in 1805, to serve an indenture of 70 years, and then to Missouri.[14] Included in Milly's petition were her children, 4 year old Eliza and 2 year old Bob.[15] (Again, although Milly's petition was based on her 16-year residence in

Rules

No charge less than One Dollar

All Negroes entrusted to my care for sale, or otherwise must be at the Risk of the Owners.

A charge of 37½ cents will be made per Day for board of Negroes, & 2½ per cent on all Sales of Slaves.

My usual care will be taken to avoid escapes, or accidents but will not be made Responsible should they occur

I only promise to give the same protection to other Negroes that I do to my own, I bar all pretexts, to want of diligence.

These must be the acknowledged terms of all Negroes found in my care, as they will not be received on any other

As these Rules will be placed in a public place in my Office That all can see, that will see: The pretence of ignorance shall not be a plea.

1st January 1858.   B. M. Lynch

N° 100 Locust St.

This notice was posted to inform and instruct prospective buyers or sellers of slaves at Lynch's Slave Pen in St. Louis.

Indiana and Illinois, during which time she was held as a slave, our interest here is in the westward movement of slaves.[16])

The ensuing mass migration of Americans west, many of whom journeyed specifically to expand plantation cultivation of cotton or sugar, and so either took numbers of slaves with them or purchased them at some point along the way for that specific purpose also bolstered the trade.[17] In 1828, Suzette (alias Judith) finally sued for her freedom after being sold to the territory of Illinois, where she changed hands through separate sales four times.[18] Suzette claimed her three children were free, based on their birth in free territory, and filed companion suits on their behalf.[19] The 1850 freedom suit of Mary, a free woman of color who claimed she had been sold west from Kentucky, provided testimony of the participation of the St. Louis–based slave trading firm of Bernard Lynch in detaining Mary and "various other persons, all negro" for the purpose of sale.[20] Indeed, although whites often perceived slave ownership as indissolubly linked to prosperity in the west, they also understood the value of slaves as investment commodities, which might be skillfully dispersed to fund each leg of westward movement.[21]

Casual discussion of entering into the business of selling slaves was fairly common. An 1816 letter proposed a partnership to trade in "convict negroes," although "prohibited under severe penalties in Louisiana."[22] Newspapers such as the *St. Louis Democrat* trumpeted the good news that the State was the seat of a "rapidly increasing commerce in blacks between Missouri and the South."[23] At times, the movement of slave property west represented what was considered the most efficient method of transporting "wealth" across the country.[24]

An informal trade also existed between friends and extended family, but the buying and selling of slaves routinely disrupted any family life slaves might attempt to create or maintain. At times, slave owners purchased or gave slaves as gifts, including, ironically, on the occasion of a marriage and the establishment of a new home for the adult children or near relatives of a slave owner. Slave owners perceived slaves as essential elements for the appropriate and even essential furnishing of the households of the slaveholding class. For example, in 1807, Will Carr of St. Louis wrote a letter to his brother, Charles Carr, in Kentucky, in which he announced his intention to marry and requested a "negro woman for the kitchen" in anticipation of his imminent marriage to Ann Maria Elliott of Connecticut.[25] William Carr estimated the cost of procuring a "suitable" kitchen slave at $500, which he advanced to John Lowrey of Lexington for that purpose.[26] (Carr also wrote in the letter that he'd recently purchased "a horse and a negro boy."[27]) He asked his brother to evaluate the slave woman, even though he expected Lowrey to be successful in locating one, and assure him of the woman's "age and qualities" for his purposes before any money changed hands.[28]

In September 1807, Carr wrote to his brother again and expressed not only dissatisfaction with a slave couple purchased for him, but also his feeling of the necessity of selling them because they did not meet his requirements. Carr claimed he found the slave trade "abhorrent," but that what must be done must be done, and added he expected the two slaves "would not be willing to be separated" and would "be obliged" to be sold together.[29] He went on to say he trusted his brother to continue his search and find a slave woman that would "please" him as he knew Will Carr's "situation." Carr emphasized that he would be "willing to give a liberal price" for the "right" kitchen slave.[30]

With the increasing probability of Missouri statehood, slaveholders' questions about the possible impact of statehood on slavery and the trade and the potential methods for safeguarding the institutions also increased. An amendment by New Yorker DeWitt Clinton proposed that "the further introduction of slavery or involuntary servitude be prohibited," and further, "all children of slaves, born within the said state" after statehood "be free at the age of twenty-five years."[31] Some legislators believed legitimacy of such a requirement was supported by Constitutional authorization to Congress to any "needful" rules or regulations regarding the territory and prohibition against slavery in the Northwest Territory, Illinois, and Indiana.[32]

Some slave owners expressed anxiety at the possibility that the end result of debate over Missouri statehood might halt the extension of slavery into the region. George Graham wrote to his brother regarding a loan for $1,000, that he'd undertaken to "get [his] negroes out" before Congress passed a law that blocked slavery in the territory, which would "ruin" him. However, Graham did not reveal how many slaves or where he planned to take them. (Graham stated in the same letter that he was planning to go to the Ohio country to deliver "annuities" to Indians there, although nothing in the letter precisely connected the discussion of slaves and the discussion of Indian annuities.[33])

Slaves were privy to their owners' agitated whispers about whether slavery would remain secure after statehood, of course, which fueled their hope and expectation that the pending legislation might mean the end of slavery. But even before the imminent compromise, recalcitrant slaves were often sold south as punishment for perceived disobedience. In the run-up to formalization of Statehood and what some considered the infamous Missouri Compromise, Auguste Chouteau began what became a time-consuming exertion to sell Charles, a persistent runaway. Francois Menard, Chouteau's long-time emissary in slave sales, wrote to him in July of 1820, detailing Charles' attempts to run away once he learned plans were afoot to sell him for his wanderlust. Frustrated by Charles' refusal to simply wait and be sold, Menard told Chouteau he'd finally put him in jail and awaited Chouteau's agreement to an auction at which Menard would "mak[e] known [Charles'] defects."[34]

Chouteau's reply was to the point.

> I had the pleasure recently of receiving your letter.... I am sorry to see the delays and difficulties you have up to now undergone for the sale of my slave Charles. Please get rid of him as soon as possible, either at public sale or private sale, for whatever price you can; I approve in advance all you will do in this regard and will be satisfied. As to the remarks he makes: they are wholly without foundation; I do not know that he has

any child, and he has surely none at my place; and to my knowledge he has never complained of pains; his health is at this time very good, as I told you in my earlier letter. This negro behaved so badly here and misuses my kindness so that I decided to get rid of him. I ought to even for the example he sets my other slaves and to maintain them in proper subjection, and I wish you, sir, even in the deed that you give for his sale to specify as an express condition that this negro may never be sent back into our territory; this condition will in one sense be bad for my interests, but in another, it is presently necessary for an example for my other slaves.[35]

This letter provides clues to the complicated relationships between owners and slaves as well as the ever-present possibility of duplicity on all sides. For example, Charles apparently importuned Chouteau for a "stay" of sale because he had fathered a child he wanted to be near, while Chouteau at least averred he knew nothing about a child, and all things considered, both statements could have been true: Charles might indeed have fathered a child, and Chouteau might in fact have known nothing about it. Despite his protests, Chouteau was adamant and Charles was placed in jail. Fees for Charles' "board" in jail were $29.75, from November 1820, through February of 1821.[36]

Incarceration did not dull Charles' ardor for freedom and the persistence of Charles, Auguste Chouteau and his agent, Francois Menard, provide telling insight into the dynamics of selling slaves, relations (as well as relationships) between slaves and slave owners, and the consistent determination of blacks to live free. It is clear from the level of frustration in Menard's missive to Chouteau that Charles meant to move heaven and earth to avoid being sold. The reasons are not as clear as Charles' determination, however, for at no point did either Menard or Chouteau mention details of Charles' personality, family life, craft or skills, birthplace, age, or other elements, which might provide insight into his desires or goals. Rather, Menard attempted to reduce Charles' dilemma to the level of a matter of inconvenience for Menard and Chouteau.

Sir,
After having undergone inconceivable worries and anxieties by the different escapes of your negro Charles, who escaped twice even though shackled, I finally succeeded in selling him at auction at the end of last month for the price of $480, not accounting in the sale for the faults which I knew he had, but only the ownership, and I was ready to send you the account for the sale when I was stopped from doing it by a letter that just came to me addressed by the lawyer of Mr. Laville, the purchaser of the said negro, in which this gentleman had me informed that if I refused to take back the negro, since I knew when he was sold that he was a runaway, he was going to bring the action against me in order to void this sale; and as I do not think I can take it upon myself, without your compliance, to break off this sale, I hasten to inform you of these disagreeable circumstances, so that you can tell me as soon as possible what you think I should do.
While waiting I will let Mr. Laville continue his proceedings and if we are condemned to take back the negro, whom he has temporarily committed to jail, I very

much fear that in view of the publicity of this affair and because of the bad qualities of this wicked slave, I will never succeed in selling him again.

    I am sorry, sir, that up to this time I have not been able to write you except to inform you of disagreeable things, but what eases me in regard to this is that I have done my best to be useful to you, and I only regret that the first business you have commissioned me to do was of such a disagreeable nature, since it deprives me of the pleasure I would have had in having been successfully useful.

    Impatiently awaiting news of you, I repeat to you, sir, the assurances of my respectful devotion, I have the honor to salute you.

Fr. Menard[37]

Menard apparently wrote two drafts of the letter, which do not differ substantially in tone, although he edited and revised his thoughts, including reference "to the article of the [New Orleans civil code] law that protects" purchasers by requiring sellers of slaves to "declare ... all defects he knows him to have." (An inarguable slave "defect" from the point of view of slave owners was evidence that a slave was a persistent runaway. In addition, as we have seen, the law defined a slave runaway as "stealing" himself or herself.) Menard also edited "wicked negro" to read "cursed negro."[38]

In May, Menard informed Chouteau the matter had been settled with Chouteau to receive $238.16-¾, and that Menard was eager to serve Chouteau in the future, in which case he hoped to achieve a "more fortunate" result. Menard stated that he would not charge Chouteau a commission on the sale of Charles.[39] (In later years, the Chouteau-Menard connection produced evidence of the seemingly casual manner in which slaves passed back and forth across the line demarcating slavery and freedom. For example, in 1831, Pierre Menard wrote to Pierre Chouteau, Jr., known, as were most Creole second sons, as "Cadet," to request that Chouteau send certain supplies from St. Louis to Menard in Kaskaskia by "mon negre" [my negro]. The supplies are named—"good coffee," "six bottles of good claret," "a few dried figs ... if only a pound" and "herb-tea," but Menard's "negro" is not.[40])

In fairly short order, Missouri politicians offered rebuttal to the Missouri Compromise of 1820, by prohibiting black settlement in the state.[41] But trade in slaves remained brisk after finalization of the Missouri Compromise. In 1822, an emissary for Auguste Chouteau wrote from New Orleans that he had had difficulty in selling three of Chouteau's slaves there:

Unfortunately today I have no better news to give you relative to the sale of your three slaves ... to place them at this time one would need to sell them for almost nothing; this difficulty in selling, even at very moderate prices, has three reasons that are very important, the failure of several harvests, the consequent poverty, and *the tremendous importation of slaves from the north that has taken place in the last 18 months* [emphasis added].[42]

The slaves Chouteau had earmarked for sale included Francoise, aged 19, and Adelaide, aged 16, two female mulattoes, who had arrived in New Orleans aboard the *Dolphin* in the care of Chouteau's agent, Louis Menard, for the purpose of being sold. Apparently, it took more than six months for Menard to effect the sale.[43]

Throughout the period, slaves were transported on the Mississippi River from St. Louis to New Orleans, both cities were ports with vigorous sales in slaves. An 1829 receipt to B. Pratte and Company shows proof of the delivery of a slave man named Andrew aboard the steamboat *Oregon* to [signature not legible] for further delivery to John G. Stevenson in New Orleans.[44]

The trade in slaves west to St. Louis also continued in the wake of the Missouri Compromise. Brothers John Granville and Lewis Bibb reported that six of their siblings were sold apart from their mother in 1830; the children were transported to Missouri from Kentucky, where the three were immediately sold to three different owners.[45] In 1832, John Ware sold a 20-year-old Virginia slave named Peter to Sylvester Labadie; James Bell of Tennessee sold Dehlia to Howell Hinds for $1,000; I. and T. Holliday of Mississippi sold 22-year-old Sarah to Thomas Morse for $800; Elizabeth Hewitt of Mississippi sold 27-year-old Fannie for $1,200 to Sarah A. Morse; and William G [illegible] wrote of his uneventful transport west of "negroes through the free states" from Columbus to St. Louis.[46]

The Chouteaus' role in the movement of slaves in and out of St. Louis was not insignificant. In 1828, Pierre Chouteau, Jr., wrote to J. Mager in New Orleans regarding a "mulatto named Isidore," whom Chouteau "fear[ed]" would fall ill because he was "not accustomed to [the] climate." Despite Chouteau's solicitation, he added that "necessary dispositions to prevent [Isidore's] escape" be made.[47] (This notation provides further evidence of the frequent and consistent efforts of slaves' attempts to "escape" to freedom, that slave owners recognized the constant possibility, and that they made their own efforts to prevent it.)

In July of 1832, M. Giraud wrote to J.B. Sarpy (a business associate of the Chouteaus) that he'd purchased "a negresse" who was "23 or 24 years old, very clean and clever at cooking." The context of the note, which discussed buying two "strong, almost new" wagons "for the company" and receiving and organizing trade goods ("red and blue blankets, wampum, and silver trinkets") for dispensing to the Osages on a journey that would begin from Independence, suggests that this slave woman might have been part of that planned trek.[48]

Another case in point involved the 1838 sale of two female slaves named Nancy and Mariane by Pierre Chouteau through an intermediary, John A. Merle. In a note from New Orleans, Merle informed Chouteau that he had set a price of $1,800 "for the two of them" and even if "some may fear their acclimatization" he would try to keep the women "from falling into bad hands." Merle further wrote,

> The captain of the *Selma* offered $1200 which I refused. They are in my house and except for their bad humor to others they are doing all they can to make themselves useful and agreeable.[49]

One week later, Merle wrote to Chouteau again, stating that "two others" were "interested in the negresses" for a total price of $2,200, and he had arranged to move them "from one house to the other and if they work well I hope to obtain the price asked."[50]

The next communication recovered is from Merle to Chouteau that October to inform him that "the two negresses have recovered their health and there is now no obstacle to their sale." A week or two later, Merle triumphantly informed Chouteau that the women had been sold for $2,000, and that they will "have a good master." Merle reported shortly after that "the two negresses [were] satisfied with their new master."[51]

While Illinois was a free state, slaves were sold from Missouri to buyers in Illinois so frequently the high number of slave freedom suits based on slaves' residence in Illinois is not surprising. Correspondence seeking or negotiating the sale or delivery of slaves provides substantial evidence of the volume of slave sales in the region and, again, the sometimes delicate or tricky arrangements where slave families—perhaps especially slave mothers with slave children—were concerned. The reliance of slave owners and *their* families on the presence and labor of slave families is also a striking component of some of the communications. For example, in June of 1834, T.F. Smith wrote to Henry Chouteau twice in one week apparently continuing an ongoing discussion between the two men about finding a suitable female "servant" for Smith.

> Dear Henry
>   ... it is impossible to [illegible] one [servant] here at any price—this is a free state and the people are as proud, vulgar and lazy as they are free.... I see advertised in the *Republican* of the 2d June by a Mr. Triplett *a woman 28 years old with two children the one three the other seven years old* [emphasis added] if the woman possesses the qualities he states her to possess it is all I want [*sic*]. I would rather have one without children but if I cannot get one I must do the best I can if his price is not two [*sic*] high purchase her and her children for me ... *tell the woman if you buy her that I will not separate her from her children & please write to me immediately as I cannot be without one & if I cannot get one I will be forced to send my family back to St. Louis* ... [emphasis added]
>
>   Your friend
>   T. F. Smith[52]

Dear Henry

... let me call your attention earnestly to my own business. *I have no female servant about the house and it is impossible to get one here unless I can get one from St. Louis and that without further delay I will be compelled to send my family away from here.* [emphasis added] Cholera or no cholera. You informed me that Auguste will sell Matilda for $400. I would not take her as a present but do not say so to Auguste for he will never forgive me for it. I think Mr. Clark asks too much for his woman, it is certainly a very high price and I like the age and description of Triplett's woman best, besides I prefer a servant who has lived in the country, so if she is healthy, good natured and honest, buy her for me provided his price is not too extravagant and send her up either in the *Warrior* or *Galenian*.

Your newspapers are constantly full of advertisements of negros [*sic*] women for sale. My last *Republican* shows two for sale by Mr. Rundlett and Horace informs me that a man by the name of Duncan has a woman that he thinks can be had and from his description of her I would like to get her. She was formerly hired at your neighbors in the cross street by the [illegible] Mr. Wiggins the ferryman. The woman I understand is known by your mother's servant—Mary Ann and I think your brother Edward knows Duncan, with these landmarks I think you may be able to trace her out, but for God's sake and more particularly for mine do not let another Galenian or the *Warrior* pass without sending me a servant of some kind.

Your friend

T.F. Smith[53]

On July 20, 1834, Smith sent a letter to Chouteau noting he'd "received the servant woman Milly by the steamboat *Winnebago*," and "thus far am very well pleased with her." After requesting a rocking chair and one of the "new patent washing machines" the ladies had "made such a long certificate about in the *Republican*," Smith returned to the subject of slaves, specifically, the new servant woman, Milly.

Milly did not bring all her cloths [*sic*] and she says they are with her husband whose name is Alfred and belongs and lives at the Widow Walker's near the Court House on the hill. Will you oblige by sending Belmont with a message to him to send them by Paul on the *Galenian*.

It is difficult to avoid the conclusion that the "Paul" referred to several times in Smith's letter—to bring "spirits" to Smith by putting them in "Paul's" suitcase, the answer to this message that Paul will bring on the *Galenian* from St. Louis to Rock Island, and "blossoms" and "sand" secreted in a "little red trunk" to which Paul has the key—is not the same Paul, a slave, Smith expressed frustration at because of his persistent running away.[54]

In an October 1834 letter to Chouteau, Smith still seemed agitated by his dealings in slaves. He lamented escape attempts by his slave, Paul, although he admitted he wasn't surprised and had proposed his half-brother exchange Paul and another perennial run-away named Horace for "a family of negroes" his brother recently inherited from their mother. Smith requested the woman and her eldest son sent ahead and "the ballance [*sic*] of the family I would be glad if you would dispose of ... there are two girls

Receipts were typically provided to buyers of slaves like this one signed by Bernard Lynch.

large enough for nurses, and if they will be serviceable to you keep them for your own use." Smith added, "they are of a fine and valuable family" and he hoped Paul and Horace wouldn't "get wind" of the pending sale and "make their escape."[55]

On May 28, 1835, T.F. Smith wrote to Henry Chouteau to keep an eye on the slave Paul, whom the riverboat Captain Crosby had informed him was "trying to get on the Illinois River."[56]

A slave named "Dick" was sold west from Virginia to Missouri, where he ended up in the hands of Henry Chouteau in St. Louis in 1839. It's not clear from the packet of receipts how much time elapsed between Dick's departure from Virginia westward, although it appears from the record that Dick was sold by John Taggart (who stated he received Dick from "Pinchard at Vicksburg") to Samuel H. Lyon in Lafayette County, who then sold Dick to Henry Chouteau in St. Louis in May of 1839. A further notation suggests Dick was sold again in 1847. Almost no specific information is provided about Dick, for example, his physical description or any skills he might have possessed; his age was estimated at "about twenty-one years of age."[57]

In 1855, Henry Chouteau bought a mulatto woman named Therese from Henry Papin for $1,000. Papin provided Chouteau a written "guarantee" that he could "return" the slave if he was "dissatisfied" "within six months barring death and accidents."[58] The price paid seemed in keeping with prices quoted in an 1855, letter to the *Missouri Republican*:

SHERIFF'S SALE.

John Warburton and others, vs. Robert Taylor.
Attachment in the St. Louis Circuit Court.
Whereas, on the 14th day of April, 1845, an order was made in the above entitled cause, by the Hon. John M. Krum, Judge of the 8th Judicial Circuit of the State of Missouri, ordering and directing the undersigned, Sheriff of the County of St. Louis, to sell the property attached by virtue of the writ of attachment in this case, in the manner prescribed by law, which said property is described as follows, to wit:

1 Negro woman, named AMERICA, aged about 25 years, and her child, aged about 18 months.
Also, twin negro boys, aged about 5 years, named FRANK and WILLEY.

Now, therefore, I, the said Sheriff, will, on *Monday*, the 25th day of August, inst., between the hours of nine and five o'clock, of that day, at the east front door of the Court house, in the City and County of St. Louis, State of Missouri, sell the said attached property above described, to the highest bidder, for cash, in pursuance of said order.

WILLIAM MILBURN, Sheriff.

St. Louis, Aug. 13, 1845.

Slave women and their children were sometimes presented together for sale, although they were often purchased by different buyers.

Prairieville, Pike County, Mo.,
January 2, 1855

Mr. Editor: There must be California in North East Missouri, or the El Dorado is in the farmers' pockets. Negro men sold on yesterday at the following prices: $1,365, $1,542, $1,405, $1,215, $1,275. These men were common crop hands ranging from thirty to forty-five years of age. Women brought from eight to nine hundred dollars, and one went as high as $1,040, another as high as $1,753! These two last good house servants and seamstresses. The women bringing $800 and $900 were over middle age. All of these sales were for cash, or for bonds bearing six per cent interest from date.... The rise in the prices of agricultural products, is now telling in the value of labor, and our farmers seem to think that the "peculiar institution" is still of some account.

While negroes sold for these prices, they hired at corresponding rates. Common farm hands, young and likely, hired for $220 and $232; boys of fifteen and seventeen years of age, or thereabouts, hired for $140 and $150—in every instance the individual hiring, and not the owner, paying all charges of every description.

These items may be of interest to your readers.—They may serve to show that the people in the country still think that matters are by no means desperate, though Congress can't elect a Speaker.

Very respectfully yours, etc., P.C.[59]

In 1849, J.E. Barrow wrote to Pierre Chouteau, Jr., and Company, regarding the transfer of a "negro woman and child" from Tennessee. In his letter, Barrow indicated he was sending $250 to the Chouteau Company by steamship, to be paid as a draft for the pair of slaves.

The understanding is that the draft is not to be paid [underline in original] until the negro woman and child arrive to your care....[60]

The letter seems clearly to state that slaves would be in transit from Tennessee to Missouri, but the nature of the Chouteau Company's involvement in the transaction is less clear.

Professional slave traders also played an active role in the sale of slaves in and through St. Louis. Bernard Lynch is mentioned frequently and operated a slave pen in the city. Lynch's role as a broker was apparently respected by potential buyers. For example, in February 1849, Peter Papin transferred three slaves to Joseph Papin, for his "free use and control" and stating that Joseph Papin would not be responsible for "accidents which may happen to said slaves." Barely a month later, Joseph Papin "disposed" of two of the slaves—a "mulato [sic] woman named Lise and her son named Harris" by deed to B.M. Lynch.[61]

Slaves of all ages were routinely advertised for sale in Missouri newspapers. Slaves were offered and sold, both singly and in groups. Some ads specified that individuals described in the groups were family members, although this was not always the case. For example, in 1838, the *Missouri Republican* advertised "a likely negro Boy [sic] about 17 years of age" and also, "a negro woman aged about 30 years with 2 children, one of 3 years and the other 7 months old."[62]

At times, slaves were not sold outright, but instead mortgaged against some future, indeterminate sale or disruption. This might be referred to as sale on the installment plan. For example, in 1825, John Young received $300.11, from Isaiah Todd and Ann Strong Hart, promising to relinquish his title of ownership to "two negro boys, slaves for life, ... one named Joseph, and the other named Henry," in the event that Young was unable to repay the debt on time.[63] By his mortgage, Young warranted that the slaves were "free from the claim and claims of all and any person or persons whatever, and slaves for life."[64] For the period of the loan, Young transferred Joseph and Henry to Todd and Hart, to be reclaimed when Young repaid the loan on or before April 1, 1826.[65] Todd and Hart went to Court to file suit against John Young because as of April 2, 1826, he'd only repaid $74.56 of the total of $300.11 due.[66] Todd and Hart demanded the Court require Young to repay the balance owed or release "all his right, title and equity" in Joseph and Henry.[67] The disposition of the case is not known.

Similarly, in 1828, William Rector's loan from David Deschler was secured by the mortgage of land and slaves. In the event of Rector's default on the loan of $563.98, with interest at 10 percent per annum, Deschler would be authorized to auction a 425⅜-acre tract of land. In the event the sale of land did not cover Rector's debt, Deschler would be authorized to auction for sale a "mulatto boy slave for life named Burwell aged about fourteen." And if the sale of Burwell did not raise enough to pay Rector's debt, the agreement empowered Deschler to auction for sale "a negro woman named Martha aged about twenty years and her child." The slaves were transferred to Deschler and he was to hold them for his use as collateral for the one-year period of the loan. In the event the auctions realized more than the loan plus interest, the difference was to be returned to Rector. If Rector was able to repay Deschler, the collateral land and slaves would be returned to him.[68]

After passage of the Missouri Compromise, a number of slaves sued for freedom based on the legal foundation provided by the Compromise. This also provides additional evidence for the presence of blacks on the western frontier. The case of *Laura v. Henry B. Belt* is a case in point. In this case, the plaintiff Laura claimed to be entitled to live as "a free person" because her owner John McKenney took her out of Missouri in 1847 or 1848, to Indian Territory within the United States and "north of 36 degrees 30 minutes, in which territory slavery is prohibited." Laura stated that she remained and "resided" with McKenney "near Fort Scott and performed labour [*sic*]" there for him until September 1850, when McKenney brought her back to Missouri.[69]

After Henry Belt was served notice of the suit and during the pendency of the hearing on the matter, Belt allegedly sold Laura. Thereafter, James Riley and James Christy purchased Laura and somehow managed to "decoy" Laura "from the place at which she had been confined." Here, a line had been drawn through the words "to wit, the jail of Bernard M. Lynch, where slaves are kept for sale," however, this phrase is reinserted later in the document. Riley and Christy reportedly told Laura they were taking her to meet with her attorney, but instead, "compelled" her to board the steamboat *Isabel*, bound for New Orleans, beyond the court's jurisdiction, where they planned to sell her. Laura's attorney stated that Riley and Christy did this knowing full well that Laura had filed suit for her freedom.[70]

Henry Belt sold Laura about January 10, 1852, and she remained in "the negro jail or yard" of Bernard Lynch until her abduction by Riley and Christy about February 16, 1852. The attorney Joel Richmond said he knew nothing about this until someone claiming to be a passenger aboard the *Isabel* wrote to him about February 24, 1852.[71] Richmond then petitioned the Court to find Riley and Christy in contempt for removing Laura out of the jurisdiction of the Court during the pendency of her suit for freedom.[72]

In response, Edward Curtis filed an answer indicating he had bid on

Laura and purchased her from the St. Louis Sheriff on behalf of Riley and Christy; Curtis denied decoying or removing Laura or committing any other action that might be in contempt of Court.[73]

James Christy echoed the Curtis answer with a nearly identical answer of his own, in which he denied everything. Christy denied "decoying" Laura "from the place where she was confined." He denied removing Laura from the jurisdiction of the Court. He denied "any knowledge whatever" that the Court had ever ordered that Laura not be removed from its jurisdiction. And Christy "positively denied" "decoying" and removing Laura "beyond the jurisdiction of the Court after he had any knowledge that she was prosecuting her suit for freedom."[74]

A number of freedom suits arose from the intersection of geographic relocations and race, including the role of native Indians held as slaves. In 1848, the case of Peggy Perryman, a woman who claimed to have been kidnapped from Arkansas in December 1846, and sold into slavery to Joseph Philibert in the Spring of 1847, was registered in St. Louis Circuit Court. Perryman stated she was the daughter of a Blackfoot Indian woman and a free man of color. Perryman petitioned for freedom based on her statement that her mother's family had been "free since the memory of man." Perryman's petition was denied.[75]

As part of the Compromise of 1850, the California legislature permitted slave owners to keep their slaves when they moved to California, as long as they did not stay in the state. Compliance with the law was spotty. Alvin Coffey was "born about 1822," in St. Louis, Missouri, and remained there as a slave working for his master until 1849, when his master decided to leave Missouri and join the gold rush. By October 1849, they reached California and settled in a mining camp. Duval, the master, did not like the West and returned to Missouri. He took all the money Alvin had been able to accumulate by working on his own after hours and sold Alvin to a man named Tindle. This whole transaction was begun and completed in the state of California where slavery did not legally exist. Tindle in turn allowed Coffey to purchase his freedom for $1,500. Freed by his own purchase, Coffey devoted himself to business. He established a laundry, and in a few years accumulated about $10,000. He was so successful in his business that he was able to make a loan of $2,000, to a minister who had lost his crop. Although the loan was never repaid, Coffey was sufficiently established in business to sustain the loss without apparent injury.[76]

Although one interpretation or implication of the Missouri Compromise had been that Missouri's western boundary would also indicate the western boundary of slavery, slavery continued to expand westward across Missouri through the 1850s.[77] Indeed, the ascendancy of "free" labor ideologies restricted opportunities at least for free blacks to settle or reside along the western Missouri frontier in this period.[78] More likely, a kind of buffer zone of slave owners became entrenched along the western boundary in hopes of forestalling establishment of a free Kansas that could undermine slave owner authority by providing a lure to slaves running for freedom or a haven for anyone who might help slaves escape.[79] Evidence exists to support that slave owners' fears were valid and that anti-slavery settlers across the western border of Missouri went to great lengths to protect escaped slaves' right to live free on the western frontier, up to and including summary executions of people suspected or confirmed as slave "kidnappers."[80] This was so, even though free soilers were among those who also sometimes went to great lengths to bar settlement, and thus competition, by free blacks.[81]

On occasion, blacks also worked as slave traders. William Wells Brown was one of a number of blacks, slave and free, who worked in the trade at some level. Brown traveled regularly between St. Louis and New Orleans.[82] A former slave, Brown was employed in various labor—house servant, tavern boy, printer's assistant, tailor's helper, field hand, steamboat cabin boy and barber, and "handy man" for a Missouri slave trader named James Walker.[83]

The slave record is replete with tales of both cruelty and kindness, at times in the example of a single person. A. Leonard left a detailed record of his management of slaves over a period of decades. Leonard organized his slave account book with neat subject headings: Name (of slave), Born about, How derived (whom, when, Price or Gift), How disposed (whom, when, price), and "Remarks." Leonard noted several slaves received as gifts, although he did not include details as to the occasions prompting the gifts. Leonard also gave gifts of slaves to his daughter, Mary, and to his brother (whose name was not recorded). Leonard noted several slaves he permitted to marry other slaves on neighboring farms or plantations, slaves transferred or given to family members, or sold for "bad conduct—incorrigible." Leonard also noted slaves who died (of fever, consumption). Some details provide information about the generations of slaves in Leonard's possession, as when he noted that Lincoln, born June 13, 1862, the "child of Ann," who was born about 1835, and purchased in a "judicial sale" in 1841, had burned to death February 15, 1863. Ann's daughter Susan perhaps fared better, when, in 1854, she became the "wife of William." Leonard sold Sally, when she married "Mr. Smith's boy Luke" and requested that she be sold to Mr. Smith. Leonard did so for $500. He also noted the births of two sons (Warren in 1839, George in 1841) to Betsy, born in 1819, and whom he received as a gift in 1830.[84]

Commercial interests as well individuals profited from the slave trade. A variety of businesses depended on or grew out of the success of the slave trade. The data indicates that significant sums of money were expended on the purchase and maintenance of slaves and the protection of the material value of slave property was a logical extension. Thus, the St. Louis Insurance Company provided the following service:

> ... INSURE THE LIVES OF SLAVES, whether working on shore, or on boats navigating the rivers. To persons owning slaves, who hire them on steamboats, this affords advantages of a gravity too palpable to need insisting on.... Persons at a distance desirous of ... insurance ... on the lives of their slaves, can receive every information relative thereto by addressing a line (post paid) to R. Collet, Secretary of the Saint Louis Insurance Co....[85]

In part because of its geographical location, St. Louis served as a conduit for the movement of slave property onto the western frontier. Large numbers of those slaves had been sold west to St. Louis from the eastern seaboard slave states or from the Deep South. The establishment of fur trading forts on the frontier often relied on primary business offices in St. Louis and slaves and free blacks frequently traveled (or were sold) back and forth between St. Louis and the frontier or on errands or employment at the forts. Although slave owner anxiety increased at the prospect of statehood for Missouri, trade in slaves, sometimes conducted by professional agents, continued. Slave families, most often slave mothers and slave children, were sometimes sold together, but were also sold apart, often, ironically, to support the stability of slave owner families. Slave runaways repeatedly sought to escape at the same time that slave owners redoubled their efforts to maintain hegemony of the slave regime. And in the face of heightened political disagreements about the morality or feasibility of the United States continuing as a nation that was home to both slave and free states, the trade in slaves remained robust even on the eve of the Civil War.

> J. L. Bates, Esq.
>   This will be handed you by Mr. White, who has a lot of negroes for sale and will probably be in your vicinity. If you have not already supplied yourself, we think you would do well to look at his negroes. He has some very good boys and in buying of Mr. White we have no doubt but that you will get good sound property and good titles. We know [illegible] very well and bespeak for him any assistance you may be able to render him whilst in your neighbourhood [sic].
>   Your friend
>   Slaughter Crosby, Esq.[86]

CHAPTER 6

"Free with the world": The Strange Case of Milton Duty

On a humid evening in August of 1838, a white man named Milton Duty fell over and died. Duty was at home when he died, and a black slave named Preston was there, too. The two men had lived together for several years and had come to Missouri from Mississippi together less than two years before. Milton Duty, who was white and owned Preston, was a man who spoke plainly to intimates and acquaintances alike. He'd told those who knew him in St. Louis that what he owned was due to the hard work he and Preston and his other slaves had done, and that he didn't think anyone else should benefit because of it. He said he didn't intend that anyone would.[1] Duty had traveled to Missouri from Mississippi in order to free his slaves. He had made a will that made his intentions clear: at his death, his slaves, including Preston, Preston's brother, Braxton, and a woman named Mary were to go free.

Preston knew it, and most of the other Duty slaves knew it, too, because Milton Duty wasn't someone who kept things to himself. He said what was on his mind and said it plain. So standing on the front porch that August evening when Milton Duty breathed his last, Preston no doubt understood that whether he was that moment free, would become free, or would remain a slave was in some way connected to the man lying dead on the floor.

It happened suddenly, and yet apparently, Milton Duty did not die instantly. Duty's neighbor, James Adams, had been visiting with him only minutes before Duty died. Adams had known Duty since his arrival in St. Louis from Mississippi, and considered him a friend. Duty spent most evenings he was in town with Adams and his family, often in the Adams

107

home. Adams said that although Duty seemed financially stable, he lived "in a very plain economical unimpressive manner."[2] The location of the Duty home may be implied by documents filed with the St. Louis Recorder of Deeds in 1831, and again in 1835, to record the lease by James and Sarah Adams of "a tract or parcel of land lying near the city of St. Louis on the branch above Chouteau's Mill Pond."[3]

A few weeks before Duty died, Adams spoke with him on his return from a recent trip back to Mississippi. Almost everyone who knew Duty described him as a man who spoke his mind, and Adams was aware that on that trip Duty had brought back $5,000 in "Mississippi money" to pay George and David Coons, a father and son money managing business, what he owed them. Duty told Adams that once he'd done that, he'd be "free with the world." Others also recalled that Duty had brought a large sum of cash to Missouri on his latest trip from Mississippi.[4]

The evening he died, Duty told Adams he didn't feel well, so Adams made ready to leave so that Duty could get some rest. Duty walked Adams to the door and went out on the porch with him to say goodbye. When Adams reached the end of the drive to Duty's house, he turned and waved. Adams saw Duty reach out, and then fall backwards onto the porch. Adams ran back toward the house, hollering for his wife as he ran. When he reached the porch, Adams knelt beside Duty and cradled him in his arms. The only other living white person at the house when Milton Duty died was his teenaged nephew, George Galloway, who lived with Duty while attending school in the area. James Adams was holding Milton Duty in his arms when Duty died.[5]

The relationship Duty had with his slaves, especially with Preston, makes it likely he'd discussed his plans with them. The Duty slaves probably understood that if Milton Duty was dead, they were supposed to be free. Word of Duty's death would have spread quickly throughout the house that night, and certainly there would have been discussions among the slaves about what would happen next.

As James Adams and Preston carried Milton Duty's body into the house and laid it on his bed, Adams was startled to notice that Duty's skin had begun to darken in the minutes after his death. Adams bathed Duty's body and shaved him, and within only a few minutes, as Adams watched, Milton Duty's complexion took on a "peculiar" ruddy shade that other white witnesses also remarked on and reported to authorities. Some, like Adams, suspected foul play. Whether Preston or the other Duty slaves noticed this or whether they were asked what they thought about it is unknown because no record has yet been discovered as to what the Duty slaves thought about Duty's death or the "peculiar" shade his complexion took on in the minutes after his death.

Thus began one of the stranger freedom suit cases in antebellum Missouri. The records of this case shine a searchlight on important elements of slave and free black identities in Missouri in the period, how they were constructed and revised, and perhaps the reciprocal relationship between those identities and the identities of the place itself. Everyone involved in the case seemed to have a different recollection of what happened the night Milton Duty died, and a different idea about what should be done with the Duty property, including, or perhaps especially, what should be done about the Duty slaves.

* * *

Milton Duty had only been in St. Louis about a year and a half when he died. The previous Spring, Duty and more than two dozen of his slaves traveled north and west by overland trail and riverboat from Mississippi to Missouri. By the time Duty and his bondmen arrived in St. Louis, the former trading post had evolved into a bustling town that possessed a "self-conscious" identity as a crossroads to the West. It is likely that Preston and Braxton helped organize and supervise the Duty household for the trip; the party was composed of a mixed group of adult women and men, as well as small children, although what held them together with more force than chains was the knowledge that at some time in the future, Milton Duty planned to set them free. The record of slave births after the arrival in St. Louis suggests that one or two of the women might have been pregnant at the time of the trip.[6]

A flurry of activity preceded the journey as Duty and his slaves made ready to leave the neighborhood of Vicksburg, Mississippi, for St. Louis, Missouri. In the weeks leading up to the planned March 1837 departure, Duty sold several slaves. It is not clear why Duty, who went to such great lengths to free more than two dozen slaves, would at the same time sell others and leave them behind in Mississippi. It's possible he did so in order to settle his debts in Mississippi and finance the journey to Missouri. But it is also possible that he sold slaves in Mississippi because those slaves wanted to remain in that state with family and friends and selling them was the safest way to accomplish that in a state where free black settlement or residence was strongly discouraged and supported by statute. That this was most likely the case is supported by one of Duty's Mississippi neighbors, who testified that Milton Duty told him he'd sold some of his slaves before he left Mississippi because they had not *"wished"* to move to St. Louis.[7]

Based on this account and many others, the Duty slaves seem to have exercised a degree of autonomy that might seem inconsistent with stereotypical notions about slavery or the exercise of power in relationships between slave owners and their chattel. Their owner, Milton Duty, considered his slaves' *wishes* when making decisions about them. In addition, Preston seems to have been in charge of collecting money slaves earned from being hired out in St. Louis and transferring it to Duty's estate administrators, the Coons father and son team. Therefore, Preston exercised a kind of power that, again, seems unusual for a slave, particularly in the case of a slave who, whatever his ability with figures, also seems to have been illiterate: Preston signed court documents and depositions with an "X."[8]

The historical record on U.S. slavery, checkered though it may be, has shown that slave owners—regardless of their race—were more likely to free slaves they were related to, and to define "slavery" more loosely for slaves who were "in the family." In Amite County, Mississippi, the children of at least one white slave owner and a black slave woman, slaves under the law, nevertheless acted on their father's behalf when conducting business. Indeed, in border states like Missouri (and even Deep South states such as South Carolina and Mississippi), free blacks who owned slaves were more likely to own a spouse or other family member. In places where free black residence was discouraged or required a bond or license—in other words, almost everywhere—this "strategy" of slaveholding might protect kin from harassment or seizure. But no photograph (or even a physical description) of the Duty slaves survives, or at least none has been discovered or identified as yet, and so it is not clear whether Preston, Braxton, Mary, or any of the other Duty slaves were "black" slaves under the law, or brown or yellow slaves (*"griffe"* or "mulatto"), who had some mixture of white blood.[9]

Before he left Mississippi, Milton Duty also met with attorneys and wrote his will. In it, he spelled out his wish that all of the slaves he owned at the time of his death were to be set free. For some reason, Duty even specified that if he happened to die in Mississippi, his slaves should be manumitted and "sent out of this State into the State of Missouri" if possible, and if not possible, that they should be sent "to such other state or territory in the United States ... deemed most suitable." Whatever the circumstances and wherever it occurred, Milton Duty was clearly preparing the way for his slaves to be free.[10] (In the case of *Stephen Smith v. David Shipman,* Shipman took a group of slaves he had mortgaged against his debt along with real estate and other property out of Kentucky to Indiana and Illinois and finally to St. Louis; there, Shipman set the slaves free, although it is not clear what his motives for doing so might have been.[11])

Twenty-five slaves—including Preston, Braxton, and Mary—were listed in the final inventory of Milton Duty's possessions. When he died, Duty, a man his friends insisted had lived simply, even frugally, had also owned a feather bed, a collection of firearms (one silver-mounted rifle, as well as a rifle with a plain wood stock, a double-barreled shotgun, and a "pocket pistol"), a silk umbrella, five overcoats, three pairs of cashmere pants, and a two-volume edition of Homer's *Iliad*.[12]

Certain details of the daily lives of Preston, Braxton, Mary, and other Duty slaves, as well as of Duty himself, survive in the record. For example, Duty had kept a careful notation of the day-to-day lives of his slaves, including a record of $8 spent for the burial of a slave described as "Caroline's child." Duty also paid a servant (who, unlike Caroline, was not named in his notebook) $4 to "attend" to Caroline "in [her] sickness," and he noted that he'd lost $19.50, for the three months' time Caroline had been unable to work because she'd been sick. Duty supplied no details as to the nature of Caroline's sickness, for example, whether she had been depressed after the loss of her child or was recuperating after a difficult pregnancy. But either scenario fits Duty's solicitousness for his slaves' mental as well as physical well-being.[13]

Milton Duty's will leaves little doubt about his fondness for some of the people whose labor had helped to make him a man his neighbors described as someone in "comfortable" circumstances. Duty directed that his slave, Preston, was to receive Duty's gold watch and clothes in appreciation for Preston's "faithfulness and honesty." Duty earmarked $1,000 to be given to a slave woman named Mary, whom he'd purchased three years before. He instructed that any cash remaining be divided equally between Preston and his brother, Braxton, and that if they wanted, the two brothers should be permitted to live in Warren County, Mississippi, and that whatever bonds the state required to permit them to settle there should also be paid. Milton Duty appointed his neighbor in Mississippi, a judge named John J. Guion, executor of his will.[14]

When Duty and his household arrived in St. Louis in the spring of 1837, they joined a steady stream of white slave-owning migrants from the East who arrived in Missouri accompanied by their black slaves. Of course, the vast majority of these slave owners were part of the expansion of the institution of slavery westward, rather than part of any effort to extinguish the institution by manumitting slaves. By that time, a small but thriving free population of color lived in the region. The presence of free black competition for labor that white men might have performed sparked white resistance that occasionally resulted in violence against property—for example, the public burning of abolitionist pamphlets in 1836—and that also contributed to pro-slavery and anti-abolitionist attitudes.[15]

But the overall population of blacks, slave and free, in St. Louis in the period was small. Census figures show 1,531 slaves (9.29 percent of the population) and 531 free blacks in 1840, with an increase by 1850 to 2,636 slaves and 1,398 free blacks. By 1860, the number of black slaves had decreased to 1,542, which was not even one percent of the total 160,733 residents, but the number of free blacks in the city had increased to 1,755 (1.09 percent). By then, an 1847 Missouri law prohibited free black settlement in the state (see Chapter 2, The Color of Law), and so it has been suggested that manumissions and natural increase were the reason for that increase.[16]

In the city of St. Louis, the combined total population of color was more concentrated and throughout these years remained steady at about 20 percent. There was no "colored" neighborhood to speak of, but most free people of color lived and worked within a few blocks of each other in buildings clustered in what was for the most part a commercial center on or within blocks of the river. Free blacks were even taxed to support public schools their children were barred from attending. The City Directory for the years 1836–37, identified free residents of color as such. Free blacks listed in the directory lived within blocks of each other in the river district and followed a variety of skilled and unskilled occupations (barber, drayman, washerwoman). (It is possible, of course, there were residents of color not so identified either because they had successfully "passed" across the color line or simply due to clerical error.) The center of activity for both free blacks and slaves were independent black churches in St. Louis. Several independent black churches were located in the river district. Five black churches had been established in St. Louis by 1850 (three Baptist, two Methodist; four of the churches were referred to as "African" churches—including the African Baptist Church at Third and Almost streets—and the other as Ebenezar Methodist). It is therefore not surprising that the Directory listings included the Baptist preacher, the Reverend John Berry Meachum on Second Street. Thus, because the Duty slaves had been in the habit of being hired out, the town was small, and communications among free blacks and even slaves good, it is likely that by the time administrators of the Duty estate announced plans to sell them, the Duty slaves were not only aware that St. Louis law might allow them legally to protest their sale by the court, but may have also known which white lawyers—many of whom kept offices in the river district that was home to many blacks as well as a neighborhood where many slaves were hired out to work—to approach to ask for help.[17]

Laws increasingly restricted activities of free blacks in St. Louis over the course of the antebellum period. Free blacks who appeared in the criminal court record illustrate both this narrowing of possibilities and opportunities for free blacks according to statute at the same time that it evidences a variety of ways free blacks sought to expand their possibilities and opportunities, or at the least to hold the line. For example, William Cornelias [sic], was cited for keeping a "disorderly house" in 1824. So-called "disorderly houses" (saloons, brothels, etc.) were targeted by law enforcement officials as much for the *sub rosa* or illegal activities they encouraged as for the tendency of the unsupervised activities of such places to blur racial definitions or hierarchies. In a border city intent upon holding the line for slavery and racial segregation, it was important to police any behavior which might encourage racial mingling.[18]

Likewise, the criminal court records memorialized some of the ways slaves in Missouri actively resisted enslavement. Throughout the antebellum period, both slaves and free blacks were charged with "enticing" slaves to run away. Thus, parallel to the sprightly sales of slaves was persistent activity by slaves and others to resist or escape (or help others to escape) slavery. Numerous freedom suits were brought based on the claim that slaves had spent extended periods of time in Illinois, the Northwest Territory, or other western lands where slavery was prohibited by statute.[19]

The American military presence increased with the advance of the frontier and the expanding white population. Indeed, the military often made the way safe for the westward expansion of trade in black slaves. Military officers received an allowance for the purchase and maintenance of a "servant" to help them "uphold a certain class status" and so while the military made the West safe for slavery—even in frontier areas where slavery had been banned by legal statute—some of the officers retained slaves for their personal use, and St. Louis was a pre-eminent crossroads of this trade.[20]

The free community of color co-existed with a vigorous trade in black slaves. "Negro traders" or slave dealers—among them McAfee & Blakey on Olive Street; James Bridges on Pine; E. Thompson on Pine; John R. White; and the infamous Bernard Lynch—also established places of business in the St. Louis river district, so that, side by side with the advancement of free people of color was the parallel advancement of the trade in slaves. During the pendency of a number of the slave freedom suit cases, blacks were sometimes detained in Bernard Lynch's "negro jail" or "negro yard." A man named Peter Hutson was listed as a "Child Hunter" in the 1857 city directory, and likely tried to trace the whereabouts of children of color sold away from their parents as slaves. So, the Duty men and women of color, like others intent on suing for their freedom, no doubt knew it might be possible to sue and win their freedom, but also knew there were people who earned their livelihoods by selling people like them further into slavery. (An 1837 ad in *The Republican* posting a $10 reward for the return of an "indentured girl" of about ten, and another posting a $100 reward for the return of a 17-year-old "indented negro boy" to be free at age 21, may confuse the issue of who or what a slave was.[21])

Milton Duty took such pains to see that his slaves would be cared for after his death, that, in fact, they should not be slaves anymore at all, it makes sense to ask who the Duty slaves were. Why would a white man in Mississippi in the 1830s liquidate his assets, sell everything he owned (including other slaves) to personally take more than two dozen slaves to Missouri to set them free? Were some of the Duty slaves his relatives? Were some of the Duty slaves his children? And what about the witnesses who noticed that Duty's complexion seemed "darker" after he died? Is it even possible that Milton Duty wasn't white at all?

* * *

Milton Duty died, and the night wore on.

For some reason, that night, Preston went to get George Coons, the local administrator of the Duty estate. Because Preston had been in charge of collecting money slaves earned and handing it over to Coons, he might have thought Coons would be the one to get the plan for the Duty slaves' manumission underway. Hugh Gallagher was staying at Coons' house, and both men were asleep when Preston arrived. Coons said Preston woke him up, and that on hearing the news of Duty's death, he and Gallagher immediately got out of bed, dressed, and went to Duty's house. Traveling on horseback or by buggy, the two men arrived at the house after midnight, which Coons believed was an hour or so after Duty died. Coons said that when Duty was taken ill, the only living white person at the house had been Duty's nephew, George Galloway, who was a minor.[22]

Coons said the first thing he did when he got to the house was examine Milton Duty's body. He said Duty's skin looked "very dark." He used the word "remarkable" to describe it. He said Duty's skin looked *remarkable*. Coons said he asked Adams and Galloway what had happened. Galloway told the men his uncle hadn't been feeling well for the past few days and had taken Calomel. He told Coons Duty had drunk "cold water" earlier that day.[23]

Coons said that while he was staring at Duty's body, Preston approached him and told him that Mr. Duty had some trunks and things in the house, and asked him to please take charge of them. Coons said Duty's nephew asked him the same thing. Coons said he didn't ask for the trunks, even after Preston and Galloway brought them to his attention, but said Preston brought them to him on his own, and Coons then examined them in the presence of everyone at the house at that time. Coons seemed to take it in stride that Preston took it upon himself to initiate that action; that is, Coons didn't mention that he found that unusual or impertinent, or that he had remarked on the inappropriateness of the action to Preston. Coons said the trunks were not locked, and he kept an inventory of the trunks' contents as he went through them. Coons said he didn't tear up any papers or destroy anything in the trunks and hadn't seen anyone else do anything like that either. He said he didn't destroy any receipts Duty might have had for anything. Coons said he took the trunks and papers away with him when he left because there were no grown white men at the house to look after them; the only people there were slaves.[24]

James Adams remembered the events of that evening somewhat differently. Adams said the first thing Coons did when he came in was tell Preston to fetch Duty's trunks. In fact, Adams said he got angry when Coons began to "ransack" the trunks and he had told Coons it was "primitive" to attend to business when the corpse had not been laid out yet. Adams said he was so focused on trying to help Duty that at first he hadn't noticed what Coons was doing, and by the time he did notice, Coons had already torn up several sheets of paper and thrown them on the floor. He said that in a matter of only 10 or 15 minutes, Coons had ransacked Duty's trunks, grabbed some papers and cash from them, and left the house.[25]

Sam Farnandis, another neighbor of Milton Duty's, also recalled events unfolding differently than the description of them given by George Coons. Farnandis said Coons came to the house while Duty's friends and neighbors were preparing his body for burial. He said Coons' bookkeeper, George Gallagher, was with him. He said as soon as Coons and Gallagher established for sure that Duty was "certainly dead," George Coons ordered Preston to bring him trunks containing papers and money that belonged to Milton Duty. And Farnandis said Preston did what Coons told him to do. Farnandis remembered that Adams was the only person who said anything to Coons about what he was doing, and he said Coons' response was something like he "couldn't help it." Farnandis said the way Coons acted the night Milton Duty died made him think that he and his father, David Coons, meant to perpetuate a giant fraud on the Duty estate. He speculated that the papers Coons destroyed might have contained proof that Milton Duty had already paid any debt he owed to Coons, and that Duty's estate was free and clear when he died.[26]

Duty's neighbor Thomas P. Follis not only recalled that Duty spoke freely about his affairs, but said Duty had told him he had made no arrangements to leave anything to any of his "kin," but had made a will that would set "all of his negroes" free. Follis said Duty told him he was leaving his watch and chain to Preston, and meant for Preston to wear them. Follis said that because Duty was always "truthful," he believed him absolutely. He went to Duty's house the night he died, but only stayed about ten minutes. Follis said that when he left, George Coons was still there.[27]

Of course, the bottom line in the Duty case was money.

Gallagher said his recollection of the state of the Coons' books was that Duty owed Coons about $1,200, although he didn't know what the debt was for unless it was for a cash advance. He said he was sure Duty must have had receipts for that amount, but when he and Coons looked through Duty's papers the night Duty died, there weren't any receipts in the trunk.[28]

Almost immediately, notices began to appear in local newspapers advertising an administrator's sale of Duty's effects—including the gold watch Duty intended for Preston and specifically "excepting" the slaves Duty had owned at his death—and a separate notice advertising those same slaves for "hire at auction."[29]

*   *   *

In the sultry summer of 1840, while the squabbling over Duty's estate escalated into a court fight, slaves continued to be auctioned on the steps of the St. Louis courthouse under the east portico. A slave woman named Mary along with her small son and daughter, were purchased by John Shelton from Asa Thompson for $830.

It turned out that Asa Thompson had sneaked this slave family out of Arkansas and brought them to Missouri, not, like Milton Duty, in order to free them, but because a mortgage Thompson had taken out on them was due and he couldn't pay it. The law referred to this as "fraud," and seized Mary and her children to make good Thompson's debt to the mortgage company, Williams and Blevins.

Because Thompson had sneaked away again for "parts unknown," that left Shelton holding the bag for $830, and no way to get his money back.

So Shelton filed petition for injunction in Chancery Court to block the transfer of Mary and her children to Williams and Blevins. Shelton claimed the men holding the mortgage knew all along that Thompson had sold him the slaves—even though technically they weren't his to sell—because they were about to get their property back. The Judge mediating the case was none other than Luke Lawless, who granted the injunction. It was just another day in the Chancery Court.[30]

In November of 1840, St. Louis County Clerk Henry Chouteau, an heir of the city's founding family, finally recorded the will Milton Duty had filed in Mississippi several years before, but Chouteau nevertheless found that Duty had died intestate—meaning without a valid will filed in the court—and appointed George Coons administrator of the Duty estate. It was common for slaves who were part of estates being contested in the Chancery Court to be hired out during the pendency of such cases, some-times for several years, and in all likelihood, that is what became of Pres-ton, Braxton, Mary, and the other Duty slaves. While the court took its time deciding their fate, they continued to be slaves.[31]

* * *

St. Louisans remembered the summer of 1841, not because of the Duty cases, but because of events that led to the execution, decapitation, and display of the severed heads of four black men found guilty of robbery, the murder of two white men, and arson. The confessions of a slave named Madison Henderson, and his three free black companions, Charles Brown, James Seward, and Amos Warrick, were transcribed by St. Louis newspa-per editor Adam Chambers, who probably paid jailer George Moody for access to the prisoners. All of the men had worked on the river in a variety of occupations, a way of life which was one of the few in which black men had the opportunity to exert independence in their lives and to construct their own definition of masculinity and authority. Not least in this con-struction was the life of mobility, a rare element in black life, slave or free, in the antebellum era. Doubtless, many, if not the vast majority of black men who worked on the river refrained from participating in illegal activ-ities; but Henderson, Brown, Seward and Warrick seemed on the make for the easy dollar, and eventually things went very wrong.[32]

Madison Henderson not only enjoyed his life of mobility working on steamboats traveling between St. Louis and New Orleans, he was also lit-erate, and apparently made use of this ability to forge a variety of docu-ments he used to obtain merchandise he sold on the black market. Some items the men sold (most often food, but also jewelry or silverware) were obtained from slaves along the way, which means that at least a few slaves on their river route earned some money their owners were not aware of. It is also likely that Henderson and Charles Brown, who was also literate, forged manumission papers and used their knowledge of ports and river cities to help runaway slaves. The story they told—which was corroborated by slave owners who admitted the absence or loss of the slaves that Henderson and Brown described in their confessions—suggested the existence of underground railroad activity with routes leading north and west through St. Louis, as well as of a complicated trade network that involved a kind of entrepreneurship practiced by both slave and free blacks.[33]

By the end of 1840, Henderson, Brown, Seward, and Warrick moved to St. Louis, often working off of the steamboat *Angus*. The following Spring, the men attempted to rob the Pettus Bank in Galena, Illinois, a town where they had pulled off successful robberies in the past. But this time, one thing after the other went wrong: a tip indicating the bank had just received a huge shipment of silver wasn't true; the men couldn't open the safe in the bank; and two clerks interrupted them while they were in the bank. The river men beat both clerks to death, then torched the bank in an effort to cover up what they had done.[34]

The St. Louis militia was called out to defend the city against the perceived threat and to calm white residents' anxiety, a general search of the city was mounted and continued for a month to ferret out "every suspicious person," and a $5,000 reward was posted by the mayor. The four men being sought scattered in different directions, each attempting to vanish into the labyrinthine world of river traffic, but the steamboat network circulated news of the murders throughout the region. At least one slave along the route was whipped to force him to give information, but the miscreants' undoing was the man who had given them the "tip" about the Pettus Bank in the first place, and who gave a tip to authorities about where they'd headed to avoid being arrested himself. Sensational news of the attempted escape, trial and execution of Madison Henderson, Charles Brown, James Seward, and Amos Warrick filled the newspapers of the region and fueled gossip through the summer and into the fall. Among the attorneys for the men were Hamilton Gamble and John Darby. Whether the men acted according to a particular abolitionist, political, or economic strategy is not clear, but whatever their specific designs, it is almost certain that white attitudes in St. Louis toward free black and slave mobility hardened in the wake of these events.[35]

*   *   *

In September of 1841, more than three years after the death of Milton Duty, George Coons petitioned St. Louis Probate Court for permission to sell the Duty slaves to get back $7,203.63, he claimed the estate owed him, plus an additional $1,422.23, as his fee for acting as Administrator of the Duty estate. Coons said even if the slaves were hired out, whatever money they earned wouldn't be enough to pay off the estate's debts. Thus, it seems certain that over the years the case was litigated, the Duty slaves continued to work. As administrator of the Duty estate, Coons was in charge of how money the Duty slaves earned was spent, but clearly, he wanted a final reading on who would ultimately get the money the Duty slaves earned.

The Court agreed that Coons could announce the sale of the Duty slaves to take place on October 12, 1841, between "nine o'clock in the forenoon and six o'clock in the afternoon" under the east portico on the St. Louis Courthouse steps. The 26 slaves, including 11 children, were to be sold to the highest bidder to pay the debts Coons said the estate owed.[36]

That same month, Preston, Braxton, and the other Duty slaves filed their own petition in the St. Louis Chancery Court for an injunction to block the attempt to sell them. Ferdinand W. Risque, an attorney well known for his involvement in petitions for freedom on behalf of St. Louis people of color, represented the Duty slaves.[37]

In March 1842, David Coons died. His wife, Mary, was executrix of his estate along with executor Andrew Christy.

The Duty case is striking for many reasons, not least because in it, so many slaves simultaneously, and collectively, sued to be free. It represented a kind of antebellum class action suit. Unlike cases in the civil, or even in the criminal courts, the Chancery Court oversaw disposition of estates, and so it was probably just a matter of time before a large group of slaves who had been part of an estate banded together to sue for their freedom. Even so, it was not until May 16, 1843, that a notice appeared in a St. Louis newspaper declaring outright that the years of writs, subpoenas, and petitions had had a single purpose: *"the object and general nature of which is for complainants to obtain their freedom."* That same year, the Missouri legislature amended its laws to prohibit anyone from bringing slaves to Missouri from other states with the intention of setting them free at a later date. (However, this legislation had no chilling effect on white slave owners heading west for Texas and beyond and who traveled through St. Louis with their slaves.) If the Duty case did not directly inspire this new phrasing of laws respecting slaves, it is a peculiar coincidence that the Duty slaves' intent and the law surfaced about the same time.[38]

When Milton Duty died, the adult slaves he had hoped to set free were young men and women, and some of them had children. Preston had been 26 years old at the time, and his brother, Braxton, had been 27. The woman identified in the will as Mary was 35. Although Milton Duty's will might make Preston seem the natural leader, his brother Braxton was more outspoken. At least, based on the record, a picture of Braxton, the older brother, emerged as a man who was bright, self-assured, and determined.[39]

In his deposition, Braxton stated that he thought George Coons was lying when Coons said the debts owed the Duty estate in Mississippi could not be paid. Braxton said he had traveled with Milton Duty back to Mississippi on more than one occasion and Duty had told him that he felt he could collect what was owed him by the year 1838, which was also the year that Milton Duty died. And Braxton said that Duty told him he was in the process of buying land in the Soulard Addition of St. Louis to build homes for his "negroes," so they would have places to live when he died. Because Missouri statute required owners to provide for manumitted slaves, this may also have been Duty's way of adhering strictly to the letter of the law in order to reduce legal impediments to his goal of setting his slaves free.[40]

Like his brother Preston, Braxton signed his deposition with an "X."[41]

Thus, these people, who had been listed as Milton Duty's personal effects, came forward, at first in small groups, and petitioned the Court not to sell them. Preston sued on behalf of himself and, as their next friend, for the minor children, Henderson and Harry (although it is not clear whether he was their father, or who their mother was). Braxton sued for himself and for his own minor children, Jackson and Mary. Malinda appeared for herself and for her sons, Howard and James. Searcy sued for herself and for her children Lewis and Margaret. Clarissa sued for herself and for her children Ann Eliza and Beverly. Caroline, who had convalesced for a few months presumably after the birth and death of a child and for whom Milton Duty had paid money out of his own pocket to hire a nurse to attend her, appeared for herself and her daughter Lucy Ellen. By the time the Duty slaves filed their petitions, estate administrator George Coons had already advertised the sale of these slaves in the *Missouri Republican* newspaper.[42]

Hearings in what would become a long court case got underway in the city's two-story brick courthouse building with its pillars supporting a roof and cupola, and continued in the copper-sheathed dome of the new, enlarged courthouse raised in 1843. As hearings continued, a limestone floor was laid in the court building's rotunda in 1844, and the building was finally opened for business on Washington's birthday in 1845.

The courthouse building was an impressive landmark sitting atop a slight rise facing the Mississippi River. Brick sidewalks framed and led up to the courthouse, and there was a wrought iron fence surrounding it as well as a border of locust trees. Despite its perhaps deceptively pretty exterior, water had to be brought into the building from pumps or a well, and the building's public privies were only swept out once a day, except on Sunday. During the years the Duty cases dragged on, public debates were held at the courthouse on the questions of U.S. expansion west and war with Mexico, the California gold rush, and slavery and race. And in the midst of the preparation for the case to finally get underway, and organized sentiment against slavery coalesced and reached fever pitch around the country, a prospectus for publication of *The African, an Anti-Abolition Monthly,* to be published by J.W. Hedenberg was circulated in St. Louis. Thus, the cases unfolded during a time when tempers were high, and getting higher, about the question of slavery.[43]

* * *

Subpoenas had been issued ordering a number of men Milton Duty had known either socially or in his business affairs to come to St. Louis to testify. In November of 1843, several men who could not or would not make the trip to St. Louis were deposed in Vicksburg, Mississippi, before Mayor Miles Folkes.

A Mississippian named Egbert Sessions said Duty had stayed with him on his last visit to Mississippi. Sessions said Duty had lived plainly and was known to be free of debt, although during that last visit, Sessions said he had witnessed a quarrel over a debt between Duty and a man named John Henderson. Sessions said he understood Duty had sold all of his stock and farming utensils (including a horse he'd sold to a local legislator, John Harris) before he left Mississippi for Missouri, although he didn't know how much Duty made from those sales. He said it was widely known that Duty left the state in the company of "at least twenty negroes."[44]

While Coons had argued about who should get the money the Duty slaves earned, Henry Chouteau quibbled over salt. Chouteau said he had delivered two shipments of salt to Duty from his firm, Risley & Chouteau. The first shipment was 6,360 pounds at a cost of $95.45, and the second was 3,360 pounds at $50.40. Chouteau said Duty used the salt to pack pork for shipment, and that the shipment of pork went to the bottom of the Mississippi when the keelboat it was on sank putting off from the landing at St. Louis. According to Chouteau, that was neither here nor there, because Duty still owed him $145.85 for the salt, and he wanted the Court to give it to him from the Duty estate.[45] (As we have seen, Henry Chouteau and his relatives bought and sold slaves, as well as fought prodigiously and persistently in St. Louis Courts to hang onto their slave properties.)

*   *   *

Part of Coons' petition to the Court was a request that the Duty slaves be hired out so that he could collect money Duty owed him. Coons said that, at the time of Duty's death, the slaves had been appraised at $7,725, Duty had $1,141.73 in cash on hand, and $2,564.61 due him for the hire of his slaves (of which $965 could not be collected because the people who owed it didn't have it). Coons said Duty owned no other real estate, and the value of his slaves had depreciated 30–50 percent, and therefore would not bring more than $5,000.[46]

The Court ordered all of Milton Duty's property except his slaves sold to pay any debts of the estate before moving on to consideration of whether to permit sale of the Duty's slaves, and that when and if the slaves were sold, Preston, Braxton, and Mary were not to be sold.[47]

*   *   *

By May of 1845, there was still no resolution to the case. At that point, the Duty slaves filed petitions demanding specific information about the status of Milton Duty's estate. In these petitions, they used Duty as their own last name. Although as property, slaves had no last names (nor, it was assumed, any need for them), once they became free, some slaves created their own last names or used the last name of an owner before their most recent owner. It was also fairly typical for freed slaves to use an owner's last name once they became free. Preston was now "Preston Duty," although he continued to sign the complaint with an "X." Henderson and Harry had turned 21 since the filing of the original complaint on October 12, 1841. And to mark the irony of the inexorable, even inescapable, quality of economic returns on the investment in slave property, a new name had been added to the list of slaves owned by Milton Duty, who were suing for their freedom: James, who had been born since the original petition was filed.[48]

In this new petition, Preston Duty—who had been in charge of collecting money for Milton Duty—asked the Court to compel George Coons to appear in Court and bring with him all of his original account books containing entries about the Duty estate and that Coons be compelled to show with receipts exactly how the Duty estate was indebted to him. The Duty slaves also asked that a special commission be appointed to settle the estate and that George Coons be compelled to pay the estate all that he owed. They asked that the order for the sale be continued.[49]

Trader's copy

☞ $2,500 ☜
REWARD!

RANAWAY, from the Subscriber, residing in Mississippi county, Mo., on Monday the 5th inst., my

Negro Man named GEORGE.

Said negro is five feet ten inches high, of dark complexion, he plays well on the Violin and several other instruments. He is a shrewd, smart fellow and of a very affable countenance, and is twenty-five years of age. If said negro is taken and confined in St. Louis Jail, or brought to this county so that I get him, the above reward of $1,000 will be promptly paid.

JOHN MEANS.

Also, from Radford E. Stanley,

A NEGRO MAN SLAVE, NAMED NOAH,

Full 6 feet high; black complexion; full eyes; free spoken and intelligent; will weigh about 180 pounds; 32 years old; had with him 2 or 3 suits of clothes, white hat, short blue blanket coat, a pair of saddle bags, a pocket compass, and supposed to have $350 or $400 with him.

ALSO--- A NEGRO MAN NAMED HAMP,

Of dark copper color, big thick lips, about 6 feet high, weighs about 175 pounds, 36 years old, with a scar in the forehead from the kick of a horse; had a lump on one of his wrists and is left-handed. Had with him two suits of clothes, one a casinet or cloth coat and grey pants.

Also, Negro Man Slave named BOB,

Copper color, high cheek bones, 5 feet 11 inches high, weighs about 150 pounds, 22 years old, very white teeth and a space between the centre of the upper teeth Had a blue blanket sack coat with red striped linsey lining. Supposed to have two suits of clothes with him; is a litte lame in one ancle.

$1,000 will be given for George----$600 for Noah---$450 for Hamp---$450 for Bob; if caught in a free State, or a reasonable compensation if caught in a Slave State, if delivered to the Subscribers in Miss. Co., Mo., or confined in Jail in St. Lonis, so that we get them Refer to

**JOHN MEANS &
R. E. STANLEY.**

ST. LOUIS, August 23, 1852. (PLEASE STICK UP.)

Reward posters illustrate the persistence of slaves who sought their freedom by running away.

Perhaps most interesting of all is that Preston Duty and the other Duty slaves petitioned the Court to give an accounting of property they considered belonged to them. Preston claimed some of the property Coons was selling belonged to them. For example, a horse and dray sold by Coons was listed as "the individual property" of Jesse, which he'd owned "with the knowledge and by the consent of" Milton Duty. They asked that Coons give them an accounting of the monies they'd earned while being hired out. And they asked that those Milton Duty had named in his will to receive legacies be given them now.[50]

Ultimately, Preston Duty and the others asked the Court to set them free according to the provisions of Duty's will. They even offered the Court a suggestion on how to find a resolution and settle the case: they be hired out for a limited number of years, sold to pay what was owed by the Duty estate, and after a certain time determined by the Court, declared free.[51]

In 1850, Preston, Braxton, and Mary Duty, and the other Duty slaves filed further petitions for freedom in the St. Louis Civil Courts. This time, they claimed they were free people held illegally as slaves because their owner, Milton Duty, had freed them in his will.[52]

In 1854, a document purporting to be the last will and testament of the late Milton Duty was produced in the Probate Court of the City of St. Louis, and was finally found by the Court "proved" as Duty's will.[53]

No documents specifically stating what became of Preston Duty and the other Duty slaves have as yet been found. But one document has surfaced which shows once again the many connections among slaves and slave owners in antebellum St. Louis.

Taylor Blow, who may be more well-known for purchasing Dred Scott after the Supreme Court declared Scott forever a slave, and then setting

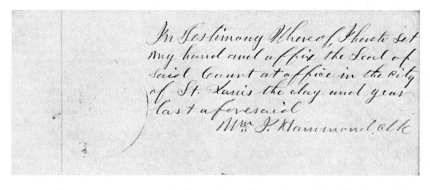

Nicene Clark, a slave once owned by Milton Duty, was bought and manumitted by Taylor Blow, who also purchased and freed Dred Scott.

him free, also played a role in the Duty case. In 1854, Blow freed a black woman slave named Nicene Clark, whom he described as about 5'2" tall and approximately 30 years old. According to Blow, he had purchased Clark from the Milton Duty estate.[54]

Sixteen years after Milton Duty died, at least one of the people he had planned to set free was finally "free with the world."

CHAPTER 7

"As far as Kansas":
Slave Resistance in the Gateway[1]

In St. Louis, recognition of the ever present possibility of slave resistance was encoded in its earliest laws. Newspaper articles in the *Missouri Republican* in September and October 1831, provided graphic details in the chronology of events of the insurrection planned and carried out in Southampton, Virginia by the slave "Baptist preacher" Nat Turner (although Turner's name was not mentioned). The newspaper recounted the discovery of intelligence about identities of conspirators, the capture and execution of ten slaves involved in the uprising, rumors that the insurrection had "extended to neighboring states," including reports of an insurrection in North Carolina, and a warning that the "terrible vengeance" meted out by the "friends and relations of the murdered families ... will operate as a salutary lesson upon this unfortunate and misguided race."[2] Despite such spectacular exceptions of collective violent action by slaves, resistance to slavery—and resistance there was, continuous, persistent— was typically perpetrated by individual slaves rather than by groups; and these gnawing incidents of refusal to accept enslavement disrupted, but did not derail, the institution of slavery.[3]

From its earliest years, St. Louis was the site of slave resistance that took many forms. But perhaps the most iconic example of slave resistance is the runaway. Even though running was usually attempted or accomplished by individual slaves, slave owners recognized the act as rebellion against the institution. Running was described by at least one slave trader as "an act of revolt on the part of the Negroes."[4] Slaves ran away from every locale within the slave regime, however, the presence of the river and the frontier were doubtless irresistible enticements to St. Louis slaves to run.[5] A pattern

126

of westward movement of slaves seeking to escape slavery is evidenced throughout the historical record. In addition, the urban environment of St. Louis with many slaves hired out in a variety of occupations in town and on the river provided opportunity if not outright encouragement to run.[6]

As early as 1810, the *Missouri Gazette* newspaper included reward postings for the return of runaway slaves, such as this one offering $30, for the return of

Three Negro Men;

All brothers, the oldest named *Jack* about 24 years of age; the next named *Dick,* about 22 years of age, and the youngest named *Stephen* about 20 years of age; each of them are [sic] about 5 feet 10 inches high, *not very* black but too black to be called dark mulattoes, they all appear to be active and sensible; the oldest and youngest are tolerably slender made, the other something [sic] larger built; they took with them a small *Shot gun* which has a piece of tin tacked about half way round the stock and lock, to hold on the lock, they have each a new black furr [sic] hat, a pair of dressed buckskin overalls, and a homespun blue cotton coat; the oldest has also an old brown-ish cloth coat and a blue cloth waistcoat; each of the others have one homespun striped cotton waistcoat and brown thickset waistcoat; *Dick* has an old blue cloth surtout [sic] coat, and Stephen an old gray cloth coat; they have no particular flesh marks, and *no* marks of being whipped.

The above reward will be given for their delivery to the subscriber in St. Charles, or for securing them in *any* gaol [jail] so that I can *get them* again; or 10 dollars will be given for securing each or either of them.

James Journey.
St. Charles, 8th Feb. 1810[7]

These aptly named Journey slaves were described in some detail, including their ages, height, as well as what they were wearing. Skin color of slaves was important to slave owners and was typically included in almost any news-paper account regarding slaves. This posting also provides evidence of famil-ial connections among slaves—the runaways were "all brothers," as well as of the unusual instance of a group of runaways, rather than an individual.

Anecdotal evidence supports the oft-made conclusion that runaway slaves' destinations tended north, but the free territories and states of the West also exerted a powerful lure.

Lexington, Mo. Augt 7th 1855

Dear Bob,

Agreeable to promise I have undertaken to write you, but have nothing to commu-nicate. I know of no negroes for sale except a Boy 10 or 12 years old belonging to Tom Graves, which he will either sell or swap for a Girl about the same age. I sold at auction yesterday a negro man 24 years old, belonging to a man in Pettis County for $810.00 cash. I also sold a Yellow Man 22 years old, belonging to a man in Cass County (Pri-vately) for $1075.00 on six months time, both of the boys had run off previously, and *one had got as far as Kansas* [emphasis added].

...

Respectfully yrs
Wm Anderson[8]

Residence in the free state of Illinois was also frequently the basis of slave freedom suits, although the status of blacks in that state was sometimes ambiguous.

$100 REWARD

RAN AWAY from the subscriber on the 18th day of April last, my negro boy, *Jack*, aged about 17 years. The said boy is indented to me until he 21 years of age [*sic*]. Jack left his home in a very mysterious manner without any cause or provocation. Jack has also a sister indented to me which [*sic*] will be free about the same time. Jack took no clothing with him except what he wore away; it is also ascertained that the boy Jack had considerable of money [*sic*] in his possession a few days before he went away. It is supposed that Jack has been decoyed away with the intention of selling him in the lower country. Jack is small of his age [*sic*], a dark mulatto or light negro; he may be easily known by removing his clothes by a large scar on his left side, from the lower part of the thigh to nearly the arm pit, occasioned by a burn. Jack is very fond of horses and an excellent rider. I will give ten dollars if Jack is confined in any jail so that I get him [*sic*], or I will give twenty dollars for his apprehension and delivery to me in Lebanon, St. Clair County, Illinois; and on proof and conviction of the offender who took off said boy, I will give fifty dollars; and should it appear that said negro Jack has been kidnapped and sold, I will give an hundred dollars [*sic*] for the apprehension and conviction of the offender.

L. ADAMS[9]

Slave runaways sometimes received assistance from free blacks, as well as from whites. When free people (black or white) who helped slaves to escape were discovered, they were often charged with theft of property. In 1821, William Flake was charged with the crime of stealing Timothy, a "negro man slave valued at $400" and the property of Mathias McGirk "against the peace and dignity of the State." A grand jury was impaneled to consider the matter. The charge described Flake as "not having the fear of God before his eyes but being moved and seduced by the instigation of the Devil." The charge referred to Flake's act as setting an "evil example."[10] A *writ of habeas corpus* was issued for a "man now in custody whose name is unknown and who refuses to disclose his name." The man was charged with "having stolen and attempted to smuggle" a negro out of Missouri and into Illinois for the purpose of "aiding and assisting the said negro to run away."[11]

William Smith was deposed and stated that the "unknown" white man had crossed the Mississippi River on a ferryboat in the company of the black man, Timothy. Smith said he overheard Timothy refer to the white man as "master," but that when the ferry reached the Illinois side of the river, the white man paid their fares and whispered to the black man to "escape." Smith said both men started running away from the boat, but both were caught and detained. Smith said Timothy told him the white man had told him to address him as "master" as part of the plan to help him escape.[12] William Farmer was also deposed, but stated the unknown white man had told Farmer that he had seen Timothy steal a spade or shovel and that the negro had told Farmer that he was free.[13]

A substantial backlog of reward posters and notices in newspaper classifieds dating from the period before Missouri statehood indicate the persistence of slaves to claim freedom by any means necessary. For example, in 1815, a reward of $25 was offered for the return of Sam, a 24-year-old "Negro man" described as having "an intelligent face" and wearing a new cape and new deerskin overalls.[14] The owner wrote that Sam was "the same fellow who roamed about two years ago" and that it was "probable" Sam had obtained "a forged pass as a free Negro."[15] The owner promised to pay both the reward of $25 and "all reasonable expenses incurred in conveying" Sam back to St. Louis in the Missouri Territory.[16] On rare occasions, entire families ran away together.

ONE HUNDRED DOLLARS REWARD

I will give the above reward for the apprehension of the following described negroes who left my residence ... in Saline County on Saturday night the first of the present month. The negro man named Antony is aged about 25 years. He is tall and well made ... black ... countenance sour and forbidding ... reserved and sullen; his habit of speaking slow and cautious.... The woman who accompanied him is his wife; her name is Alcey—she is short and heavy for her height—her complexion yellow—her countenance pleasant—her manner mild.... Sheila twenty years old very handsome. Their child ... is a fine looking boy three years of age.... A very black young negro ... heavy built, belonging to James Remines of Saline County is supposed to be ... with them. His age is twenty-three ... a scar on one of his feet, whether right or left not known. Mr. Romines will give fifty dollars for ... said boy in addition to the reward above offered.

It is believed the ... negroes carried with them what purports to be free papers.... It is thought ... they may be ... traveling under the protection of some white person.... I will give $200 if they are taken out of the State, and secured until I can get possession of them.

DE WITT McNUTT[17]

In his ad, DeWitt McNutt described the couple as married, even though marriage as such was not recognized in civil law where slaves were concerned. Beyond the somewhat casual mention of a slave man and his "wife," there is also mention of a young woman who is mother to a three-year-old child, and another adult male; the familial connections of the larger group, if any, was not noted. The ad mentions the "negroes carried with them *what purports to be free papers*"—as well as the possibility that a white man was traveling with them as "protection." These kinds of details, accurate or not, fed rumors of "abolitionist" activity in the region; and such rumors increased in the decades before the Civil War.

The Mississippi River was a frequent avenue of escape. Slaves forged or purchased free papers or passes that identified them as authorized to hire out on the river.[18] Others attempted to stow away and get off at the first urban stop on the river.[19] Although free blacks working on the river often provided help to runaway slaves, some free blacks informed on runaways to cement their own positions.[20] As for white participation, the interest and participation in westward movement by whites included an increased presence in Missouri by whites of every political stripe, including abolitionists. Such individuals engaged in a variety of activities intended to precipitate the end of slavery—manumission of slaves (sometimes purchase of slaves for the express purpose of manumitting them or, as has been shown in the case of Milton Duty, the relocation of slaves for the purpose of manumitting them); membership in and activism in colonization societies; participation in Underground Railroad activities; and on occasion, guerrilla activities (especially in the lead-up to and wake of Kansas-Nebraska). For example, in 1856, Walker Shumate, who identified himself as "an agent" of the Missouri Colonization Society, manumitted six slaves who appeared to be a family, although they were not specifically identified as such in the manumission document. They included Philip, "about forty-three years old," Jemima, "about forty," Amanda, "about nineteen," Jane, "about fourteen," Harry, "about nine," Elvira, "about five," and Eveline, "about three."[21] It is not clear whether the slaves manumitted by Walker Shumate were in any way connected to the transport of "about 26 negroes" from Virginia to Missouri in July 1846. On July 29, 1846, R. C. Nicholas wrote to G. W. Goode, Esq., in St. Louis, describing in circumspect terms the relocation of the slaves from Richmond to Fauquier County, Missouri.[22]

An 1852 letter from R. Dexter Tiffany of Worcester to John Darby of St. Louis for the most part represented a routine exchange of family news (pregnant wives, speculation as to whether the Mississippi would be navigable by March), but also an accounting of Tiffany's presence at a concert given by the "Black Swan." Tiffany was aghast:

> I went to hear the Black Swan sing last night, and what do you think she is. Why I will tell you, a stout fat Dutch built, fellow, who looks like Mike Sutter, the Butcher, has picked up one of the coarsest, Dutch built short-necked-homely looking, black negro wenches, you most ever saw, calls her the Black Swan, and talked around among those free soilers, abolitionist and niggers to make money. I went and of all the mixed audiences, for a concert, that beat all. There were the real stripe of abolitionists, free soilers, and all the radicals mixed up. On the same [illegible] where I was was [sic] two strapping negresses and behind me on the next were five others. I think this concert was rather more of the Elephant than anything I have before seen in Massachusetts. But by paying the press and carting round this negress, this chap makes a good easy living and I [illegible] be surprised that he takes her to England and makes something of a noise about her. She has just compass of voice but not much volume and no intermediate notes and has had no training and I doubt from her appearance whether she has intellect enough to be trained.[23]

Having delivered his cultural critique, Tiffany returned to musings about the weather. Tiffany's discussion, and similar others, may shed light on how abolitionist activities, not to mention cultural attainments of free blacks, were viewed by some whites in the period leading to the passage of the Kansas-Nebraska Act.

Slave owners were most fearful of the possibility of armed slave rebellion and the criminal court record at St. Louis provides ample evidence that this concern was a reasonable one. Whether the prospect of collective resistance demonstrated by reports of an 1816, effort by deputy constable William Morris to "suppress a riot among the negroes, slaves and mulattoes"—an incident which suggests not only slave unrest, but alliances between slaves and free people of color, or the 1818, arrest of a slave named Elijah and owned by John B.N. Smith, for the suspected poisoning of "his mistress and the family by arsenic," it seems clear that slave resistance in and around St. Louis sometimes took violent form.[24] In the former case, St. Louis Grand Jurors ruled on the August 4, 1816, arrest of a laborer named Bazile Bissounet, apparently for interfering with Deputy Constable Morris' efforts to suppress a slave "riot," although Bissounet's race and status were not noted.[25] In 1826, a warrant was issued in St. Louis based on information supplied to a "justice of the law" regarding a possible slave "riot." And in the midst of the Civil War, in 1863, Timothy F. Slattery was charged with "inciting slaves to insurrection" and indicted for "murder."[26] The record indicates a change of venue from St. Charles Circuit Court, and the defendant was discharged.[27]

The record also notes the role of free blacks in anti-slavery activities in the region. Moses Dickson was born free in Cincinnati in 1824, and worked as a shipboard barber from the age of 16. It was while traveling through the South by steamboat that Dickson observed and was deeply affected by what he referred to as the "horrors" of slavery. In 1846, Dickson moved to St. Louis, where he assembled a group of 12 anti-slavery men who met in a building at Green (Lucas) Avenue and Seventh streets to discuss Dickson's plans to overturn southern slavery. While Dickson remained in St. Louis, after swearing to an oath of secrecy, he directed his 12 associates to return to their southern home states (South Carolina, Mississippi, Virginia, Louisiana, North Carolina, Georgia, Tennessee) and recruit men to take part in the violent overthrow of slavery scheduled for 1856. While his men were ostensibly putting together an army of resistance, Dickson worked to perfect the Underground Railroad, so that runaway slaves could be more safely and efficiently smuggled out of the south. Dickson claimed spectacular success with his personal contribution that resulted in an exponential increase in the number of successful slave run-ways and he had postponed unleashing his 47,000 recruits to destroy slav-ery when clues—John Brown's 1859 raid at Harper's Ferry and Lincoln's 1860 election—convinced him the Civil War would soon break out.[28]

After publication of the Emancipation Proclamation, instead of going forward with his plan for armed resistance against slavery by blacks, Dick-son enlisted in the Union Army, and after the war, he joined the Missouri Equal Rights League. The organization was made up of 94 African Amer-icans sympathetic to Radical Republican support of black suffrage, who were further inspired when Missouri defeated a black suffrage clause in its 1865 Constitution. But Radical Republicans chose the politically expe-dient course in demanding only that blacks be granted civil rights short of the vote and elected office.[29] The League's organization in St. Louis on the heels of that defeat and, a decade later, the mass migration of blacks into the West as free "Exodusters," signaled a new relationship between people of color in the region and the advancing frontier.

CHAPTER 8

Standing Ground: Free People of Color and the St. Louis Land Court

It was about the land.

The goal of the founders of St. Louis had been to create an important trading center, and they were even more successful than they had anticipated when the trading center became a major cosmopolitan city. The settlement had quickly become a crossroads of exploration, trade, and settlement in what was then considered "the west." Missouri was a slave state and, as we have seen, a small but reliable segment of trade in St. Louis was the purchase, sale, and transportation of slaves. Thus, the growing village on the river benefitted from and stood at the crest of a far-reaching wave of westward activity involving a variety of people, livestock, and goods.

The essential physical plan of St. Louis did not change markedly over the years. The city began at the edge of the Mississippi River at the place that was most accessible for expedient landing and loading and unloading of boats, and construction of the first buildings began on the bank of the river. Commercial establishments competed for land that would give them most convenient access to the waterway and residential and other buildings were constructed in what was left over. Both commercial and residential buildings housing the town's most prosperous citizens shared space on First or Main Street.[1] The founding families built their own homes close to their places of business and often owned "country" estates a mile or two west of the river. The din of construction—felling of trees with axes and hatchets, cutting and planing of hardwood panels, cutting and hauling of limestone blocks from the river bluffs and dragging supplies uphill from the banks of the river, and the calls and shouts directing it all—continued for decades as the forested banks of the Mississippi were gradually tamed or cleared and stone or whitewashed buildings with painted shutters or awnings took their place. Buildings on the east side of Main Street did not face those on the west side of Main Street, but rather, they were built to face west, their whitewashed backs to the first row of buildings on the river and the river itself.[2]

St. Louis was built low to the ground. In the early years, colonial huts were built on stilts and platforms high enough off the ground for a man to walk easily underneath, and therefore it was hoped, to keep wild animals at bay. But as the town matured and settled into itself, houses were constructed either flush to the ground or over a root cellar or crawl space, where valuables could be hidden or where one could take refuge in the event of sudden attack by Indians.[3]

The city founders and others who profited early from the fur trade built imposing two-story dwellings of native Missouri limestone and the region's prized pink granite; the houses favored adjoining courtyards enclosed by high stone walls, and frame wooden houses weren't common even 40 years after the founding of the town. In the settlement's wild early days, the stone enclosures were more about protection than luxury, and holes carved into the high walls were used to mount rifles to defend the town. Domestic animals and buggies were kept in pens in the enclosures, and sometimes there was room for a root cellar or private garden.[4]

St. Louis houses were typically constructed with a gallery or porch on one or two or even on all four sides. The summer heat was punishing and a porch was one way to keep the sun from bearing down directly on the stone sides of the houses, which created a kiln that dramatically raised the temperature inside the rooms. Amenities included planed and polished walnut floors, and many houses of the prosperous installed imported, glazed glass windows, which were sold by Clamorgan, Loisel and Company, and shutters painted with colors available from the same store. Ceilings in the dwellings were not high; at roughly eight feet, typical ceilings were only a couple of feet above the heads of the tallest men. Although most houses included a fireplace to cook and heat the house, many also included a separate kitchen in the back of the house. Houses in town were built on adjoining lots, and each owner was responsible for putting up a fence, usually wood stakes with sharpened points on top. Residents engaged in reading or after-dinner conversation late in the evening by candlelight or grease lamps.[5]

A natural wall of limestone separated the broad main street of the settlement from the river. Roy's Tower, a windmill with a revolving top and canvas sails, was a landmark that stood on the riverfront near Mullanphy Street at the north end of town. South of the main village, the commons extended seven miles and for a generation was bounded by a fence. The sounds of the town included the bellowing of cattle, neighing of horses, and grunts of hogs grazing on the commons or, in the early years, of animals wandering free on the roads of the town. South and west of the original settlement and commercial district was Chouteau's Pond. In 1767, Pierre Laclède purchased the lake and surrounding lands from Joseph Taillon, who had dammed the water to construct a small mill, which turned out to be too small to meet the town's needs. Laclède improved and expanded the operation, which his stepson Auguste Chouteau purchased in 1779, from the company formed by Laclède and Maxent after Laclède's death. Chouteau razed the standing mill and ultimately built a two-story stone mill in its place, which became a thriving business.[6]

As for the pond itself, in summer, locals fished and swam there and picnicked on its banks, and in winter, skated on the frozen surface of the pond. The free black preacher John Berry Meachum baptized converts in the waters of the pond. After his father's death, Gabriel Chouteau continued to operate the mill and shared control of the property with his brothers, Henry and Edward, providing the city with high quality flour from his mill built at a dam on the pond. (Slaves seeking their freedom sued both men in the city's civil court.[7]) Men raced their horses along the river road and over the hard-packed dirt roads of the village to cheering crowds for fun, sport, or a gentlemanly wager.[8]

The city developed into a commercial and cultural center of some importance, a phenomenon that complemented the progress of the nation. For example, on April 22, 1857, the Ohio and Mississippi Railroad reached Illinois Town, just across the river from St. Louis, connecting the Atlantic Ocean to the Mississippi River, and several weeks later, a great celebration in St. Louis commemorated this event. But the city was also not immune to a variety of disasters that struck over the years. On the night of May 17, 1849, the steamboat *White Cloud* caught fire while docked at the landing in St. Louis. It was a windy night and the fire leapt ashore and ignited gunpowder stored in warehouses along the main street. The commercial district and 23 boats tied up for a mile along the waterfront were soon engulfed in flames, but somehow, the city's nearby courthouse was spared. Then in 1853, Chouteau's Pond, long a landmark and repository of town tradition, was drained. The cholera epidemic of 1849 and 1850, prompted fears that unsanitary conditions created by the standing water of the pond had contributed to it. That same year, Roy's Tower was demolished.[9]

* * *

Free people of color owned land, houses, and other buildings in the vicinity of St. Louis, and court records reveal a variety of patterns of ownership and ways in which free colored landowners improved or expanded their properties. The law did not specifically prescribe a separate black or colored neighborhood. Free people of color lived in town in houses they rented or owned, often near businesses they owned or which were their places of employment. While some free people of color had once been slaves, others were the children and grandchildren of free blacks. Most lived in relative anonymity, but there were occasional, spectacular exceptions, including the owners of Clamorgan's, a barbershop and importer of perfumes and other luxury items, located on 4th and Pine streets, three brothers who were free men of color.

Social events occasionally "shared" entertainment. Beginning in the 1840s, and continuing through the end of the Civil War, the free black composer and musician Joseph William Postlewaite composed music and performed for dances held separately by whites, free blacks, and slaves.[10] (Postlewaite continued to play for dances after the war.) He was a successful entrepreneur with operating partnerships in a local coffeehouse and agency representing musical acts; he also owned a music publishing company.[11] Postlewaite played music for elite free people of color, but in keeping with the rigid class distinctions recognized by elites of all colors, was not considered one of them.[12]

City landmarks on or near the river included the Cathedral on Walnut Street, the Courthouse on 4th Street between Chestnut and Market, and the American Fur Company. Free people of color lived in rented rooms or houses they owned in the vicinity of the Cathedral and the city's founding families on streets named for the city's first political elite: Chouteau, Soulard, Papin, and Biddle among them. In the 1840s, a free black riverboat pilot named David Desaray lived at the corner of 3rd and Almond streets, John Davis owned a billiards parlor on Morgan Street, a free woman of color named Elizabeth Drummond kept a hotel on Wash Avenue, and a dressmaker named Martha Smith lived on 6th and Washington. A free black midwife named Hannah Courtney delivered free babies of color from her home on 9th Street, and in 1859, the free woman of color and dressmaker Elizabeth Keckley lived with her son James on 5th Street, while a free black teacher named William Carter lived—and perhaps taught free black students—on 7th Street between Carr and Franklin. In 1860, Dred Scott's widow, Harriet, lived in rooms in an alley between Franklin and Wash. Free people of color were shoemakers, butchers, milkmen, tobacconists, plumbers, saddle makers, and Joseph Willes on Hazel Street was even a "matchmaker," and they lived and practiced their occupations in every quarter of the city. By the 1850s, there were also over two dozen dealers of slaves in the city, buying and selling at auctions on the courthouse steps, and the offices of men who traded in slaves were also close by (James Bridges at 1st and Pine, McAfee & Blakey at 91 Olive Street, in an upstairs office at 61 Pine Street, "E. Thompson," and Bernard Lynch negro traders across the street from the city jail). Thus, the tension between freedom and slavery was always present, and the importance to free people of color of shoring up free status part of the daily landscape.[13]

The first great change in the appearance and culture of the city came with the official transfer of the village to the United States in 1804, just one year after the Louisiana Purchase. After the transfer, frame and brick houses and log cabins—American innovations—became more common. There was also an effort to enforce laws (against horse racing through the city streets, arresting slaves who were drunk on the streets, and prohibiting black slaves from attending the fancy dress balls given by free people of color). Men who broke the law might be publicly whipped at the whipping post in the public square, a cause for gawking and gossip if not actual deterrence of crime. A volunteer patrol consisting primarily of white men who owned property in the village returned slaves found on the streets after 9:00 p.m. to their owners and turned vagrant Indians over to the Indian agent. Dead animals were ordered removed by their owners as soon as possible in the interest of public health.[14]

As early as 1808, a commission formed to discuss and settle claims to the lands of the Louisiana Territory. Resolving such questions was so important the commission met every day except Sunday. What the commissioners decided was published in the newspapers, sometimes for as long as nine weeks running. Thus, at least everyone who could read would know the outcome, and those who couldn't read would find out by the grapevine.[15]

Discussion of land also occupied a great deal of column space in local newspapers. The *Missouri Gazette* began publishing while St. Louis was officially still Louisiana, and advertised houses for rent and land for sale. Readers could easily find a room or storage space to rent or a building or lot to purchase by studying the pages of the city's newspapers. In 1831, lots "situated for warehouses and stores" were listed for sale on Main, Cross,

Pine, and Front streets, as well as a house on the "bank of the river." Three-story stone warehouses near the steamboat landing were also for rent that year, and in demand for use as storage for dry goods, feed or clothing. Joseph Benjamin had houses for sale on the outskirts of the main settlement "near the pond"—one brick and one frame, one with a lot and the other with a "good well of water in the yard." When "R. Webster" opened the Eagle Tavern as "a house of entertainment," he advertised in the newspaper for "genteel borders." There seemed to be something for everyone.[16]

The classifieds section of newspapers also showed who had recently purchased or opened stores in the commercial district. Descriptions were detailed but succinct: for example, a new iron store opened by Bates & Hicks was described as being near the steamboat landing in a corner of a large stone building below the American Fur Company, but above Scott & Rule's Warehouse. Charles Collins opened a livery stable near the Missouri Hotel, and for those looking to outfit their stables, the Harness, Trunk, and Military Accoutrement Manufactory opened at 52 Main Street. It was also possible to follow the movements, up and down the economic and social ladders, of St. Louis business leaders by reading the classifieds: a small brick building near the courthouse that had once been the law office of Judge Luke Lawless was listed for rent by John F. Darby, who had occupied the building but was moving his own office to Main Street.[17]

Despite what passed for peaceful co-existence, or perhaps grudging acceptance, the fragile rapport between the races was sometimes shattered suddenly in ways that led to fatal consequences for some. The city jail was also located in the commercial district at 6th and Chestnut streets. In 1836, a free mulatto named Francis McIntosh was burned to death by a lynch mob. In those years before slavery ended, it was rare for a slave to be killed by a mob. They were considered much too valuable. But free blacks were another matter. McIntosh, a steamboat steward, was arrested at the steamboat landing for involving himself in sheriff's business being conducted by deputies and was taken to the jail. Along the way, the deputies "joked" between themselves, though loudly enough for McIntosh to hear, that he would be hanged. Terrified, McIntosh broke free of the men, and stabbed both of them. One of the deputies died. A mob estimated in the thousands dragged McIntosh through the streets before burning him at the stake. Horrified, activist newspaper editor Elijah Lovejoy moved to the other side of the river, where he was killed a year later while trying to defend his press from another mob.[18]

The monstrous burning to death of Francis McIntosh by a mob followed a year later by the murder of Elijah Lovejoy also by a mob illustrated the color-blind tenacity of race and slave politics in the area, but the slave trade itself continued unabated. Public auctions of slaves traditionally took place on the steps of the courthouse, and slaves were confined in the city jail until they could be sold. The east portico of the courthouse faced the river, providing scant shade during the late morning or early afternoon hours when slave auctions were typically conducted. While the business of slave buying and selling was almost always conducted by white men, on occasion, entire white families gathered on the knoll above the river for the events, sometimes equipped with camp seats, parasols and refreshments and often accompanied by slaves who drove their buggies or wagons. Thus, gentlemen and their families could enjoy relative comfort while bidding on chattel released to settle debts on an estate—as was the case when 15 "women, boys, girls and children" from the estate of Auguste Chouteau were auctioned at high noon on October 26, 1831—or recently offloaded from a steamboat up from New Orleans. Black or white-skinned mulatto slaves stood in the blinding sun that reflected off the limestone of the east face of the courthouse awaiting inspection, sale or rejection. The call of the auctioneer quieted the crowd and at least momentarily attracted the attention of passersby before they continued with the routine of their days. After all, it was a commonplace event, not one that was shocking, unusual, or unexpected. Among those observing, and occasionally participating in, the slave sales were members of the city's free black population.[19]

Free blacks paid taxes for public schools, even though an 1847 Missouri law prohibited educating blacks. Free people of color with the means sent their children out of state to private schools; Pennsylvania was a favored location, but there were also schools that accepted students of color in other states, including New York and Massachusetts. Free people of color had actually founded some of the schools, while others were segregated schools run by whites. It is likely that racial discrimination or exclusion was not the only reason free people of color who could afford it might have sent their children out of state to be educated, since well into the 19th century there seems to have been a studied inattention to establishing educational institutions for working whites or blacks. Like their black counterparts, whites with money often sent their children to schools out of state, or patronized small, privately run academies around St. Louis.[20]

Then there were those free blacks who took matters into their own hands and set up schools for the education of blacks themselves, against great odds, at great risk, and sometimes even against the law. In the 1820s,

John Mason Peck taught black children religion and "the three R's," while the free black preacher John Berry Meachum oversaw a day school for blacks, which apparently had a racially integrated staff for several years before the city sheriff arrested one of its white teachers and closed the school down. (In 1859, Peck was still listed in the city directory as a clergyman living in an alley between Carr and Wash streets, and it is possible this was also the location of his classroom.) In 1845, the Catholic Sisters of St. Joseph of Carondelet taught the basics, French and needlework to black girls, but in 1847, the school was destroyed by a mob. It had long been against the law to teach slaves to read and write, and finally, in 1847, white fear and anger exacerbated by the increasingly strident national debate over slavery prompted the Missouri Legislature to make it a crime even to teach free people of color.[21]

Some of the free people of color who taught in St. Louis later went on to careers on the national public stage. Elizabeth Keckley reportedly taught sewing, which might have acted as a cover for lessons she provided in reading and writing, before leaving the area to become dressmaker to Mary Todd Lincoln. The city's five black churches convened classes in their basements, and in 1860, Hiram H. Revels (who later became the first black United States senator from Mississippi) opened a school on the levee. Blanche K. Bruce, the second black elected U.S. Senator, took it over in 1861. In May 1863, the American Missionary Society organized a school for fugitive slaves in the Missouri Hotel, which outgrew its rooms in the hotel and moved to the Ebenezer Church on Washington Avenue. Two days later, one of the city's ubiquitous white mobs, which haunted the city during the Civil War, burned the church down. But the school relocated as the "American Freedom School" and soon grew to over 100 pupils. Despite the clear commitment and the consistent effort of St. Louis blacks to attain formal education, by late 1863, only 10 percent of the city's black children were enrolled in schools. (However, one reason for this might have been that the city's free black residents did not want their children to mix with "contrabands"—slaves who fled the Deep South and followed the advancing Union line to St. Louis.[22])

*   *   *

The free population of color in St. Louis was small and fairly stable. The majority of free blacks who owned land in St. Louis were not former slaves, and certainly not slaves who had sued to be free. By 1847, free persons of color were prohibited from emigrating to Missouri for any reason whatever at the risk of a prison sentence of no less than ten years. But some of the most poignant and powerful of the freedom suit stories are those lived by slaves who, after winning their freedom in the courts, bought land which they also had to fight to hold onto in courts of law.

Questions about who owned land or disputes over who owned land were addressed in the Land Court, which was organized in 1853, specifically to handle such disputes. Before that, disputes over land titles were also resolved in civil, criminal, or probate courts. Squire Brown, a slave who sued for his freedom and won, was one of those free black St. Louisans who fought first for title to himself, and then for title to his land, but even before the Land Court was organized, free people of color battled for title to lands on which they staked their free identity.

In 1845, a free woman of color named Elizabeth Dickinson was sued by Thomas M. Knox, who claimed Dickinson "entered into ... land and premises" he occupied near Olive and Third streets in the city of St. Louis and "ejected" him. Knox sought $1,000 in damages. Dickinson later purchased her daughter, Laura Lewis, and her grandson, George, to provide them with some protection in the sometimes volatile environment of slave St. Louis. Free women of color also sometimes purchased their slave husbands to provide them protection from being sold away. But in the case of Dickinson's daughter, the strategy seems to have failed because in 1860, Lewis sued a man named Henry Hart for her freedom. Her case went to the state Supreme Court in 1863.[23]

One of the more intriguing disputes over legal ownership of land involved a slave woman named Ester and a West Indian adventurer named Jacques Clamorgan who also gave birth to one branch of St. Louis' free colored elite. Ester was described as a "mulatto" and came west from Virginia first to Kaskaskia, and later, in 1784, to St. Louis.[24] She was transferred to Jacques Clamorgan as payment for a debt.[25]

Dashing and dark, there remains speculation about Clamorgan's racial origins, but whatever they were, he operated at the highest levels of economic power in early St. Louis. The rumor is that Clamorgan had read some law, but whatever the case, he seems to have been equally persuasive in several languages, and his confidence and charm greatly impressed the Spaniards who came to the Mississippi Valley before the Creole French. Clamorgan's innovative ideas in trade were eagerly sought after, but his penchant for mulatto women meant he was not received socially at the highest levels.[26]

Jacques Clamorgan was one of the visionaries who imagined there must be a shortcut to India and a fabled Oriental trade, and it might even go right through St. Louis. He was one of the prime movers of the Missouri

Company, which campaigned for investors to underwrite a team to enter the race for a river route to the Pacific setting out on the Missouri River and trading furs with the Indians along the way. Clamorgan claimed to have been deeded a grant of half a million arpents of land (more than half the size of present-day Rhode Island) from the King of Spain in what became the Louisiana Territory, and the Spanish were mesmerized enough by the man to have made such a grant. By 1797, Clamorgan's Missouri Company already explored a large portion of the western territory that was not crossed until several years later by the Lewis and Clark expedition. But the company did not make money for its investors in its quest for a passage to India, and through attrition, Clamorgan and Regis Loisel ultimately became the company's sole partners. However, the company did manage a successful trade with Indians in furs.[27]

After the official transfer of the Louisiana Territory to the United States, many of the Spanish land grants were contested and disallowed despite a provision in the sale of the territory that guaranteed inhabitants would be "maintained in the full enjoyment of their property." It was no doubt with an eye to appease the Creole founders of St. Louis that many of those with substantial land claims were appointed to positions of influence in the new American government. Jacques Clamorgan was appointed a justice of the Court of the Quarter Sessions.[28]

A tug of war over some of the land once owned by Jacques Clamorgan lasted for generations of one free family of color in St. Louis. Ester, one of the slave women Clamorgan was romantically involved with, was his match in many ways. The two had a child together named Seleé. Jacques Clamorgan freed them both in 1793. Clamorgan also gave Ester deeds to several plots of land. But for some reason, about 1808, he changed his mind and asked Ester to return the land to him. When she refused, Clamorgan beat her, but Ester still wouldn't change her mind. Then Clamorgan threatened to sell Seleé and Ester's four other children south. Enraged, Ester did a bit of investigating on her own and was astonished by what she discovered.[29]

Apparently, Jacques Clamorgan had forged deeds giving him ownership of land he'd previously deeded to Ester and that she'd refused to return to him. But for Ester, the straw that broke the camel's back was a deed Jacques apparently forged giving him ownership of her daughter, Seleé. She had been angry before, but now Ester was also frightened. This man who had once been her lover, and whom she had continued to think of as a friend, had gone behind her back and written himself a deed for their child. What else had he done? Had he also written a deed for her?

If he had, what would become of her and her child and grandchildren? She didn't know what to do, and someone recommended that she speak with a lawyer named William C. Carr. She was told Carr knew the law well and was honest besides.[30]

Carr, who would later be a powerful clerk of the St. Louis court and a judge, was just beginning his career and struggling to make ends meet when Ester Clamorgan approached him. He listened to her story, and then enthusiastically agreed that what Jacques Clamorgan had done was an outrage. Carr promised Ester he would represent her as if she were his own mother. The payment Carr required was that Ester Clamorgan transfer one of her town lots to him. Carr also asked her to give him all of the deeds she felt were in question, so that he could study them and figure out what to do.[31]

The papers Ester Clamorgan turned over to William C. Carr included the deeds to town lots in St. Louis and Jacques Clamorgan's I.O.U. to Ester in the amount of $750. The papers also included manumission certificates for Ester's daughter, Seleé, and her grandson, Edward, a house and land deeded to Edward, and the deeds for two slaves named Ben and Charlotte. Ester Clamorgan also handed over to Carr the deed to herself, the manumission papers by which Jacques Clamorgan had set her free. Carr studied the papers eagerly, then exclaimed to Ester Clamorgan, "You have a great deal of land!"[32]

Carr revised his original estimate of his fee and told Clamorgan his services would cost her not one, but two of her town lots. He told her that on a Monday and told her to check in with him again the following Wednesday.

The gossip around town in the space of that 48 hours was that William Carr had been seen spending a lot of time with Jacques Clamorgan. On Wednesday, Carr sent a message to Ester Clamorgan reminding her of their appointment. Ester went to the office, and Carr told her he'd given her case a good deal of thought and decided the effort he'd have to put into her case was worth *all* of her town lots. Ester was speechless for only a moment or two, then said quickly that Carr could keep everything she owned if he would only protect her child and her grandchildren. Carr just as quickly agreed, and said to her, "Don't worry, just trust me."[33]

Between 1809 and 1811, Carr went to court and requested over and over again that the case be continued. Ester Clamorgan heard that Carr had been given a judgment of $800 from Jacques, and had kept the money for himself. Ester had sold one of the lots in her grandson Edward's name to Carr for $300, but he hadn't paid her that money either. In addition, one of the lots Ester Clamorgan claimed belonged to her was sold by Jacques Clamorgan during this time to Peter Chouteau, and then deeded to William Carr; and Carr was living on this estate by June 1809. Ester charged the deed of land to Carr was a "reward" from Jacques Clamorgan for Carr's role in quashing her claim to the land. Ester said that when she met William Carr, he was "a poor young man without property and in embarrassed circumstances," but thanks to her he'd become a wealthy man. Ester Clamorgan said that because Carr hadn't done a thing for her and had even accepted a "reward" to *not* help her, in good conscience, he didn't deserve a penny for the so-called services he'd rendered, and furthermore, she should get back what she'd already given him. In 1811, Carr apparently walked away from the Ester Clamorgan suit, "abandoning the suit without bringing it to trial."[34]

Ester Clamorgan also sued to try to find out where her land was and who claimed to own it because Carr, in cahoots with Jacques Clamorgan and Peter Chouteau, had made her lands virtually disappear. In their mad shuffle of deeds and I.O.U.'s and legal writs, physical land boundaries were made to bend or overlap, manifesting a flexibility more common to abstract notions. It is no wonder at all that in time, Ester Clamorgan might have doubted the land she knew and had stood on with her own feet did not exist at all.

In response to Ester's petitions, on November 5, 1830, the court issued a subpoena ordering William Carr to appear and explain himself.[35]

In 1838, the court was still sending out summonses to witnesses for testimony in the case. A free black woman named Rachel Camp, who lived on 6th Street that year, was one of the witnesses who received a court summons to give testimony in the case. But Sheriff Marshall Brotherton's deputy, Joseph McClurg, said he couldn't find Camp.[36]

Ester Clamorgan apparently understood a fair amount about the law, and on November 9, 1831, she made a will. In her will, Ester left land to Charles DeWard and Margaret S. McNair, to her granddaughters, Teresa Speers and Agatha (Mrs. Thomas) Butcher, and to her grandsons, Joseph Scavener and Francis. These were the children of Ester's daughter, Seleé. When Ester Clamorgan died in October of 1833, the question of title to her land had still not been resolved. Her grandson, Francis, died shortly after, and his portion of his grandmother's "very considerable estate" "became vested in his two sisters and one brother."[37]

Ester's granddaughter, Thérèse Speers, took up her grandmother's cause. In 1837, Speers and her husband, George, hired the well-known slave freedom suits advocate, Ferdinand Risque, to represent her in her petition demanding the payment of rents and other benefits she claimed were rightfully due her on property at Fifth and Myrtle streets in St. Louis. Speers stated the land had been left to her "in trust" for her "use and benefit ... during her life with the remainder to her children and their descendants forever." It is legalese reminiscent of that particular vocabulary reserved to the bequeathing of slaves to the heirs of slave owners "forever." Speers signed the plea with her mark, and it is possible her husband, George, had been named administrator of her grandmother's estate because he was literate.[38]

Speers either witnessed or had heard that Jacques Clamorgan beat her grandmother, and that city court clerk Marie Leduc had seen him do it. Her grandmother had revealed that Jacques Clamorgan, "who had formerly been her friend and benefactor, had become her enemy" and while hitting her, ranted that she had "neither land nor property." Clamorgan told Ester that "all she ever had and claimed belonged to him." He threatened that if Ester did not give him back the deeds to the land, he'd sell her children and grandchildren in the slave markets of New Orleans. Speers knew that part of the land Clamorgan turned over to her grandmother included property deeded to him by the "Spanish government" with an eastern boundary referred to as the King's Road, lots in the old French quarter bounded by the Mississippi River, Third, Oak and Church streets, and another parcel that Jacques Clamorgan was still living on near Church Street in the city. Ester Clamorgan had stated that because she was "ignorant" of the law, and a person of color only recently freed from slavery and therefore not sure what her rights might be, she'd been "almost in despair" over the situation. When William Carr had been recommended to her as an "able and honest" man, Ester Clamorgan thought her troubles were over.[39]

Thérèse Speers not only agreed with her grandmother that Carr did not deserve "one cent" for his so-called representation of her, but that because he had done her and her family "irreparable injury," he should pay them damages for it. The injury was not only that Carr had pretty much stolen their inheritance, but had also colluded with Jacques Clamorgan to steal it and had used fraud to do it. Speers said Carr had had her grandmother sign documents which transferred land to him, but that her grandmother did not understood that because Carr told Ester Clamorgan the papers she was signing were deeds to land she was transferring to him in payment for his services. In the first years of the presumed suit, when Ester Clamorgan trusted Carr was pursuing and protecting her interests, he'd apparently been able not only to "prove" that Jacques Clamorgan forged deeds to land she owned, but that Clamorgan owed Ester "wages." It had been around that same time that Carr began to make a habit of applying for continuances in the court before finally abandoning the suit altogether. Speers charged that in the intervening years, Carr reaped benefits of rents and leases charged on the properties in addition to the flat value of the properties, and that he had accepted land from Jacques Clamorgan in exchange for "concealing" that Clamorgan forged titles to Ester Clamorgan's land. Speers said she and her family contacted Carr many times to try to solve the matter in a "peaceable and friendly manner" to no avail.[40]

At least one element of the benefit of free identity for blacks was self-respect and self-confidence, which Thérèse Speers demonstrated throughout the pendency of these cases. Speers also apparently inherited her grandmother's drive and determination because she next set her sites on Peter Chouteau, an heir of the city father, whom she believed was as culpable in the matter as Jacques Clamorgan. Speers and her husband sued Chouteau, too, charging he had "connived" with Carr to cheat Ester Clamorgan out of a tract of land known as "La Grange de Terre." And they said there were probably other "confederates" involved in this deceit. Speers asked the court to be willing to insert into the suit the names of any additional "confederates" if and when they were discovered. As she had done with Carr, Speers said that she and her family had tried to get in touch with Peter Chouteau to try to settle the matter in a friendly way, but Chouteau hadn't responded. Speers wanted Chouteau to produce the original deed signed by her grandmother to reveal if they'd sold any of the original tracts of land and, if so, to whom they'd sold it. She said even if Chouteau said he wasn't guilty because he hadn't known Jacques Clamorgan had cheated Ester Clamorgan out of her land at the time, he surely knew it by now. Speers said she just wanted Chouteau to tell the truth about what had happened.[41]

The ultimate disposition of the case is not part of the extant record.

By the time the Land Court was created in 1853, a significant minority of free people of color owned land and occasionally sought to resolve disputes over their land in the courts. These cases offer a window into the lives of ordinary working people who sought to establish and maintain their free identity through land ownership, and sometimes, as in the case of Fanny Jackson, the cases also provide insights or raise questions about gender relationships within the free community of color.

In 1857, a free woman of color named Fanny Jackson sued a free man of color named Randolph Taylor in the Land Court over the question of who was the rightful owner of a city lot on 8th Street between Biddle and O'Fallon streets. Jackson had inherited the land from a man named Henry Taylor. After Jackson inherited the land, Randolph Taylor and another free man of color named Levi Dust apparently approached Jackson and promised to take care of her if she would write a will naming them owners of the lot when she died. The men also promised Jackson they would pay all taxes, assessments, and costs connected to maintaining the lot.[42]

Jackson was an old lady and fragile. She was not in a position to take care of the property, not to mention herself, and it was common practice for members of the colored community (both free and slave) with no kin to form close relationships with non-relatives for their mutual benefit. Taylor and Dust took Jackson to the law office of A. J. P. Garesche, and even though Jackson was illiterate and not able to understand the writing on the papers the men offered her, she took the men's word that the documents represented confirmation of their agreement, and put her mark on it.[43]

The paper Jackson signed turned out to be a transfer of the deed to her property, but although clearly fraudulent, the transaction might have had some benevolent aspects for her. For example, the deed permitted Jackson to remain on the property until she died and to collect rents on it. On the other hand, the deed also bound Jackson to pay all taxes, assessments, and costs connected to the property. And it prohibited her from selling the property. Jackson asked the court to rule the document null and void because it was fraudulent, and on top of that asked the judge to fine the men $1,000 for the injury she suffered because of the fraud. Whether Jackson herself came up with the idea of monetary restitution or had sound legal advice isn't indicated in the record.[44]

Levi Dust told a different story.

Dust told the court he'd known Henry and Maria Taylor for about five years before "the old man" died. He said Maria had wanted to will the property to him and to Randolph Taylor. Dust said Fanny Jackson was "70 or 80 years old" and "couldn't read or print." He said he had supported her since the old man died, but Randolph Taylor "has not paid five cents" toward it. Dust said he wasn't married to Fanny and hadn't been there when the deed was signed, although he admitted he'd agreed with Taylor to take half of the property and "shut up about it." Dust said he couldn't help it.[45]

A woman named Martha Keller also testified in the case. Her testimony highlights the insularity of the St. Louis community of color. Keller said she'd known Fanny Jackson about ten years, knew Randolph Taylor "by sight," and also knew Levi Dust. Keller said she had heard Taylor use the word "will" when discussing the paper Fanny Jackson signed. Keller said the men told Fanny Jackson not to bring anybody with her when she came to sign the "will." According to Keller, Fanny Jackson was about "forty years old."[46]

A man named Sam Wills reported to the court that Fanny Jackson "once belonged to him," and he knew the defendants. Wills said he went with Jackson when she went to the lawyer's office to complain about the document. He said the lawyer, whose name was Garesche, told Fanny Jackson he'd given the property back, and his "brother or cousin" would draw up the papers to make it right. Wills then went to Randolph and asked him to give him the papers, but Randolph refused and told Wills he hadn't paid Jackson anything for the property, so things could just be as they had been before.[47]

Leicester Babcock told the court he had drawn up a written agreement between Randolph Taylor and Levi Dust. Babcock said "a black man named Johnstone" came to him and asked him to examine the records of the property owned by Fanny Jackson, and he found a deed from Jackson to Randolph Taylor. Babcock said Johnstone left, but came back a few days later with Fanny, Levi Dust, and Randolph Taylor. Jackson wanted to know if the document Babcock had found in the record was a deed or a will. Babcock said when he told Jackson it was a deed, she was surprised, but Dust was "incensed." Babcock got the impression that Jackson had "at one time been very friendly" with Taylor and "willing to do whatever he wished."[48]

Some months passed, then Randolph Taylor and Levi Dust returned to Leicester Babcock and asked him to draw up a deed that split the property between them. Babcock did that.[49]

John Phillips said he overheard Fanny Jackson tell Randolph Taylor to divide the property equally with Levi Dust. Phillips said that was Jackson's idea. Phillips said after Randolph Taylor agreed, he and Fanny Jackson "went traveling."[50]

Peter Johnstone testified that when he had business with people who could not read or write, he always read any documents they discussed out loud to them. He said he read the documents to Fanny Jackson, and she was satisfied with them based on what he read to her.[51]

The attorney Alexander J. P. Garesche said the deed he'd drawn up for Fanny Jackson was in his own handwriting. Garesche said he told Jackson himself the document was a deed, then gave the deed to Johnstone to read to her. The only other Johnstone mentioned in the case was the Johnstone Leicester Babcock described as "a black man," which could lead one to conclude that Garesche had a black legal apprentice or clerk. Garesche testified he'd also drawn up a will for Jackson at the same time, but the will did not concern leaving any property other than the lot to Randolph Taylor. Garesche said he had known Taylor a long time, but didn't know Fanny Jackson. He said he'd only seen her once before, when he made out her freedom papers.[52]

A variety of documents were presented in court to support these varied versions of the story about Fanny Jackson's land. A deed entered into evidence had been written on February 6, 1854, and conveyed a city lot on 8th Street from Fanny Jackson equally to Randolph Taylor and Levi Dust. This deed noted a previous deed that had conveyed the lot to Taylor alone. This document also required Levi Dust to pay Randolph Taylor one dollar. And the document permitted Fanny Jackson to remain on the property for her lifetime. The deed was signed "John R. Taylor," above the printed name "J. Randolph Taylor."[53]

A second version of the deed stated that Fanny Jackson had two aliases: Taylor and Willy. This version described both Jackson and Randolph Taylor as "emancipated slaves." This deed stated that Jackson conveyed the land to Taylor because he was her friend, but also in exchange for $100 from Taylor. This deed acknowledged that Jackson inherited the property from Henry Taylor, would have use of the property for her natural life, would be able to collect rents and other profits from the property, but would also have to pay any taxes on the property. Fanny Jackson had signed the deed with an "X," and Peter W. Johnstone, as justice of the peace, witnessed that the woman who signed the deed was the woman he knew as Fanny Jackson.[54]

A written agreement between Randolph Taylor and Levi Dust was also presented as evidence. The agreement described the men as "free men of color" and equal owners of a property they received from Fanny Jackson, and that Jackson then occupied. The men stated they wanted to build "small dwelling houses" in the back of the lot, and the rent they collected from these houses would go to Fanny Jackson as long as she lived. In addition, the men promised to contribute to Jackson's support. Taylor and Dust promised to contribute up to $800 between them to build the houses, and to complete the houses within six months' time. The rent Jackson would collect from the houses was to be considered payment for the lot when she died. Dust promised to provide Jackson with "protection" and support just as he had for the "last three or four years." Dust promised that if Jackson became "dissatisfied" with him and wanted him to leave her premises, he would do so, and his "successor" would take over her care, but Dust would still be half-owner of the property when she died. Randolph Taylor was given permission to occupy one room of one of the new dwellings, but would have to pay rent and taxes on the room to Jackson and Dust. It appears that Taylor signed his name to the document, and that Dust made an "X" to it. The document is dated July 24, 1855.[55]

In 1859, Fanny Jackson was listed in the St. Louis directory with "[col.]" after her name. Her address at that time was 180 North 8th Street. Levi Dust was listed as living at the same address on 8th Street in both 1859 and 1860.

The Fanny Jackson story is not the only example of the sometimes labyrinthine connections among free people of color, slaves, and whites found in the Land Court and other civil records. Another case in point is that of Squire Brown, a slave who sued for freedom in the St. Louis courts, and won. Between 1841 and 1843, Brown filed three separate petitions for freedom in St. Louis Civil Court. Perhaps his experience in the courts led him to seek justice in the courts again, but whatever the reason, having won the right to own himself, Brown also filed suits in the St. Louis Land Court to keep other property he had accumulated.

The Land Court had jurisdiction over all matters relating to land, including disputes over ownership, partition, or dower rights of land, landlord and tenant disputes over leases or rents, and settlement of liens brought by builders, mechanics, furnishers or artisans.[56]

Squire Brown admitted he had once been a slave, and that his former owner, Henry Brown, had owned him for about eight years. During 1839 and 1841, Squire Brown took the ferry from the landing on the Mississippi River and crossed the river to work in St. Clair County, Illinois, sometimes for months at a time. His owner sent him there. Because he had lived in free territory, consistently over a period of years, Brown believed that made him a free man. At the least, he figured his residence in the State of Illinois, even working for hire as a slave of Henry Brown, entitled him to sue for his freedom. Henry Brown sold Squire Brown to William Anderson before the first of May, a month before Squire Brown sued. Brown signed his first petition for freedom on June 26, 1841, with an "X."[57]

In June of 1841, the Court granted Squire Brown authority to sue to recover his freedom from his then-owner William C. Anderson. The Court (Judge Bryan Mullanphy) appointed attorneys John Davis and Benjamin B. Dayton to act as counsel for Brown, and the attorneys filed a case seeking $500 in damages. The Court made clear that Squire Brown was not to be taken out of the jurisdiction of the court, and that he "not be subjected to any severity" because he had sued for his freedom. However, before a final decision was reached in the case, William C. Anderson sold Brown to Charles Anderson, who either threatened or made actual plans to sell Brown somewhere beyond the court's jurisdiction. Brown then also filed suit against Charles Anderson.[58]

Squire Brown's testimony provides insights into the everyday lives of some of the slaves who lived on or near the Mississippi River—as has been documented, slaves in the region were hired out to do a variety of jobs on both the Missouri and Illinois sides of the river and, when they worked on steamboats, even at ports north and south of St. Louis. Brown's deposition implied that profits from his own labors did not necessarily adequately support him. He told the Court he was in desperate need of clothing, but that Charles Anderson, who hired Brown out and received everything he earned, refused to buy him any clothing unless or until he withdrew his suit for freedom. Once Brown filed suit against Charles Anderson, Anderson demanded that Brown be put in jail, and he was. But the judge seemed convinced that Anderson would spirit Brown out of the jurisdiction of the Court, and he issued a writ of *habeas corpus* demanding that Brown be produced before the bench. The Court also ordered that Brown be hired out during the case to pay costs of the proceeding.[59]

It took a few years, but Squire Brown finally won his freedom in the St. Louis court. Nearly a generation later, in the midst of the Civil War, Squire Brown resurfaced, this time in the city's Land Court, apparently as a free landowner suing to maintain the right to his property.[60]

Although only one or two slave freedom suits were actually brought during the course of the Civil War, the St. Louis courts remained in session, and a number of cases pursued in the war years involved people of color. In 1862, Squire Brown sued Isaac Breckenridge, another free man of color, over a house and lot near Scott Avenue in St. Louis. Breckenridge believed the property belonged to him, so he moved into it, and refused to let Brown in. Brown told the Court he rented the property out for $5 a month, and wanted the rent paid every month until he got his property back, and $25 in damages besides. Squire Brown had not learned to write his name yet, and signed the Land Court petition with an "X."[61]

The legal definition of the petition Brown filed was an "ejectment," which meant he just wanted Breckenridge removed from his property. (Breckenridge lived on the north side of Scott Avenue near Pratte, two blocks north of the Pacific Railroad line in a one-story frame house with two rooms and a chimney in the middle.) On March 14, 1862, Breckenridge asked the Court to make a white man named Joseph T. Brown his co-defendant, because he claimed he only rented the property from Brown.[62]

On April 26, 1862, after being made co-defendant, Joseph Brown told the Court the property in question belonged to him because of an "agreement" his slave, "Lanzy," had with Squire Brown. Two days later, on April 28, Breckenridge told the Court he was broke and asked that Joseph Brown be held responsible for court costs. A lawyer named Robert S. Voorhis represented both Breckenridge and Thomas Brown. On May 2, 1862, Voorhis recorded what he'd found out about the case in an affidavit supporting his petition on behalf of his clients for a new trial.[63]

Voorhis spoke with the slave man named "Lanzy," and, probably because of laws against persons of color testifying in court against whites, asked Lanzy if he knew of any white men who might have known what was going on. Lanzy told Voorhis he thought a white man named Charles Miller and someone he referred to as "Mr. Billough" knew the facts. Voorhis asked Charles Miller about the case. If the story Voorhis related was true, it provides intriguing information about the relationships between slaves and free people of color in St. Louis during the Civil War, when slave and free status sometimes shifted from day to day.[64]

According to Miller, Squire Brown had not purchased the lot at all. Apparently, the slave named Lanzy had paid for the property, and Brown merely put his name on it because he was free and Lanzy wasn't. Miller told the lawyer that Lanzy made the first installment on the property, and another payment, and he never saw Squire Brown at all until a year after the property was sold. In the meantime, Miller also continued to search all over town for the "Mr. Billough," but couldn't find him.[65]

When he gave his own affidavit before the Court, the defendant Isaac Breckenridge swore that personally he didn't know any of the details of the case. He said he didn't know any white men who knew all of the facts of the case, either. He'd asked a Charles Hall, who was Joseph T. Brown's "business agent," if he knew anything about this case, but Hall said that he didn't and he didn't know anyone who did.[66]

A "surprise" witness named Charles A. Smith appeared before the Court and stated he'd known Squire Brown for about a year, because Brown came into the store that Smith owned with his partner, John P. Pilkey. (The store had closed in 1861.) Neither Isaac Breckenridge nor his lawyer Robert Voorhis had known about the existence of Smith and swore to that in their own affidavits. Smith said Brown often talked to Pilkey, but in those conversations never claimed to own the land in question, and in fact, Brown had said the opposite, that he didn't own the land. Smith said he'd overheard Brown talk about the land in the store he had with his partner, John P. Pilkey. According to Smith, Brown had said flat out that the property belonged to Lanzy, but that because Brown was a free man and slaves were forbidden to own land, he'd put his name on the deed. Confusing the matter even more, Brown reportedly said he'd given Lanzy some money to keep up his payments on the property.[67]

In February 1862, Joseph Brown filed a suit in Land Court against Squire Brown and George W. Berkeley. This was a Petition to Foreclose Mortgage. (Joseph Brown lived on the corner of Chouteau and Pratte.) According to Joseph Brown, Squire Brown borrowed money from George Berkeley in 1856, and used the property in question as collateral. It was a five-year loan, and if Squire Brown didn't pay Berkeley back, Berkeley could auction the property on the courthouse steps to reclaim his money. Any profit above and beyond what Brown owed to Berkeley would go to Brown after the sale.[68]

Joseph Brown claimed Squire Brown never repaid the loan. Joseph Brown claimed that any profit from transactions involving the land he said was his belonged to him, and the money Squire Brown owed Berkeley, including interest, belonged to him, too, so the land should be sold and the profits given to him.[69]

The Court ruled that any contract made with the slave Lanzy was void, because as property, slaves obviously did not have the right to make contracts. In a ruling eerily echoing the Supreme Court decision in *Dred Scott* a few years before, the Court ruled that it was as if Lanzy "had not existed at all." The Court also found that if the property did belong to Joseph Brown, he could not file a petition that was in effect a lien, since no man can have a lien on his own property.[70]

Beginning with the founding of St. Louis, free and slave people of color entered into a range of relationships with each other (and sometimes with the courts) using the cover of law. Squire Brown, a slave who mounted a legal suit to gain his own freedom seems to have used the triumph of that freedom to shield from scrutiny the legal ownership of land by a slave named Lanzy. In such cases, the bond of color seems to have transcended free or slave status. And as the Squire Brown cases came to an end, the Civil War had taken the question of slavery, freedom, and the equality bequeathed by the west beyond the boundaries of the courts.

CHAPTER 9

The Civil War

By the time of the Squire Brown land case, Missouri was already in the midst of war, and for much of that war, the state was governed by martial law.[1] The state's borders failed to stop blacks from fleeing west beyond the boundaries of slavery at the same time that a counter-migration south by slave owners fleeing with their slave property was under way. But in the early days of the war, it appears that at least initially, the status quo prevailed. The slave holding elite continued to enjoy entertainments available when not scouting for the best deal on amenities needed to clothe and maintain their slaves. In May 1861, 12-year-old musical prodigy "Blind Tom" toured the region and performed using a Steinway grand piano. Although someone broke into his hotel room and stole $180, Blind Tom earned rave reviews as a performer.

> This more than wonderful little negro gave his first concert last evening to a large, discriminating and delighted audience. Seldom does an entertainment of any kind equal the glowing announcement of bills and programmes, but, in this instance, the expectations of his hearers, high as they had been worked up, were more than realized. He is indeed a marvel.[2]

Local favorite Thomas Postlewaite also continued to perform during the war, at one point in 1862, playing aboard a Chouteau-owned riverboat.[3] Missouri slave owners continued to seek the best bargain available to obtain quantities of "shoes for negroes."

> St. Genevieve, Mo.—
> November 1st 1861—
>
> James C. Edwards Esq
> Dear Sir
> I wish you would send me 1 dozen heavy, well made brogan shoes, for Negroes—the numbers to be as follows, to wit 2 pairs of No 13—3 pairs of No 11—2 pairs of No 8—3 pairs of No 6—1 pair of No 10—and 1 pair of No 4—get me as good a bargain

as you can for such shoes—Mr. Coffman my Brother in law got such shoes when we were up for 18 per doz—do the best you can, send me the shoes at Ste Genevieve and the bill and I will return you voucher by mail—

Very Respectfully

N. Blackledge[4]

Late in the war, in 1864, the Western Sanitary Commission sponsored a concert in which both black and white musicians participated to raise money "for hospitals, for aid to the black freedmen, and for support of orphans."[5]

Much has been made of the magnetic attraction the advancing Union line south held for slaves, who, almost immediately following publication of the Emancipation Proclamation on January 1, 1863, headed north for the presumed shelter of that Union line; however, their reception by Union officers was mixed, although slaves were often put immediately to work in jobs ranging from outdoor physical labor to domestic chores, such as cooking and laundry duties.[6] The Commander of the Missouri forces, General Henry W. Halleck, issued General Orders, No. 3, on November 20, 1861, which sought to "remedy the evil" of admitting fugitive slaves within their lines by ordering that fugitive slaves and any other "unauthorized persons of every description" "be immediately excluded therefrom."[7] Halleck proffered the possibility that slaves were "spies" for the Confederacy.[8]

In Missouri, the arrival of runaway slaves in large numbers was followed by the slaves' energetic efforts to obtain legal freedom. A direct result was the December 1862, implementation of General Order 35, requiring provost marshals to issue certificates of freedom to slaves who escaped from Confederate-held territory and to "protect the freedom and persons" of people set free by the Second Confiscation Act.[9] This was despite reassurance from President Lincoln himself that, in the interest of preserving the Union, the "property" of people in border states such as Missouri would be protected.[10] Not surprisingly, Lincoln's views were neither universally respected nor complied with in the state. In the summer of 1863, the *Daily Missouri Democrat* published an editorial highlighting the sport of "negro hunting" by diehard pro-slavery men in Missouri.

Potosi, July 26th, 1863

Last Saturday we had an example of what it means to have regard for "law and order." I mean one of those old fashioned negro hunts. Some half a dozen slaves, who had deserted their rebel masters and were in possession of their regular protection papers, issued by a Provost Marshal, under General Order No. 35, Department of the Missouri, were hunted down like wild deers, [sic] handcuffed, and on a wagon hauled to jail in Potosi…. You could see men who never show their faces except on an occasion of this kind. By "law and order men" I understand that class which hold only as law

Head Quarters, District of St. Louis.

Office of Superintendent of Contrabands.

St. Louis, Mo., October 26th 1863.

Lucinda Walker a negro, aged _29_ years, _3—6_ height, _brown_ color, whose last master was _Berry Prince_ of the County of _Washington_ State of _Mississippi_ is hereby declared to be an emancipated Slave, and a freedman, by virtue of the Proclamation of the President of the United States, made 1st January, 1863, under the provisions of the Act of Congress of 17th July, 1862.

Emancipation of Lucinda Walker. During the Civil War, the St. Louis Office of Contrabands freed some of the slaves who escaped from the Deep South and made it to the city. Lucinda Walker and her two young daughters escaped from Mississippi and were freed in St. Louis during the Civil War. Each family member's description and age, as well as his/her "last master" was included on the emancipation documents.

the fugitive slave law, the black laws of the State of Missouri and the laws of the Confederacy; they don't consider the laws of our Congress as binding on them.... For the purpose of "law and order" they set all law aside. We will see what our Provost Marshall does in the matter. These negroes are promised in their papers the protection of all officers of the United States ... we have just come again to the barbarous state of affairs where we were at the beginning, and near the end of the nineteenth century, in the midst of a civilized community, we see ... [h]uman beings are treated like beasts....[11]

By the end of 1863, however, slaves who had been declared "contraband" of war had begun to be freed by the Union, as was the case of Alice M., Lucinda, and Winnie Walker, who had arrived in St. Louis from Mississippi and were emancipated by the local Office of Superintendent of Contrabands.[12]

Observers reported the arrival of countless slaves, who had walked many miles to Kansas, some walking on the frozen Missouri River or swimming it, "carrying all of their earthly possessions in little bags or bundles,

Emancipation of Winnie Walker.

sometimes in red bandana handkerchiefs."[13] The Union Army also relocated hundreds of black slaves from the South to Kansas as contraband of war.[14] General James Lee was among those who took immediate advantage of the first Confiscation Act to actively disrupt slavery in western Missouri, which facilitated migrations of blacks into Kansas.[15] An African American man named "Sam Marshall" crossed the border from Kansas to Missouri in March 1864, to retrieve his children and return with them to

Head Quarters, District of St. Louis.

Office of Superintendent of Contrabands.

St. Louis, Mo., October 26th 1863.

Alice M. Walker a negro, aged 8 years, Child height, brown color, whose last master was Berry Prince of the County of Washington State of Mississippi is hereby declared to be an emancipated Slave, and a free man by virtue of the Proclamation of the President of the United States, made 1st January, 1863, under the provisions of the Act of Congress of 17th July, 1862.

By Order of Brig. General STRONG,

H. C. Fillebrown
Capt. and Chief of Staff.

Witness:

Chaplain and Superintendent of Contrabands.

Emancipation of Alice M. Walker.

freedom in Kansas; he was waylaid by members of the federal militia.[16] Uniformed militiamen tied Marshall to a tree and whipped him before dragging him back to the border.[17]

In addition, black men escaping slavery in Missouri and points South also found the Kansas corridor a means for enlisting in the Union Army.[18] Incentives to enlist included pay of $10 per month, clothing, rations and housing, but perhaps more to the point, a certificate of freedom for the soldier plus freedom to his wife and children, and his mother.[19] In fact, the epic migrations of slaves northward were likewise exacerbated by the succession of "compromises" (such as the Kansas-Nebraska Act in 1854) engineered in an attempt to keep the Union together. However, many of those slaves were as attracted to the western boundary and flooded the Kansas-Nebraska Territories well before the Civil War.[20] It must also be kept in mind that slaveholders themselves, beginning with the 1841 Preemption Act opening lands for settlement in the territory, moved west with their slaves in tow with the design to create a slave state.[21] By 1863, the slave population of Missouri had decreased from its 1860 high of 114,931 to 73,811.[22] The corollary can be seen in the exponential increase of the Kansas black population from 627 in 1860 to 12,527 by 1865.[23]

The decree summarily enacted by Major General John C. Frémont has been called "The First Emancipation Proclamation." Nearly two years before Lincoln's decree, on August 30, 1861, General Frémont ordered St. Louis placed under martial law, confiscated the property of supporters of the Confederacy (even if they were not using their slaves to support war against the Union), ordered armed rebels "court-martialed and shot," and declared slaves of Missourians in rebellion to be free.[24] Frémont also refused to return fugitive slaves to their owners.[25] Fearing secession of slave states that had remained in the Union until that time, the President overturned Frémont's order and relieved the general of his command despite the general's insistence that his decision was based on "military necessity."[26] But some Missourians vociferously protested what seemed to them the arbitrary appropriation of their property.

> Jackson City, Mo.
> December 10, 1861
>
> Major Gen Halleck
> Sir
> Having been very lately troubled and as we think unjustifiably so, I appeal to you for redress....
> On the sixth of October, a band of armed men, one calling himself a United States officer, of Gen Lane's Brigade came up to the house, and without asking a question, demanded of my husband his negroes, and without telling him for what reason, merely saying he supposed he had read Fremont's proclamation, took ten of our negroes, and five of my fathers [sic], that were left in our charge, he being sick in St. Louis. They took our wagons, sixteen head of horses and mules.... My father is an old man upwards of seventy and has been in St. Louis for the last eighteen months waiting to die.... My husband is a Southern man in his feeling but has never had any thing [sic] to do with the army in any way.... Gen. Lane ... gave him a receipt for some of the horses and mules.... He would give no receipt for my fathers [sic] property, and I think he by all means should be remunerated, for he was bitterly opposed to secession, as was my husband.... Besides the ten negroes that they took from us, they have four valuable men who ran off the day before, and went to them.
>
> Respectfully yours,
> Anne E. Mason[27]

Journalist Horace Greeley was among those who thought it might prove problematic for the President to reverse emancipation of slaves.[28]

Jefferson Barracks was eight miles south of St. Louis, then the eighth largest city in the United States, and its federal arsenal housed the largest cache of weapons and ammunition west of the Mississippi.[29]

Despite Lincoln's efforts to keep the Union intact, some slave owners especially feared the political compromises that had maintained it were unraveling. White slave owners fled west with their chattel in the hope of being able to keep them.[30] Adeline Henderson spoke of her Virginia owner telling the slaves to pack everything for their move to Missouri in the early days of the war. Henderson recounted a three-month walk with over 100 slaves, as well as cattle and horses. She and her family ran away almost immediately after arriving in Missouri in 1862.[31] A Missouri slave named Jerry testified to the Provost Marshall's Office that in 1863, his owner, "Dr. Harris," had told him they were taking him to Texas "to get out the way of the Abolitionist."[32]

As the war wore on, the small free black population of St. Louis grew in size. Many were "contraband," or slaves fleeing slave territory as the Union Army made its way south. An 1862 letter suggests that from the perspective of certain elements within the military in Missouri, the state had become a veritable "general depot of the Underground Railroad," based on the numbers of "Negroes flowing in from all directions."[33] Famously, General James Lane commanded Missouri Union troops who cut a swath through secessionist areas of the state in the fall of 1861, attracting hundreds of slaves seeking refuge and freedom. Many of the former slaves worked for the Army as domestics.[34]

The number of blacks fleeing slave territory increased even more after the announcement of President Lincoln's Emancipation Proclamation on New Year's Day, 1863, which promised freedom to those still held as slaves in Confederate territory. Five hundred freed people from Arkansas arrived in St. Louis aboard the *Jesse K. Bell* that March. The first contraband camp was in the Missouri Hotel at Main and Morgan streets. Because learning to read was a priority for many of the freed people, classes for them in reading and writing were immediately convened at the Hotel. Another camp of contraband free blacks assembled at St. Louis was dubbed "Camp Ethiopia." The freed people were put to work repairing the city's fortifications and unloading supplies at the landing on the river. They worked like slaves all day long, and often dispersed without pay at nightfall to wander along the river. Runaway slaves established their own makeshift camps in the woods near St. Louis, and some contracted frostbite in the cold, winter months.[35]

It has already been documented that slaves in some parts of the Confederacy took advantage of civil war in the larger society to organize armed resistance movements of their own.[36] Although the Congressional grant of presidential authority to quell rebellions was primarily directed at white insurgents against the Union, the authority extended and expanded the legal definition of slave insurrection to treason against the United States.[37] Although people of color could not testify in courts of law, in 1863, the military prosecutor accepted the testimony of a black woman named Rachel Johnson in the court martial of a white Union soldier who was found guilty of murder.[38]

The Emancipation Proclamation may have freed only a fraction of slaves in Confederate territory, if any, but at least as importantly, the edict authorized the formation of black military units in the Union Army. Union officers traveled throughout the border states specifically to inspire black enlistment in the 62nd Colored Infantry; in some cases, white officers were accompanied by companies of armed blacks wearing the uniform of the Union Army to provide even more inspiration.[39] Some of the officers offered coupons for later compensation from the government for the lost service to owners of black men who wanted to enlist.[40] In 1863, a number of free men of color enlisted in Missouri. They included Isaac Slakeman, a 21-year-old laborer, Wesley Logan, a 36-year-old laborer, Charles Alston, a 26-year-old laborer, James Wilson, an 18-year-old laborer, and Isaac Scott, a 36-year-old laborer. The men signed enlistment papers with an "X," and were part of a regiment of colored volunteers assembled at Fort Smith, Arkansas, in October and November of 1863.[41] As early as June 1863, Missouri whites wrote of their distress at the presence of Union Army recruiters circulating among the state's blacks and the mixed feelings of blacks, who were excited by the prospect of fighting to end slavery, although some expressed concern about leaving their families.[42]

War Department General Order 329 authorized enlistment of slaves with the permission of their owners (Union owners would be compensated), and extending enlistment to slaves without owner consent if enlistments sufficient to form a regiment could not be raised among free or freed blacks and slaves unable to obtain their owner's permission. Although the October 1863, Order was implemented first for the State of Maryland, it was extended for use in Missouri, as well.[43] In November 1863, General Order 135, provided for the enlistment of "any able-bodied man of African descent, slave or free, regardless of the owner's loyalty or consent, with freedom for slave enlistees and compensation for loyal owners."[44] In February 1864, Major General W. S. Rosecrans received a petition enumerating some of the ways black men had been kept from enlisting in the Union Army by their owners, including "actual violence, … threats of violence, … locking up the clothing, and … promising rewards of bounties *not* to enlist"[45] [emphasis added]. Slave men reported that their families had been "abused, beaten, seized and driven" out "deprived of reasonable food & clothing because of their Enlistment" and "in the deliberate shooting" of one of the men.[46]

Black men enlisted despite the certain danger that awaited them, the natural horrors of war exponentially increased by Confederate racism which interpreted black military participation as an affront and fueled southern white determination to punish blacks for taking up arms against the South.[47] Indeed, the danger began perhaps with the decision and resolution to enlist; for example, Aaron Mitchell was among three Missouri slaves who ran away to join the Union Army, one was killed and the other two men were beaten for their efforts.[48] There seemed to have been an unspoken understanding throughout Confederate regiments that few black prisoners of war were to be taken and widespread killing of black troops away from the battlefield—or for that matter, any black working for the Union in any capacity or simply seeking Union sanctuary—was routine.[49] In fact, one southern newspaper editorialized:

> We cannot treat negroes … as prisoners of war without a destruction of the social system for which we contend…. We must claim the full control of all negroes who may fall into our hands, to punish with death, or any other penalty.[50]

Such sentiments were formalized by Confederate President Jefferson Davis' December 23, 1862, proclamation ordering black Union soldiers handled the same way as runaway slaves.[51] Davis went further in a January 1863, address to Congress, in which he directed that black Union Army prisoners be sold as slaves or charged with and tried for insurrection, which warranted a death sentence.[52] In addition, slave owners opposed recruitment of their slaves and at times physically restrained, whipped, or killed them to keep them from enlisting in the Union Army.[53]

> [Louisiana, Mo.] Janry 4 1864.
> Aaron Mitchell, colored man, belongs to Thomas Waugh, Says, I was present last October, about the 8th or 10th, when Alfred a colored man of James Stewart was Shot. Alfred, myself, Mrs Beasley's Henry and a girl named Malvina had Started to Hannibal a few days before to Enlist. We were arrested near Frankford, by George Tate, Joseph Brown, Robert Huff and John Cash taken to Frankford, kept there all night, and the next day we were taken back to our homes near Prairieville. They took Henry home to Mrs. Beasly and whipped him. They then took me and Alfred [*sic*] to Stewarts, and whipped us both. I was first taken home to Mr Waugh's & learning that Mr Waugh was at Stewarts, they took me there. Just before we got to the house I heard a pistol fired I was about 200 yards off when I heard it. When I got there, I saw Alfred lying

in a little icehouse in the yard. He was dead. He had been Shot through the heart, the ball coming to the Skin on his back. Jas Stewart, Henry Pollord, James Calvin Mr. Gee, the overseer, Wm Richardson, Thos Waugh, Samel [sic] Richardson, Walker Johnson, Geo Tate, and Bob Huff were standing, looking at him.[54]

An army investigation uncovered information that Alfred had been badly beaten first and then

the owner (who I am informed is a widow woman) offered to give anyone five dollars who would kill the negro, whereupon one of the party steped [sic] forward and drew his Revolver and Shot him through the heart, killing the boy almost instantly.[55]

Family members of black men who enlisted were also often mistreated or abused by owners who knew or discovered that a black male relative had run off to join the Union Army. Despite the fact that she was mistreated by their owner after her husband ran away to enlist in the Union Army, Ann, of Paris, Missouri, wrote to him, pleading with him not to write to her or send money because his letter might be discovered and taken by their owner, who would certainly keep the money; Ann told her husband that "it wont [sic] be long before I will be free and then all we make will be ours."[56]

Violent abuse of slave women and children left behind when black men enlisted in the Union Army, as well as of female contrabands, was brutal and commonplace. In some cases, family members of black soldiers were brutalized or murdered. In March 1864, when a slave woman was intercepted by her owner when trying to run away to find her soldier husband, records show that, furious because the woman refused to disclose the location of her children, the owner

stripped and beat ... [her] on the bare back with a band saw until large blisters formed, and then the wretch sawed them open, under which treatment the poor woman died.[57]

Martin Patterson of the 2nd Missouri Volunteers of African Descent informed his recruiting officer, Lieutenant William P. Deming, that his owner (James Patterson of Fayette in Howard County) had "compelled" his wife

to do out door [sic] work,—such as chop wood, husk corn &c. and ... one of his children has been suffered to freese, [sic] and has sinc [sic] died....[58]

Deming had also received complaints from William Brooks that his owner, Jack Sutter, had mistreated his wife in Fayette (Howard County), and that both Patterson and Brooks asked military authorities that their families be removed to Jefferson City.[59]

At least one general in the St. Louis area protested the abuse of the families of black soldiers and, in 1864, petitioned the military commander at Benton Barracks to provide protection to those families. General James

A. Pile drew the commander's particular attention to the case of Richard Glover, whose pregnant wife had been beaten with a buggy whip to persuade her to be moved to Kentucky. Understanding practical concerns, Pile also pointed out that black men would be more likely to enlist if they thought their families would be safe from slave owner retaliation.[60]

In 1864, Missouri state legislators suggested forced enlistment of slaves who had taken advantage of wartime edicts and the chaos of war to seize their freedom and "work for them Selves."[61] In a letter dated February 13, 1864, the legislators complained of "a large number" of slaves who had "left their masters" and were "wandering about" unemployed, "in a destitute condition" and "likely to become a nuisance" in the region.[62] The legislators suggested that "steps be taken as will force every colored man who is suitable for service, and who has left his own, to *enlist* [sic]" as a remedy.[63] Former owners simultaneously evicted slave women, some of whom were the wives, mothers, or daughters of these men; slave owners pleaded their inability to raise enough food to feed the dependents of men who had run off.[64]

It is likely that most African American men who enlisted in the Union Army did so with their eyes wide open; that is, they foresaw and understood the possible, even probable consequences not only for themselves, but for their families.[65] In some instances, black soldiers found themselves in the unenviable task of digging graves for the burial of the bones of their comrades left in the wake of battle.[66] At times, the burials were in fact "reburials" of Union soldiers buried quickly on Southern soil and retrieved after the war ended to be reinterred for the most part by black freedmen or former Union soldiers.[67] Some of the war dead had been African American soldiers, but the majority were white, all fallen in the Union cause.[68]

Racial discrimination against black soldiers also resulted in their assignment to the least pleasant or appealing, if not downright dangerous, chores. Heavy labor and long hours were not the only obstacles in the military quest for freedom, which also often included substandard rations and exacerbated the ratio of black soldiers who died of disease (one out of five compared to one out of 12 among white soldiers).[69] In addition, in Southern and border states, families of black men known to have gone to Union lines and to participate in the Union war effort were subject to punitive treatment, including forcing women to do the kind of heavy labor typically assigned to men.[70]

Archer Alexander was born in 1813 on a Virginia plantation. Alexander's father was sold and his mother died while he was still young. As often happened at the death of a slave owner, Alexander found himself transported west to St. Charles, Missouri, suddenly the property of his owner's son, Thomas Delaney. Alexander married a woman named Louisa, a slave of the Hollman family, who later owned Alexander as well. During the Civil War, Alexander provided information about Hollman's Confederate sympathies and guerrilla activities to Union authorities and likely escaped to St. Louis just before being discovered. Employed by the Rev. William Greenleaf Whittier, Alexander contacted his wife to tell her he was prepared to buy her and their children, but Hollman wouldn't hear of it. A sympathetic German neighbor helped his family to escape.[71]

During the Civil War, former slave Archer Alexander provided information to Union forces in exchange for protection for himself and his family.

Archer Alexander was not alone in bartering information for protection and even freedom granted by the Union. Especially in the widespread guerrilla warfare conducted by white Confederate sympathizers in Missouri, black slaves proved to be invaluable as "spies" for the Union. It should not go unspoken that Union soldiers learned that black slaves were often more reliable than whites when trying to get the lay of the land. As the war wore on, Union officers extended both protection and freedom to blacks who provided information often at the risk of their own lives.[72]

Black soldiers who left families behind at home in slave states were made aware of hardships their families were subjected to by letters which reached them along the way.

Mexico Mo Dec 30th 1863

My Dear Husband I have received your last kind letter a few days ago and was much pleased to hear from you once more. It seems like a long time since you left me. I have had nothing but trouble since you left. You recollect what I told you how they would do after you was [sic] gone. They abuse me because you went & say they will not take care of our children & do nothing but quarrel with me all the time and beat me scandalously the day before yesterday—Oh I never thought you would give me so much trouble as I have got to bear now. You ought not to left me in the fix I am in & all these little helpless children to take care of.... I wish you could get a furlough & come to see us once more. We want to see you worse than we ever did before ... write & tell me when you are coming.

...You need not tell me to beg any more married men to go. I see too much trouble to try to get any more into trouble too—Write to me & do not forget me & my children—farewell my dear husband from your wife

Martha[73]

Within weeks after this letter was written, the Superintendent of black recruitment in Missouri had to step in to block the sale of Martha Glover and her children south.[74] Despite the understandably fearful and angry tone of Martha Glover's letter, large numbers of African American women and their children followed their husbands and other male family members to recruiting posts in Jefferson and Mexico and throughout the state of Missouri.[75] For fear of losing not only slave men, but entire slave families, many owners considered moving their slaves farther south. Such forced migrations were sometimes accompanied by extreme duress, violence, and murder: after the war, Fanny Ann Flood testified that she and her family had been forcibly moved out of Missouri to Kentucky, during which move, her husband, Peter, had been beaten to death by their then owner, when her husband prepared to run away to return to Missouri.[76]

And whatever the odds might seem against them, most African American Union soldiers fought with the courage and confidence that theirs was an honorable cause and they would prevail.

A Union Army officer authorized Archer Alexander to remain in the St. Louis area during the war.

Benton Barracks Hospital, St. Louis, MO, September 3, 1864

My Children I take my pen in hand to rite [sic] you A few lines to let you know that I have not forgot you ... be assured that I will have you if it cost me my life on the 28th of the mounth. [*sic*] 8 hundred White and 8 hundred blacke [*sic*] solders [*sic*] expects to start up the rivore [*sic*] to Glasgow and above there that's to be jeneraled [*sic*] by a jeneral [*sic*] that will give me both of you.... Don't be uneasy children I expect to have you.... Your Miss Kaitty [*sic*] said that I tried to steal you But I'll let her know that god never intended for man to steal his own flesh and blood....

Give my love to all enquiring friends ... and Corra [*sic*] and Mary receive the greater part of it you sefves [*sic*] ... Oh! My Dear children how I do want to see you.

[Spotswood Rice][77]

A watch owned by former slave Archer Alexander.

Having written to his children, Spotswood Rice, a black soldier no doubt empowered by his military service and the certainty that he fought on the right side, confronted his former owner. His letter suggests a claim to citizenship rights by fiat.

Benton Barracks Hospital, St. Louis, Mo., September 3, 1864
I received a leteter [*sic*] from Cariline [*sic*] telling me that you say I tried to steal to plunder my child away from you now I want you to understand that mary [*sic*] is my Child and she is a God given rite of my own and you may hold on to hear [*sic*] as long as you can but I want you to remembor [*sic*] this one thing that the longor [*sic*] you keep my Child from me the longor [*sic*] you will have to burn in hell and the qwicer [*sic*] youll [*sic*] get their for we are now making up a bout one thoughsand [*sic*] blacke [*sic*] troops to Come up tharough [*sic*] and wont to come through Glasgow and when we come wo [*sic*] be to Copperhood [*sic*] rabbels [*sic*] and to the Slaveholding rebbels [*sic*] for we don't expect to leave them there root neor [*sic*] branch.... I want you to understand kitty diggs [*sic*] that where ever you and I meets we are enmays [*sic*] to each orthere [*sic*] I offered once to pay you forty dollars for my own Child but I am glad now that you did not accept it ... now you call my children your pro[*per*]ty [*sic*] not so with me my Children is my own and I expect to get tem and when I get ready to come after mary [*sic*] I will have bout a powrer [*sic*] and autherit [*sic*] to bring hear [*sic*] away and to exacute [*sic*] vengencens [*sic*] on them that holds my Child you will then know how to talke [*sic*] to me.... I have no fears about getting mary [*sic*] out of your hands this whole Government gives chear [*sic*] to me and you cannot help your self
Spotswood Rice[78]

Born free in Kentucky, Charlton Tandy moved west to St. Louis in 1857, where he worked odd jobs until being hired as a messenger at Jefferson Barracks during the war. Tandy volunteered for the militia, then recruited and assumed command of "Tandy's St. Louis Guard." After the war, Tandy was active in Republican Party politics, continued his work in a political patronage job as a messenger at the St. Louis Customs House, and assisted freed blacks who were part of the Exodusters movement to settle in the west.[79]

Although patients at the hospital at Benton Barracks north of the city at first included both blacks and whites, by April of 1864, a separate colored hospital was opened there. White nurses not only soothed the bodies of wounded blacks, but their minds as well, teaching them to "read, write and cipher." The white nurses also tried to train black women as nurses, a task they reported was "difficult," although the Colored Ladies' Union Aid Society organized by free colored women cared for wounded black Union soldiers, some of whom had enlisted at St. Louis. Although some free people of color were concerned about the influx of southern blacks with strange habits and ideas, and even Missouri slaves segregated themselves from Mississippi slaves in contraband camps, some free people came forward to support the newly arrived. The Rev. Edward Woodson said the city's six black churches (three Baptist and three Methodist) had 600 members between them, and volunteered the churches' "poor funds" to help out. (Woodson lived on 7th Street between Market and Walnut in 1860, and at 120 Clark Avenue in 1865.[80])

In the Spring of 1864, Sarah King arrived in St. Louis among a group of contrabands from Alabama. Because her infant was found to be clutching a ten-dollar gold piece, King was sentenced to two years in the penitentiary at Jefferson City. But after one year, Lavina P. Jorden petitioned for King's release on probation so that King could work for her as a domestic. Jorden described King as "good ... trusty ... patient and faithful" with a husband in the Union Army and a child who needed her. It has been suggested that King was part of a group of slaves who left the South for the West in search of social, economic, and political rights, but in the years of the Civil War and immediately after. For blacks, the West remained a "new" frontier where they could experience full freedoms of American citizenship.[81]

In fact, Jorden disavowed any specific, factual knowledge of the case itself and clearly stated in her petition that she did not "assert that the said prisoner is innocent of the crime," but rather, was part of a group of Alabama contraband, who had been "hurdled [sic] together in some miserable hut." It was during that time that the gold piece went missing and turned up in King's child's possession. Jorden offered as mitigating circumstances the fact that King's husband was "in the Federal Army" and King's incarceration reduced their child to the status of an orphan. The

Register of Inmates listed Sarah King as a "very light" negro and pardoned by Governor Thomas C. Fletcher on March 4, 1865.[82]

The black population both increased and evolved different identities in the period of the war. In 1860, about 3,297 blacks lived in St. Louis, but by 1870, the influx of migrants dramatically increased that number to 22,088.[83]

One of the first goals of free blacks in the city was demanding appropriate application of their tax dollars for the establishment of schools for free children.

St. Louis, Aug 4th 1864

Hon Steven D. Barlow
President of the Board of School Directors

We wish to call your attention to the fact that there are a large number of Free Colored children now in this city who are being educated by the voluntary contributions of individuals. This should not be, especially when we consider that there is quite a respectable sum derived annually from the tax on the property of Free Negroes for school purposes.

We respectfully and earnestly petition your Board, that the sum thus derived shall be appropriated to the education of our free colored children. This is so manifestly just, that no argument is required to convince you of the propriety of such an appropriation, and we deem it only necessary to bring the subject to your attention to ensure its prompt recognition and your favorable action. Temporary places for schools will have to be provided until permanent buildings can be erected in convenient localities.

Requesting your early consideration to our petition with the hope that you will adopt suitable measures to open schools for our free colored population at the commencement of our next school term. The spirit of the age, common justice, and an enlightened humanity alike demand it.

We remain
Very Respectfully
Your [illegible]
James E. Yeatman
W.G. Eliot
C.S. Geiley
Geo. Partridge[84]

Although the owner of Andrew Evans moved him, his mother, and siblings during the Civil War in an attempt to protect his slave property, Evans ran away because he wanted to join the Union Army. He was promptly caught and brought back, but in 1865, when he was 18, Evans and a friend walked to St. Louis and tried again to join the Union Army. He said he was rejected because of his age, but was finally successful in joining up when he crossed the river to Illinois and days before the end of the war, signed up there with the Seventeenth United States Colored Infantry.[85] By the end of the war, approximately 180,000 black men had fought with the Union Army to end slavery and gain their freedom.

Casual mention of the end of slavery crept into personal letters exchanged to congratulate a relative on the birth of a new baby, although the sentiments conveyed were hardly in favor of the turn of events.

> ...you will hardly consider this a real letter without some news, so I must think of some to tell you. First, the state conventions passed a law setting free all the slaves in the state, so now Missouri is a free state. It is said up home that Aunt Harriet, when she heard the news jumped up and cracked her heels together three times and cried "Bress [sic] the Lord"! What a chattering of dry bones there must have been, for Harriet is so old and dried up there is scarcely anything left but bones. [Illegible] is talking of leaving.... Cassa, I suppose will remain, as she is too lazy to go away.[86]

Despite the fact that the Missouri State Constitutional Convention abolished slavery in the state on January 11, 1865, and without compensation to owners, pro-slavery forces in the state refused to concede and threatened to kill every black who did not leave the state within ten days and continued to agitate against farmers' hiring free blacks.[87] But the next day, the *Daily Missouri Democrat* published a jubilant editorial celebrating the end of slavery in Missouri.

> Missouri is free. Emancipation, real, genuine, radical emancipation is achieved. This is a victory equal to any event won upon the field of battle, and as such deserves to be commemorated.... The deliverance of the State from slavery ought not to be passed over as an ordinary occurrence. There should be some public manifestation of rejoicing....[88]

But not all was merrymaking. Shortly after the announcement, lynching of freedmen and indiscriminate raping of freedwomen in Missouri began.[89] Many whites threatened to hang any freed blacks, who did not leave the state immediately.[90] In some areas, a savage segregation was implemented and maintained with violence and threats of violence.[91]

Over 100 freed slaves signed a petition to the Convention on January 31, 1865, indicating their competence to read (including the U.S. Constitution) and write. The signatories noted their patriotism as indicated by their readiness to take up arms in the war and to pay their taxes.[92]

In the vortex of war, slaves from the Deep South were drawn into the disparate free community of color of St. Louis, which, once again, was about to undergo changes that went to the heart of their collective and individual identities.

The Bond of Color: St. Louis People of Color and the West

African Americans contributed to the implementation of American "manifest destiny" to claim and define "the West" as slaves and as free people. It may seem a peculiar irony, but free black men arrived with the first French Creole founders and helped raise St. Louis from the ground in its founding period; and they contributed to the establishment of the fur trading fort that became both a large cosmopolitan city and a capital of the slave trade. Black men and women alike were pioneers in the unsettled territories west of St, Louis and worked as fur traders and trappers as well as interpreters for Indian trappers in the prosperous fur trade. In addition, people of color worked in a variety of river occupations on the Mississippi and by their presence ultimately challenged and forced the revision of laws, and through their family and cultural lives added to American social structure and identities. Perhaps the majority of African American actors in the drama of westward expansion were not willing participants, but rather, pushed along as involuntary members of an American migration to the frontier.

Dred Scott, whose name and legal cases became synonymous with the black slave effort to tie the process of American advancement in the west to their right to freedom, remains one of the most well-known of those involuntary migrants. His story inadvertently invites curiosity into the presence and role of blacks in that historical period, as well as further scrutiny. Between 1818 and 1830, Scott's owners moved from Virginia to Alabama to Missouri, a series of moves the owners doubtless intended to

171

improve their own circumstances, but which proved fateful not only in their lives, including the life of their slave, Dred Scott, but in national legal and political history.[1] Like Scott, hundreds of people of color in the gateway city of St. Louis refused to be mute witnesses to their participation in the migration and settlement, and memorialized their stories in correspondence, newspapers, and legal writ, including hundreds of lawsuits for freedom filed by slaves in the St. Louis courts.

St. Louis acted as a gateway through which African Americans acculturated to French, Spanish, and American mores came together to fashion new identities. American and African American migrations were both impetus and culmination of the centuries-long obsession with the western frontier and its promise of individual freedom, land ownership, and treasure. Exploration and expansion were abetted by the peculiar marriage of slavery and laws, and their bastard offspring, the far-flung and profitable commerce in slaves. The serendipitous juxtaposition of St. Louis to the west also supported the growth of a small but sturdy free population of color and persistent resistance by slaves to their enslavement, including by means of alliances between slaves and free blacks (at the risk of their own liberty) and through use of the extraordinary method of formal lawsuits filed by slaves. Against this tumultuous backdrop, statehood gained by fragile political compromise rendered Missouri an outpost, which faced the promise of freedom on the western frontier, but within which the institution of slavery was still protected. The resulting political, economic, and cultural tensions slowly but surely fractured the nation along the fault line of race, slavery, and western expansion, a breach that bisected the state and the city.

As St. Louis had been the jumping off place for westward expansion of American political, economic, and cultural enterprises, in the wake of the Civil War, African Americans as individuals, families, and en masse as "Exodusters" continued the movement west. Often, post-war newcomers joined or took advantage of the pioneer and early settlement efforts of blacks who had worked in the fur trading outposts, runaway slaves, or free blacks who were among those to build cities on the Pacific coast. St. Louis, Missouri, as the gateway, funneled countless thousands of blacks into the West; in the founding years, blacks with French, Spanish, and finally, American cultural allegiances contributed to an early "melting pot" of African American and American identities. It is in this context that Dred Scott became, not merely a slave who sued for his freedom and lost, but rather, a complex symbol of blacks who encountered the West from St. Louis and through their experiences actively shaped what we came to know as "the west" through pioneer settlement and law, all the while remaining invisible to history. Blacks on the frontier, especially those who later pointed to their residence in areas that prohibited slavery as the basis for challenging their legal status as slaves sounded the first notes of the "firebell" that eventually erupted in civil war. Dred Scott symbolized the burgeoning trade in slaves west from St. Louis at the same time that he became an iconic symbol of free people of color, especially those who created free identity using the law and the courts.

Almost instantly, a phenomenon unique to the peculiar institution in the region was born: by ones and twos and threes, then dozens, then hundreds, slaves who had served time in the free western territories used that residency as leverage in the courts to begin to pry open a free space themselves at the edge of the frontier. Not yet a "firebell," but a high-pitched harbinger of some of the ways in which the west and slavery conjoined to reshape definitions of citizenship and polity. Thus, to the names Dred and Harriet Scott, we must add York, Jim Beckwith, Preston, Braxton, and Mary Duty, Fanny Jackson, and Squire Brown, and the many hundreds of named as well as anonymous people of color in St. Louis, Missouri, from its founding through the end of the Civil War.

Chapter Notes

Preface

1. Patricia Nelson Limerick, *The Legacy of Conquest: The Unbroken Past of the American West* (New York: W. W. Norton, 1987), 19.

Introduction

1. Monroe Lee Billington and Roger D. Hardaway, *African Americans on the Western Frontier* (Boulder: University of Colorado Press, 1998), 1.

2. See, for example, J. Frederick Fausz, *Founding St. Louis: First City of the New West* (Charleston: The History Press, 2011); Carl J. Ekberg, *Stealing Indian Women: Native Slavery in the Illinois Country* (Urbana: University of Illinois Press, 2007); Patricia Cleary, *The World, the Flesh, and the Devil: A History of Colonial St. Louis* (Columbia: University of Missouri Press, 2011).

3. *Missouri Gazette*, Wednesday, April 26, 1809, Vol. I, p. 2; Hodes, *Beyond the Frontier*, 221.

4. Helen Tunnicliff Catterall, "Some Antecedents of the Dred Scot Case," *The American Historical Review* 30, no. 1 (October 1924), 56–71.

5. Richard C. Wade, *The Urban Frontier: Pioneer Life in Early Pittsburgh, Cincinnati, Lexington, Louisville, and St. Louis* (Chicago: University of Chicago Press, 1959, 1968), 1.

6. David Hackett Fischer and James C. Kelly, *Bound Away: Virginia and the Westward Movement* (Charlottesville: University of Virginia Press, 2000); Ira Berlin, *The Making of African America: The Four Great Migrations* (New York: Viking Penguin, 2010).

7. Margaret Washington, "African American History and the Frontier Thesis," *Journal of the Early Republic* 13, no. 2 (Summer 1993), 230–241. Washington notes an "Implicit Thesis" of historian Peter H. Wood in his *Black Majority* (1974), which argues that frontier conditions in early South Carolina produced a society where certain economic and social opportunities existed for free Africans, but which were emphatically reversed and even "stifled" with settlement facilitated by establishment of the Carolina rice culture (Washington, 238–239).

8. *Ibid.*, 1.

9. Jay Gitlin, *The Bourgeois Frontier: French Towns, French Traders and American Expansion* (New Haven: Yale University Press, 2010), 48.

10. Fischer and Kelly, *Bound Away*, 6.

11. *Ibid.*, at 8.

12. Letter to Amos Stoddard from the Committee of the Town of St. Lewis [*sic*], August 4, 1804, Stoddard Collection, Missouri Historical Society, St. Louis, Missouri; James Neal Primm, *Lion of the Valley: St. Louis, Missouri, 1764–1980* (Missouri Historical Society Press, 1998 [1981, 1990]), 72; Stuart Banner, *Legal Systems in Conflict: Property and Sovereignty in Missouri,*

1750–1860 (Norman: University of Oklahoma Press, 2000), 95.

13. *State v. Philip Harris,* Case File Numbers 3 and 16, 1850, November Term, Criminal Case Files; *State v. Benjamin Savage,* Case File Numbers 4 and 17, 1850, September Term, Criminal Case Files.

14. Stephen Aron, *American Confluence: The Missouri Frontier from Borderland to Border State* (Bloomington: Indiana University Press, 2006), 181.

15. Nikola Baumgarten, "Education and Democracy in Frontier St. Louis: The Society of the Sacred Heart," *History of Education Quarterly* 34, no. 2 (Summer 1994); *The St. Louis University, Pltff. vs. Michael J. Crely, Jr., Et Als, Defendants,* No. 23, 1854, March Term, Office of the Circuit Clerk, City of St. Louis, Missouri, St. Louis Circuit Court.

16. *Celeste v. Mme. Chevalier,* 1805, District of Louisiana.

Prologue

1. Frederick A. Hodes, *Beyond the Frontier: A History of St. Louis to 1821* (Tucson: Patrice Press, 2004), c. 2, "The Europeans Arrive," 28–67; Patricia Cleary, *The World, the Flesh, and the Devil: A History of Colonial St. Louis* (Columbia: University of Missouri Press, 2011), 26–29.

2. Carl J. Ekberg, *Stealing Indian Women: Native Slavery in the Illinois Country* (Urbana: University of Illinois Press, 2007), 3.

3. Hall, 2, 40–41.

4. *Ibid.,* 57. (According to Carl Ekberg, Indian slaves "Continued to Be Employed Throughout the Eighteenth Century In ... St. Louis"; Ekberg, *Indian Women,* 13; in addition, Indians were exchanged for black slaves from the Caribbean to "Early French Louisiana" at a rate of 3:2 or 2:1, although the trade was not "significant" and may have been banned by French royal directive of 1726. Ekberg, *Indian Women,* 14–15.)

5. *Ibid.,* 34.

6. *Ibid.,* 160–161.

7. *Ibid.,* 188–189.

8. *Ibid.,* 29–31.

9. *Ibid.,* 38, 36.

10. *Ibid.,* 34–36.

11. *Ibid.,* 59, 62, 69.

12. *Ibid.,* 35.

13. Landon Y. Jones, *William Clark and the Shaping of the West* (New York: Hill and Wang, 2004), 149; Hall, *Africans in Colonial Louisiana,* 9–10, 25.

14. Hall, 129–130.

15. *Ibid.,* 131–132.

16. Thomas C. Buchanan, *Black Life on the Mississippi: Slaves, Free Blacks, and the Western Steamboat World* (Chapel Hill: University of North Carolina Press, 2004), 5–7, 10, 12; Jones, *William Clark,* 171. In addition to the Mississippi River, the Missouri River (with which the Mississippi formed a confluence), and nearby Illinois and Ohio Rivers made St. Louis an ideal site for commercial and residential success.

Chapter 1

1. John Craig Hammond, *Slavery, Freedom and Expansion in the Early American West* (Charlottesville: University of Virginia Press, 2007), 36.

2. Hodes, *Beyond the Frontier,* 68; Aron, *American Confluence,* 50–51; Patricia Cleary, *The World, the Flesh, and the Devil: A History of Colonial St. Louis* (Columbia: University of Missouri Press, 2011), 23–24.

3. Clyde A. Milner II, Carol A. O'Connor, Martha A. Sandweiss, *The Oxford History of the American West* (New York: Oxford University Press), 135.

4. Patricia Cleary, *The World, the Flesh, and the Devil: A History of Colonial St. Louis* (Columbia: University of Missouri Press, 2011), 19 and 19, n.29.

5. Catterall, "Some Antecedents of the Dred Scott Case," 57, 59–60; Lorenzo J. Greene, Gary R. Kremer and Antonio F. Holland, *Missouri's Black Heritage* (Columbia: University of Missouri Press, 1980), revised and updated by Gary R. Kremer and Antonio F. Holland, 1993, 9.

6. Catterall, "Antecedents," 58, 59, 61; Dennis K. Boman, "The Dred Scott Case Reconsidered: The Legal and Political Context in Missouri," *The American Journal of Legal History* 44, no. 4 (October 2000), 410–411.

7. Aron, 79.

8. Gitlin, *The Bourgeois Frontier*, 1.

9. *Ibid.*, 9, 52–53.

10. *Ibid.*, 147.

11. William E. Foley and C. David Rice, *The First Chouteaus: River Barons of Early St. Louis* (Urbana: University of Illinois Press, 1983), 2–6; Charles E. Peterson, *Colonial St. Louis: Building a Creole Capital* (Tucson: Patrice Press, 1993), 3, 8.

12. *Chouteau's Narrative*, 4; Dunne, *The Missouri Supreme Court: From Dred Scott to Nancy Cruzan*, 8.

13. Hodes, *Beyond the Frontier*, 73; *Chouteau's Narrative*, 5.

14. Susan Calafate Boyle, "French Women in Colonial Missouri, 1750–1805," in LeeAnn Whites, Mary C. Neth, and Gary R. Kremer, eds., *Women in Missouri History: In Search of Power and Influence* (Columbia: University of Missouri Press, 2004), 15–16.

15. Ekberg, *Indian Women*, xiii, 13, 29, 47–49.

16. A.P. Nasatir, *Before Lewis and Clark: Documents Illustrating the History of the Missouri, 1785–1804, Volume 1* (Lincoln: University of Nebraska Press, 1952, 1990), 62.

17. Hodes, *Beyond the Frontier*, 76–77.

18. Foley and Rice, *The First Chouteaus*; Hodes, *Beyond the Frontier*, 88–89, 126; Wilson Primm, "History of St. Louis," in Sandweiss, *Seeking St. Louis*, 90.

19. Cleary, *The World*, 31.

20. *Ibid.*, 79, 82.

21. *Ibid.*, 85–86.

22. Hode, *Beyond the Frontier*, 100, 139.

23. Ekberg, *Stealing Indian Women*, 54.

24. *Ibid.*; Catterall, "Antecedents," 58, 59, 61; Dennis K. Boman, "The Dred Scott Case Reconsidered: The Legal and Political Context in Missouri," *the American Journal of Legal History* 44, no. 4 (October 2000), 410–411.

25. Ekberg, *Indian Women*, 60–63; Cleary, *The World*, 117–118. Slave owners often maintained a ratio of two (or more) female to male slaves to maintain a profitable level of labor and production during times when female slaves might be indisposed due to pregnancy or childbirth.

26. Carl J. Ekberg and Sharon K. Person, *St. Louis Rising: The French Regime of Louis St. Ange De Bellerive* (Urbana: University of Illinois Press, 2015), 230–231.

27. Ekberg and Person, *St. Louis Rising*, at 231.

28. Hodes, *Beyond the Frontier*, 133; Cleary, *The World*, 144–145.

29. Harriet C. Frazier, *Runaway and Freed Missouri Slaves and Those Who Helped Them, 1763–1865* (Jefferson, NC: McFarland, 2004), 42–43.

30. Fernando de Leyba, "Account of the Battle of San Carlos, June 8, 1780," in Sandweiss, *Seeking St. Louis*, 21–27; Hodes, *Beyond the Frontier*, 185–187; Cleary, *The World*, 232–233.

31. Hodes, 188, 189; de Leyba, 23–24.

32. de Leyba, 25–27; Hodes, *Beyond the Frontier*, 199, 297; Cleary, *The World*, 233.

33. Aron, 79.

34. Ekberg, *Indian Women*, 91–92.

35. Petition and mediation before Zénon Trudeau, captain of the regiment attached to the Louisiana Territory and Commander in Chief of the Western part belonging to the Illinois Indians, June, 1796, Missouri Historical Society, St. Louis, Missouri; Banner, *Legal Systems in Conflict*, 25.

36. Hodes, *Beyond the Frontier*, 211, 221.

37. *Ibid.*; these figures specify slaves between the ages of 14 and 50. The race or color description of slaves over 50 was not provided, however, 19 male slaves and nine female slaves were listed in that age category.

38. Cleary, "Settlement Choices," 70; Hodes, *Beyond the Frontier*, 168.

39. "Cleary, "Settlement Choices," 70; Hodes, *Beyond the Frontier*, 168.

40. Nasatir, *Before Lewis and Clark Volume 1*, ix.

41. *Ibid.*, vol. 1, 85, "Regulations for the Illinois Trade, St. Louis, October 15, 1793," Article 17, 191, Article 19, 192; 190.

42. Nasatir, *Before Lewis and Clark, Volume 1*, 162.

43. Hodes, *Beyond the Frontier*, 237.

44. *Ibid.*, 448.

45. Frederic L. Billon, *Annals of St. Louis in Its Territorial Days from 1804 to 1821, Being a Continuation of the Author's Previous Work the Annals of the French and Spanish Period* (St. Louis: Printed for the author, 1888), 10.

46. Nasatir, *Before Lewis and Clark, Volume 1*, 366.

47. Hammond, "Slaves Accounted for Between ¼ and ⅓ of the Population of St. Louis," 32.

48. Hammond, 54, 71.

49. *Ibid.*, 56; Aron, 120, 173.

50. Hodes, *Beyond the Frontier*, 303; Banner, *Legal Systems in Conflict*, 95.

51. Gitlin, *The Bourgeois Frontier*, 57; Primm, *Lion of the Valley*, 72; Banner, *Legal Systems*, 95.

52. Hammond, *Slavery, Freedom, and Expansion in the Early American West*, 30.

53. Aron, 119.

54. Hodes, *Beyond the Frontier*, 291–292.

55. *Ibid.*, at 292.

56. Foley, 96–98; Richard E. Jensen, ed., "Last Years of the Missouri Fur Company: The Correspondence of Angus William Mcdonald," in *The Museum of the Fur Trade Quarterly* 37, Issue 2 (2001), 2, n.15 at 15; Nicolas de Finiels, "From 'An Account of Upper Louisiana,'" in Sandweiss, *Seeking St. Louis*, 30; Peterson, 8, 12–14; D.S. John Biggs, Foreman, 1805, Pierre Chouteau Collection, Missouri Historical Society, St. Louis, Missouri.

57. Aron, 160–171, 173–174.

58. *Ibid.*, 197–198.

59. Billon, 10.

60. *Ibid.*, 62.

61. Donald F. Dosch, *The Old Courthouse: Americans Build a Forum on the Frontier* (Jefferson National Expansion Historical Association, 1979), 18, 28, 29; Billon, *Annals of St. Louis*, 10.

62. *Ibid.*

63. *Ibid.*

64. Hodes, *Beyond the Frontier*, 304.

65. Stuart Banner, *Legal Systems in Conflict: Property and Sovereignty in Missouri, 1750–1860* (Norman: University of Oklahoma Press, 2000), 14; Foley, 96–98.

66. Hodes, *Beyond the Frontier*, 312.

67. *Ibid.*, at 338.

68. James Neal Primm, *Lion in the Valley: St. Louis, Missouri, 1764–1980* (Missouri Historical Society Press, 1998, third ed.), 23; Louis S. Gerteis, *Civil War St. Louis* (Lawrence: University Press of Kansas, 2001), 22, 40.

69. Foley, 95; Hodes, 134–135.

70. Frazier, *Runaway and Freed Missouri Slaves*, 24.

71. Hodes, *Beyond the Frontier*, 419.

72. *Ibid.*, at 420.

73. Foley, 93–94; Hodes, *Beyond the Frontier*, 154, 161–163.

74. Hodes, *Beyond the Frontier*, 409.

75. *Ibid.*, 123, 135–136.

76. Foley, 95; Hodes, 134–135.

77. Leonard P. Curry, *The Free Black in Urban America, 1800–1850: The Shadow of the Dream* (Chicago: University of Chicago Press, 1981), 186; Greene, Kremer, Holland, *Missouri's Black Heritage*, 67, 69; Randall M. Miller, "Black Catholics in the Slave South: Some Needs and Opportunities for Study" in *Records of the American Catholic Historical Society of Philadelphia* 86, no. 1 (1975), 93–106.

78. James Kennerly, Journals and Diaries, December 27, 1837, Missouri Historical Society and Archive, St. Louis, Missouri; P. Chouteau/Maffitt, receipts of J. B. Meachum, 3/8, 3/19/1831, Missouri Historical Society, St. Louis, Missouri; *John Berry Meachum, Free Man of Color v. William Smith*, No. 211, November Term, 1840, St. Louis Circuit Court.

79. Loren Schweninger, "Prosperous Blacks in the South, 1790–1880," *The American Historical Review* 95, no. 1 (February 1990), 43–44.

80. *Berry Metchum v. David Massey, Action of Trespass and Ejectment*, St. Louis Circuit Court, No. 33, June Term 1823, St. Louis, Missouri.

81. *Metchum v. Massey, Trespass and Ejectment*, 1823.

82. *Metchum v. Massey, Trespass and Ejectment, Summons*, 1823.

83. Answer of David Massey, October 31, 1823.

84. *Meachum v. Massey*, surveys, 1823.

85. *John Berry Meachum, Free Man of Color, v. William Smith*, No. 211, November Term 1840, St. Louis Circuit Court.

86. *Judy Alias Julia Logan vs. Berry Meachum, Petition for Assault and Battery and False Imprisonment*, No. 11, March term 1835, St. Louis Circuit Court.

87. Deposition of Benjamin Duncan, October 28, 1835.

88. *Judy Alias Julia Logan vs. Berry*

Meachum, March Term 1836, St. Louis Circuit Court.

89. *Judy Alias Julia Logan vs. Berry Meachum, Reasons for a New Trial*, March Term 1836, St. Louis Circuit Court.

90. *Berry Meachum vs. Judy Alias Julia Logan, Petition Before the Missouri Supreme Court*, 1836.

91. *Green Berry Logan, an Infant, by Judy Alias Julia Logan, His Mother and Next Friend vs. Berry Meachum, a Free Man of Color, Action of Trespass, Assault and Battery, and False Imprisonment*, No. 22, July Term 1836, St. Louis Circuit Court.

92. Hodes, *Beyond the Frontier*, 413.

93. *Ibid.*

94. *Ibid.*, 446.

95. Baumgarten, "Education and Democracy in Frontier St. Louis, 172–177.

96. Carol K. Coburn and Martha Smith, "City Sisters: The Sisters of St. Joseph in Missouri, 1836–1920," in Lee-Ann Whites, Mary C. Neth, and Gary R. Kremer, eds., *Women in Missouri History: In Search of Power and Influence* (Columbia: University of Missouri Press, 2004), 89.

97. Coburn and Smith, "City Sisters," 91.

98. *Ibid.*

99. Hodes, *Beyond the Frontier*, 393.

100. Primm, *Lion of the Valley*, 86; *Missouri Gazette*, Wednesday, September 7, 1808, Vol. I, No. 9.

101. Foley, 86; Jones, *William Clark*, 163; Hodes, *Beyond the Frontier*, 434–435.

102. Foley, 90–91.

103. Stuart Banner, *Legal Systems in Conflict*, 86, 95, 113.

104. Kolchin, *American Slavery*, 177.

Chapter 2

1. Kerr, *Petty Felony*, 4–5.

2. *Ibid.*, 43.

3. *Ibid.*, 59.

4. *Ibid.*, 129.

5. Hall, *Africans in Colonial Louisiana*, 262.

6. *Ibid.*, 304; Aron, *American Confluence*, 47.

7. Hodes, *Beyond the Frontier*, 219–220; Schafer, *Slavery, the Civil Law, and the Supreme Court of Louisiana*, 2–3.

8. *Laws of the State of Missouri*, "Freedom," Sec. 1, 1824.

9. Billington and Hardaway, *African Americans on the Western Frontier*, 9.

10. Banner, *Legal Systems*, 27; "Surgeon's Certification to Francois Cruzat Regarding Dead Negro Found in the Barn of Widow Chouteau," December 28, 1785, St. Louis, Chouteau-Papin Collection, Missouri Historical Society, St. Louis, Missouri.

11. Amos Stoddard Papers, Letter, August 4, 1804, Missouri Historical Society, St. Louis, Missouri.

12. *Ibid.*, August 6, 1804.

13. Hodes, *Beyond the Frontier*, 508.

14. *Ibid.*

15. *Ibid.*, 509.

16. *Ibid.*, 507.

17. *Ibid.*, 508.

18. *Ibid.*, 367; Dennis K. Boman, "The Dred Scott Case Reconsidered," 414.

19. Committee of Town of St. Louis, August 4, 1804, Stoddard Papers, Missouri Historical Society, St. Louis, Missouri.

20. Hodes, *Beyond the Frontier*, 398.

21. *Ibid.*, 399.

22. Sheriff Walker turned the children over to William Orr for "safekeeping" at the behest of John Carman, and Orr charged Carman a fee for "Room and Board" while the case regarding Carman's loan to Jones of approximately $380 (damages of $500) was being litigated. Orr's bill for $173.87 ½ was for food, shelter, clothing and medical care for the children from July 1831 to January 1832. A receipt for $5 for medical care provided in December 1831 for "Mary an (Black Girl)" [sic] was presented by Sheriff Walker to Merry Tiffin.

23. St. Louis Circuit Court, Articles of Agreement, November 25, 1821. Several years later, William Woods brought suit against Benjamin Jones to reclaim two slaves (one male and one female). The petition states that Margaret Jones, wife of Benjamin, agreed to care for Abner, "An Aged Man and Blind," in return for items listed in the 1821 Articles of Agreement while her husband was out of the country. Apparently, the arrangement worked well for a few years, even after Benjamin Jones' return to the United States. However, at some point, Abner Woods left the Jones'

home and refused to return, and William Woods petitioned the Court to return his slaves. St. Louis Circuit Court, Chancery, January 17, 1828.

24. Ekberg and *St. Louis Rising,* 155.

25. *Ibid.*

26. Frazier, *Runaway and Freed Missouri Slaves,* 24; Cleary, *The World,* 144.

27. Frazier, *Runaway and Freed Missouri Slaves,* 24–25.

28. Grand Jury Presentment, Slaves Hiring Themselves Out, March 1827.

29. Grand Jury Presentment, 1827.

30. Grand Jury Presentment, Slaves at Large, March 1829, Criminal Court of St. Louis.

31. *Ibid.*

32. *Ibid.*

33. Boman, "Dred Scott Case Reconsidered," 415.

34. *Ibid.,* 415–416.

35. *Ibid.,* 414–415.

36. *Ibid.,* 415.

37. Criminal Index Record Book, Index 1–4, 1831–1863, St. Louis, Missouri.

38. *Ibid.,* at Record Book 4, p. 64, Thursday, July 24, 1846; Record Book 5, p.63, Tuesday, August 1, 1848; Record Book 5, p.395, February 24, 1849; Record Book 9, Case No. 6, p. 170, Tuesday, May 12, 1857.

39. Hall, 144.

40. *Ibid.,* at 143.

41. Frazier, 26–27.

42. Harriet C. Frazier, *Death Sentences in Missouri, 1803–2005: A History and Comprehensive Registry of Legal Executions, Pardons, and Commutations* (Jefferson, NC: McFarland, 2006), 7.

43. *Ibid.*

44. *Ibid.*

45. *Ibid.*

46. *Ibid.,* 7–8.

47. *Ibid.,* 10, 31.

48. *Ibid.,* 10.

49. *Ibid.,* 12.

50. *Ibid.,* 34.

51. *Laws of the District of Louisiana* (22), 1804; Miller, "Black Catholics in the Slave South," 97.

52. *Ibid.* (6), 1804.

53. *Ibid.* (9).

54. Advertisement dated July 7, 1841, for the *Eagle* excursion to public hanging of four negroes, "Broadsides"—Transpor-

tation, Box 10, Missouri Historical Society, St. Louis, Missouri; Frazier, *Death Sentences,* 33–34.

55. *Laws of the District of Louisiana,* Chapter 35, Freedom, 1807.

56. Hodes, 398.

57. Petition and summons, St. Louis Criminal Court, July 7, 1824.

58. Summons, July 7, 1824.

59. Petition, *State v. Dennis Dolan, Jr., Assault of Dennis Dolan, Sr.,* October, 1824.

60. Petition, July Term, 1829, St. Louis Circuit Court.

61. *Nicholas Jones vs. John Gay and John Horner,* deposition, February 12, 1830, St. Louis Circuit Court.

62. Deposition, February 12, 1830, Anne Arundel County, Maryland Justice of the Peace.

63. *Ibid.*

64. Criminal Index Record Book 1, page 91, Tuesday, August 28, 1832, St. Louis, Missouri.

65. *Ibid.*

66. *"The African" Prospectus,* Saint Louis, Mo., September 16, 1843, Circulars, Missouri Historical Society, St. Louis, Missouri.

67. *Ibid.*

68. Letter from Peter Camden to Dr. George Case, June 4, 1860, Case Family Papers, Missouri Historical Society, St. Louis, Missouri.

69. Manumission, Elizabeth Keckley and George by Ann P. Garland, November 13, 1855, Missouri Historical Society, St. Louis, Missouri.

70. *Martha Drusella v. Richmond J. Curle,* Case File Number 252, 1844, November Term.

71. *Thornton Kinney vs. John F. Hatcher and Charles C. Bridges,* No. 35, November Term 1853, St. Louis Circuit Court, State of Missouri.

72. *Ibid.*

73. *Ibid.*

74. *State v. Mary Meachum,* Case File No. 137, 1853, May Term, Criminal Case Files.

75. *State v. Philip Harris,* Case File Numbers 3 and 16, 1850, November Term, Criminal Case Files; *State v. Benjamin Savage,* Case File Numbers 4 and 17, 1850, September Term, Criminal Case Files.

76. Allen E. Wagner, *Good Order and Safety: A History of the St. Louis Metropolitan Police Department, 1861–1906* (Missouri History Museum, 2008), 22–23.

77. Wagner, *Good Order and Safety*, 23.

Chapter 3

1. Ira Berlin, *The Making of African America: The Four Great Migrations* (New York: Viking Penguin, 2010), 20; Lea VanderVelde and Sandhya Subramanian, "Mrs. Dred Scott," *The Yale Law Journal* 106, no. 4 (January 1997), 1037.

2. Berlin, *The Making of African America*, 99–100.

3. *Ibid.*, 37, 45–48.

4. Quintard Taylor, "Freedmen and Slaves in Oregon Territory, 1840–1860," in Sucheng Chan, Douglas Henry Daniels, Mario T. Garcia and Terry P. Wilson, eds., *Peoples of Color in the American West* (Lexington, MA: D.C. Heath, 1994), 76.

5. Thomas P. Slaughter, *Exploring Lewis and Clark: Reflections on Men and Wilderness* (New York: Vintage Books, 2003), 39, 43, 47.

6. *Ibid.*, 102.

7. *Ibid.*, 114; Roger D. Hardaway, "The African American Frontier: Bibliographic Essay," in Billington and Hardaway, eds., *African Americans on the Western Frontier*, 235.

8. Slaughter, *Exploring Lewis and Clark*, 114–115.

9. *Ibid.*, 114.

10. VanderVelde and Subramanian, "Mrs. Dred Scott," 1040 n.18.

11. Slaughter, *Exploring Lewis and Clark*, 117.

12. *Ibid.*, 118–119.

13. *Ibid.*, 119.

14. *Ibid.*, 122.

15. *Ibid.*, 123.

16. *Ibid.*, 123–125.

17. *Ibid.*, 123.

18. *Ibid.*, 123; Aron, *American Confluence*, 174–175; Frazier, *Runaway and Freed Missouri Slaves*, 49.

19. Harriet C. Frazier, *Runaway and Freed Missouri Slaves and Those Who Helped Them, 1763–1865* (Jefferson, NC: McFarland, 2004), 49.

20. Slaughter, *Exploring Lewis and Clark*, 124, 127; Aron, *American Confluence*, 175; Frazier, *Runaway*, 49.

21. Slaughter, *Exploring Lewis and Clark*, 124.

22. *Ibid.*, 124.

23. *Ibid.*, 124–125.

24. *Ibid.*, 125.

25. *Ibid.*, 126.

26. *Ibid.*, 128–133.

27. Taylor, "Freedmen and Slaves," 79.

28. *Ibid.*, 79–80.

29. *Ibid.*, at 80.

30. *Ibid.*, at 80–81.

31. ALS Theodore Papin to P.M. Papin, June 16, 1832, translation from the French, Chouteau-Papin Collection, Missouri Historical Society, St. Louis, Missouri.

32. *Ibid.*

33. Billington and Hardaway, eds., Glenda Riley, "American Daughters,"165.

34. Monroe Lee Billington and Roger D. Hardaway, eds., *African Americans on the Western Frontier* (Boulder: University Press of Colorado, 1998), W. Sherman Savage, "Slavery in the West," 9–10, 14; Riley, "American Daughters," 165.

35. Annie Heloise Abel, *Chardon's Journal at Fort Clark, 1834–1839* (Lincoln: University of Nebraska Press, 1932, 1997), 55, 58, 60, 65, 99, 230 (n.90), and *Passim.*

36. Abel, *Chardon's Journal*, 253 (n.227).

37. *Ibid.*, 23, 70–71, 78, 208–209 (n.36), 213–214 (n.52), 215 (n.60), 229 (n.88), and *Passim.*

38. *Ibid.*, 80, 83, 145, 164, 168, 173, 186.

39. Gitlin, *The Bourgeois Frontier*, 17, 52.

40. Abel, *Chardon's Journal*, 298–299 (n.363).

41. *Ibid.*, 213 (n.51).

42. *Ibid.*, 175, 182–183.

43. VanderVelde and Subramanian, "Mrs. Dred Scott," 1052 and n.78.

44. Abel, *Chardon's Journal*, 9, 69, 72, 87, 95, 194, 267–268 (n.252), 286 (n.306); Barton H. Barbour, *Fort Union and the Upper Missouri Fur Trade* (Norman: University of Oklahoma Press, 2001), 33, 59–60.

45. Abel, *Chardon's Journal*; Barbour, *Fort Union and the Upper Missouri Fur Trade.*

46. Abel, *Chardon's Journal*, 7, 284 (n.295), 31.

47. *Ibid.,* Letter from Kenneth Mackenzie to Ramsey Crooks, December 10, 1835, 380.

48. *Ibid.,* 284 (n.295).

49. Barbour, *Fort Union and the Upper Missouri Fur Trade,* 60, 65; also Abel, *Chardon's Journal,* xiv.

50. Abel, *Chardon's Journal,* 255 (n.228).

51. A.L.S. Joshua Pilcher to Pierre Chouteau, Jr., St. Louis, June 16, 1833, Chouteau-Papin Collection, Missouri Historical Society, St. Louis, Missouri.

52. *Ibid.*

53. A.L.S. Berthold to B. Pratte and Company, December 12, 1823, St. Louis, Chouteau-Papin College, Missouri Historical Society, St. Louis, Missouri.

54. Abel, *Chardon's Journal,* xvi–xvii.

55. Barbour, *Fort Union and the Upper Missouri Fur Trade,* 116–117.

56. Abel, *Chardon's Journal,* 310 (n.427).

57. Elinor Wilson, *Jim Beckwourth: Black Mountain Man and War Chief of the Crows* (Norman: University of Oklahoma Press, 1972), 7.

58. Washington, "African American History and the Frontier Thesis," *Journal of the Early Republic* 13, no. 2 (Summer 1993), 231.

59. *Ibid.,* 233.

60. *Ibid.,* 238.

61. Wilson, *Jim Beckwourth,* 7, 11.

62. *Ibid.,* 15–16.

63. *Ibid.,* 17.

64. *Ibid.*

65. *Ibid.*

66. Wilson, *Beckwourth,* 18–19, 21.

67. Donnie D. Belamy, "The Education of Blacks in Missouri Prior to 1861," *The Journal of Negro History* 59, no. 2 (April 1974), 143–157; Baumgarten, Nikola. "Education and Democracy in Frontier St. Louis: The Society of the Sacred Heart," *History of Education Quarterly* 34, no. 2 (Summer 1994), 171–192; Elinor Mondale Gersman, "The Development of Public Education for Blacks in Nineteenth Century St. Louis, Missouri," *The Journal of Negro Education* 41, no. 1 (Winter 1972), 35–47.

68. Wilson, *Beckwourth,* 19.

69. *Ibid.,* 22–23.

70. *Ibid.,* 26–27, 28.

71. Primm, 128–129.

72. Wilson, *Beckwourth,* 27–28.

73. *Ibid.,* 28–29.

74. *Ibid.,* 29–30.

75. *Ibid.,* 44–45, 30–45.

76. Abel, *Chardon's Journal,* 310 (n.428–429).

77. Barbour, *Fort Union and the Upper Missouri Fur Trade,* 116.

78. Wilson, *Beckwourth,* 41–42.

79. Abel, *Chardon's Journal,* 255 (n.228).

80. A.L.S. F.A. Chardon to J.B. Sarpy, June 27 1837, Mandan Village, Chouteau-Papin Collection, Missouri Historical Society, St. Louis, Missouri.

81. Washington, "African American History and the Frontier Thesis," 239–240.

82. Abel, *Chardon's Journal,* 146.

83. Gitlin, *The Bourgeois Frontier,* 17.

84. Abel, *Chardon's Journal,* 153.

85. *Ibid.,* 147–149, 152.

86. *Ibid.,* 149.

87. John E. Sunder, *The Fur Trade on the Upper Missouri, 1840–1865* (Norman: University of Oklahoma Press, 1965, 1993), 105.

88. Abel, *Chardon's Journal,* 255 (n.228), 268 (n.253).

89. David J. Wishart, *The Fur Trade of the American West, 1807–1840* (Norman: University of Nebraska Press, 1979), 68.

90. Abel, *Chardon's Journal,* 123–141, 145–146, 149, 173–174, 181, 394–396.

91. *Ibid.,* xx.

92. Aron, *American Confluence,* 174–175.

93. *Ibid.,* 175; Landon Y. Jones, *William Clark and the Shaping of the West* (New York: Hill and Wang, 2004), 251; Frazier, *Runaway and Freed Missouri Slaves,* 50.

94. *Lemmon Dutton v. John Paca,* No. 116, St. Louis Circuit Court, July Term, 1834.

95. *Josiah William Dallam, to Sundry Slaves, Manumission,* Hartford County, State of Maryland, 1787.

96. *Ibid.*

97. *Dutton v. Paca.*

98. *Dutton vs. Paca, Judgment and Opinion, Supreme Court, 3d Judicial District, June Term 1835.*

99. *Ibid.,* at Judgment and Opinion.

100. Frazier, *Runaway and Freed Missouri Slaves,* 78; Edlie L. Wong, *Neither*

Fugitive Nor Free: Atlantic Slavery, Freedom Suits, and the Legal Culture of Travel (New York: New York University Press, 2009), 129.

101. Jack, *The St. Louis African American Community and the Exodusters*, 43–46.

Chapter 4

1. Jeffrey S. Adler, "Streetwalkers, Degraded Outcasts, and Good-For-Nothing Huzzies: Women and the angerous Class in Antebellum St. Louis," *Journal of Social History* 25, no. 4 (1992), 740, 742. Adler and others have analyzed the tendency to define black women as "dangerous," especially as individuals who exerted a peculiar sexual power *Vis-À-Vis White* men; Adler discusses the use by "prostitutes" to unfurl a kind of erotic sorcery, but quickly expands the well-accepted definition of "prostitute" to include women who ignored or challenged societal conventions regarding race and gender. Deborah Gray White's classic *Ar'n't I a Woman?* put the lie to the convenient white male apologia that pleaded vulnerability to black female sexual magic, laid the blame for miscegenation and immorality within the slave regime on black women, and went on to connect this particular "defense" to the deliberate construction of a pro-slavery agenda. White, *Ar'n't I a Woman*, 61.

2. Ira Berlin, *The Making of African America: The Four Great Migration* (New York: Viking Penguin, 2010), especially notes the sexual vulnerability of slaves during transport or at sale or auction, 115–116. See also Carol K. Coburn and Martha Smith, "City Sisters: The Sisters of St. Joseph in Missouri, 1836–1920," in Whites, Neth, and Kremer, eds., *Women in Missouri History*, 82–100, which considers the place of some of the first Catholic nuns in antebellum St. Louis, their religious and racial identities, and their "Interaction" as educators with girls and women of color; and Deborah Gray White, *Ar'n't I a Woman? Female Slaves in the Plantation South* (New York: W. W. Norton, 1985), 15–17.

3. A.L.S. Hyacinthe Papin to Pierre M. Papin, November 9, 1832, Chouteau-Papin Collection, Missouri Historical Society, St. Louis, Missouri.

4. *Celeste v. Mme. Chevalier,* writ of *Habeas Corpus,* June 15, 1805, District of Louisiana; answer, May Term, 1806, District of Louisiana, General Court, Missouri Historical Society, St. Louis, Missouri. Both free and slave people of color were often referred to in the legal record by their first names only. Sometimes slaves used the name of a present or former owner, and sometimes they created names of their own. The same was apparently true for free people of color.

5. William E. Foley, "Slave Freedom Suits Before Dred Scott: The Case of Marie Scypion's Descendants," *Missouri Historical Review* LXXIX (October 1984–July 1985), 5.

6. *Ibid.,* 5–6.

7. *Ibid.,* 2–3.

8. *Ibid.,* 7–9.

9. *Ibid.,* 6.

10. *Ibid.,* 9.

11. *Ibid.,* 11–23.

12. Patricia Morton, quoting Peter Kolchin on the findings of slavery studies of the 1970s, in Patricia Morton, ed., *Discovering the Women in Slavery: Emancipating Perspectives on the American Past* (Athens: University of Georgia Press, 1996), 6.

13. Petition and mediation before Zénon Trudeau, captain of the regiment attached to the Louisiana Territory and Commander in Chief of the Western part belonging to the Illinois Indians, June, 1796, Missouri Historical Society, St. Louis, Missouri.

14. Hodes, *Beyond the Frontier,* 211, 221.

15. *Ibid.,* 409.

16. *Ibid.,* 123, 135–136.

17. *Ibid.,* 133.

18. *Ibid.,* 133.

19. Martha Saxton, *Being Good: Women's Moral Values in Early America* (New York: Hill and Wang, 2003), 175.

20. Saxton, *Being Good,* 178–179.

21. *Ibid.,* 183.

22. Hodes, *Beyond the Frontier,* 413.

23. *Ibid.*

24. *Ibid.,* 446.

25. Martha Saxton, *Being Good: Women's Moral Values in Early America* (New York: Hill and Wang, 2003), 179.

26. Saxton, *Being Good,* 179, 186.

27. Nikola Baumgarten, "Education and Democracy in Frontier St. Louis: The

Society of the Sacred Heart," *History of Education Quarterly* 34, no. 2 (Summer 1994), 172–177.

28. *Jane McCray v. William R. Hopkins,* Case File No. 162, 1845, November Term.

29. Wong, 163.

30. *Mahala v. Martin Mitchell, Suit for Freedom,* No. 6, November Term 1832, St. Louis Circuit Court.

31. *Mahala v. Martin Mitchell,* 1832.

32. *Ibid.*

33. *Mahala v. Martin Mitchell, Petition for Freedom and for Habeas Corpus,* November 6, 1832.

34. *Mahala v. Martin Mitchell,* 1832.

35. *Habeas Corpus,* July 21, 1832.

36. Deposition of Ichabod Badgley, November 28, 1832, St. Louis, Missouri.

37. *Ibid.*

38. *Mahala and Others v. Martin Mitchell, Deposition of Ichabod Badgley,* filed January 1, 1833.

39. Jeffrey S. Adler, "Streetwalkers, Degraded Outcasts, and Good-For-Nothing Huzzies: Women and the Dangerous Class in Antebellum St. Louis," *Journal of Social History,* Volume 25, Number 4, 1992, 740, 742.

40. Saxton, *Being Good,* 225.

41. *Rachel Steele v. Thomas Taylor,* Statement of Charlotte P. Grimes, March 25, 1845.

42. *Rachel Steele, Coloured Woman, in Forma Pauperis, v. Thomas Taylor, Suit for Freedom,* April Term, 1845, St. Louis Circuit Court.

43. Wong, *Neither Fugitive Nor Free,* 128.

44. *Ibid.*

45. *Marie v. Auguste Chouteau,* No. 1, 1819, March Term, Superior Court Northern Circuit, City of St. Louis; *Marguerite vs. Pierre Chouteau, Sr.,* No. 26, 1825, July Term, Office of the Circuit Clerk, City of St. Louis, Missouri, St. Louis Circuit Court; *Theotiste Alias Catiche vs. Pierre Chouteau, Jr.,* No. 6, 1827, November Term, Office of the Circuit Clerk, City of St. Louis, Missouri, St. Louis Circuit Court; *Sally v. Henry Chouteau,* No. 101, 1835, July Term, Office of the Circuit Clerk, City of St. Louis, Missouri, St. Louis Circuit Court.

46. *Mary Charlotte v. Gabriel Chouteau,* No. 13, 1843, November Term, Office of the Circuit Clerk, City of St. Louis, Missouri, St. Louis Circuit Court; *Pierre, a Mulatto v. Therese Cerre Chouteau,* No. 192, 1840, November Term, Office of the Circuit Clerk, City of St. Louis, Missouri, St. Louis Circuit Court.

47. *Ibid.,* at *Mary Charlotte.*

48. *Mary Charlotte.*

49. *Mary Charlotte v. Gabriel Chouteau,* No. 13, 1843, November Term, Office of the Circuit Clerk, City of St. Louis, Missouri, St. Louis Circuit Court.

50. *Maria v. Garland Rucker,* Case File No. 14, 1829, November Term.

51. *Patrick Henry v. Garland Rucker,* Case File No. 16, 1829, November Term.

52. White, *Ar'n't I a Woman?,* 70–77; Frazier, *Runaway and Freed Missouri Slaves,* 95; Saxton, *Being Good,* 184; Johnson, *Soul by Soul,* 31–32.

53. Saxton, *Being Good,* 184–185; 348, n.4.

54. Frazier, *Runaway and Freed Missouri Slaves,* 124.

55. *Ibid.,* at 124.

56. *Ibid.,* at 87–88.

57. *Ibid.,* 125.

58. *Ibid.*

59. *Ibid.,* 126–127.

60. *Ibid.,* 128.

61. *Eliza Sly,* Enticing Slave Out of State, No. 6, May 12 and May 19, 1857, Criminal Court Record Book 9, pages 170, 174, 178–179, 184; Frazier, *Runaway and Freed Missouri Slaves,* 129. Frazier also briefly notes the incarceration for the same crime of a white woman named Marian Clements, who was pardoned after three and a half months.

62. Frazier, *Runaway,* 136.

63. *Ibid.*

64. *Elsa Hicks v. S. Burrell and James Mitchell,* Case File No. 55, 1845, April Term.

65. *Elsa Hicks v. Patrick T. McSherry Et Al.,* Case File No. 121, 1847, November Term.

66. Aron, *American Confluence,* 47.

67. Annette Gordon-Reed, "Celia's Case," in Annette Gordon-Reed, ed., *Race on Trial: Law and Justice in American History* (Oxford: Oxford University Press, 2002), 49.

68. *Ibid.,* at 49–50.

69. *Ibid.,* at 51.

70. *Ibid.*
71. *Ibid.*, at 51–52.
72. *Ibid.*
73. *Ibid.*, at 54.
74. *Ibid.*, at 55–57.
75. *Ibid.*, 57.
76. *Ibid.*, 57.
77. *Ibid.*
78. Gordon-Reed, 57.

Chapter 5

1. Ekberg, *Indian Women*, 29.
2. A.L.S. B. Duval to Benjamin Coursault, June 10, 1807, St. Pierre Martinique, Auguste Chouteau Papers, Missouri Historical Society, St. Louis, Missouri. This letter from Martinique to Philadelphia was found in the Chouteau Papers.
3. Steven Deyle, *Carry Me Back: The Domestic Slave Trade in American Life* (Oxford: Oxford University Press, 2005), 33, 39, 308n.3; Ira Berlin, *The Making of African America: The Four Great Migrations* (New York: Viking Penguin, 2010), 111–112; VanderVelde and Subramanian, "Mrs. Dred Scott," 1046.
4. *William Tarleton Otherwise Called ... vs. Jacob Horine*, Assault and battery and false imprisonment, No. 7, October 3, 1813, St. Louis Court of Common Pleas, Territory of Missouri; *Jacob Horine Ads. Billy Tarleton Otherwise Called Bill*, petition for $1,000 damages, February 22, 1814; *Tarleton v. Horine*, petition to sue, No. 7, February, 1814; Answer, June 27, 1814.
5. *Jack, a Coloured Man vs. Charles Collins*, Petition to sue in forma pauperis, March 17, 1831, St. Louis Circuit Court.
6. *Dunky, a Woman of Colour vs. Andrew T. Cay*, for liberty to sue in forma pauperis, April 6, 1831, St. Louis Circuit Court.
7. *Ibid.*
8. VanderVelde and Subramanian, "Mrs. Dred Scott," 1047–1048, 1055 n.87.
9. *Ibid.*, 1049.
10. Deyle, *Carry Me Back*, 74–76.
11. VanderVelde and Subramanian, "Mrs. Dred Scott," 1056 and n.95; 1057 n.97; 1072 and n.164, 1073, 1093 n.252.
12. *Ralph, a Man of Color vs. Coleman Duncan*, Appeal from St. Louis Circuit Court, State of Missouri Supreme Court, Third Judicial District, May Term 1833.
13. Walter Johnson, *Soul by Soul: Life Inside the Antebellum Slave Market* (Cambridge: Harvard University Press, 1999), 7, 46, 48–49.
14. *Mathias Rose Ads. Milly, a Black Woman*, Pleas, claiming freedom, August Term 1819, St. Louis Circuit Court, Missouri Territory.
15. *Milly, a Black Woman v. Mathias Rose*, Petition for Freedom, April 21, 1819, St. Louis Circuit Court.
16. *Ibid.*
17. Berlin, *The Making of African America*, 101–102, 112–114; Buchanan, *Black Life on the Mississippi*, 82–83.
18. *Suzette Alias Judith vs. John Reynolds*, Action of Trespass and False Imprisonment, July Term, 1828, St. Louis Circuit Court, State of Missouri.
19. *Angelique vs. John Reynolds*, action of trespass and false imprisonment, No. 10, July Term, 1828, St. Louis Circuit Court; *Edmund vs. John Reynolds*, No. 11, July Term, 1828, St. Louis Circuit Court. No court record was discovered with reference to Suzette's third child, John.
20. *Mary of Color and Her Children, Samuel and Edward vs. Launcelot W. Calvert*, Petition for Freedom, April Term, 1851, St. Louis Circuit Court, State of Missouri.
21. Hammond, *Slavery, Freedom and Expansion*, 61.
22. A.L.S. Wilkinson to Solomon Van Rensselaer (N.Y.), November 7, 1816, Philadelphia, Wilkinson Papers, Missouri Historical Society, St. Louis, Missouri.
23. Deyle, *Carry Me Back*, 75; VanderVelde, *Mrs. Dred Scott*.
24. VanderVelde, *Mrs. Dred Scott*.
25. ALS Will C. Carr, St. Louis, to Charles Carr, Lexington, Kentucky, 7-3-1807, William C. Carr Papers, 63-0099, Missouri Historical Society, St. Louis, Missouri.
26. *Ibid.*
27. *Ibid.*
28. *Ibid.*
29. *Ibid.*
30. *Ibid.*
31. Robert Pierce Forbes, *The Missouri Compromise and Its Aftermath: Slavery*

and the Meaning of America (Chapel Hill: University of North Carolina Press, 2007), 35–36.

32. Forbes, *The Missouri Compromise and Its Aftermath*, 37.

33. Letter from George Graham to his brother, St. Louis, September 10, 1819, R. Graham Papers, Missouri Historical Society, St. Louis, Missouri.

34. A.L.S. Fr. Menard, New Orleans to August Chouteau, Missouri Territory, July 8, 1820, August Chouteau Papers, Missouri Historical Society, St. Louis, Missouri.

35. Auguste Chouteau to Francois Menard, July 13, 1820, Chouteau Papers, Missouri Historical Society, St. Louis, Missouri.

36. Account of jailor [*sic*] with Francois Menard for board, etc., of negro Charles, February, 1821, August Chouteau Papers, Missouri Historical Society, St. Louis, Missouri.

37. A.L.S. Menard to Auguste Chouteau, March 5, 1820 (1821), New Orleans, August Chouteau Papers, Missouri Historical Society, St. Louis, Missouri.

38. A.L.S. Fr. Menard to Auguste Chouteau, March 5, 1821 (continued on March 17, 1821), New Orleans, Missouri Historical Society, St. Louis, Missouri.

39. Fr. Menard, New Orleans, to Auguste Chouteau, St. Louis, May 19, 1821, Missouri Historical Society, St. Louis, Missouri.

40. A.L.S. Pierre Menard to Pierre Chouteau, Jr., January 4, 1831, P. Chouteau Maffitt Collection, Missouri Historical Society, St. Louis, Missouri.

41. Forbes, *The Missouri Compromise and Its Aftermath*, 8.

42. A.L.S. Fr. Menard to Auguste Chouteau, May 12, 1822, New Orleans, August Chouteau Papers, Missouri Historical Society, St. Louis, Missouri.

43. Certificate of Sale, Louis Menard (for Auguste Chouteau) to Valery Jean Delassize (for Eugenie Delassize), December 20, 1822, New Orleans, LA, Missouri Historical Society.

44. Receipt, April 5, 1829, Saint Louis, Pierre Chouteau Collection, Missouri Historical Society, St. Louis, Missouri.

45. John Blassingame, ed., *Slave Testi-mony: Two Centuries of Letters, Speeches, Interviews, and Autobiographies* (Baton Rouge: Louisiana State University Press, 1977), 286–287. The brothers went on to state that, many years later, they were reunited in Canada, the place both had managed to run to a number of years after being transported west and sold.

46. Deed of sale of negro boy, Peter, by Captain John Ware to Sylvester Labadie, June 8, 1832, Pierre Chouteau Collection, Missouri Historical Society, St. Louis, Missouri; Receipt, February 15, 1836, A1518, Slaves and Slavery, Folder 3, 1834–1835, Missouri Historical Society, St. Louis; receipt, November 7, 1854, Slaves and Slavery, Folder 5, Missouri Historical Society, St. Louis; receipt, September 6, 1856, Slaves and Slavery, Folder 5, Missouri Historical Society, St. Louis; Letter, April 1, 1857, Slaves and Slavery, Folder 5, Missouri Historical Society, St. Louis.

47. A.L.S. P. Chouteau, Jr. to J. Mager, September 22, 1828, St. Louis, Chouteau-Papin Collection, Missouri Historical Society, St. Louis, Missouri.

48. A.L.S. M. Giraud to J.B. Sarpy, July 26, 1832, Marais des Cignes, P. Chouteau Maffitt Collection, Missouri Historical Society, St. Louis, Missouri.

49. A.L.S. John A. Merle to Pierre Chouteau, July 12, 1838, New Orleans, P. Chouteau Maffitt Collection; A.L.S. John A. Merle to P. Chouteau, Jr., November 15, 1838, Missouri Historical Society, St. Louis, Missouri.

50. A.L.S. John A. Merle to P. Chouteau, July 20, 1838, P. Chouteau Maffitt Collection, Missouri Historical Society, St. Louis, Missouri.

51. A.L.S. John A. Merle to P. Chouteau, Jr., October 6, 1838, Chouteau-Walsh College; A.L.S. John A. Merle to P. Chouteau, Jr., October 18, 1838, Missouri Historical Society, St. Louis, Missouri.

52. A.L.S. T.F. Smith to Henry Chouteau, June 22, 1834, Fort Armstrong, Illinois, Henry Chouteau Collection, Missouri Historical Society, St. Louis, Missouri.

53. Letter from Capt. T. F. Smith to Henry Chouteau, Rock Island, June 29, 1834, Henry Chouteau Collection, Missouri Historical Society, St. Louis, Missouri.

54. T. Smith to Henry Chouteau, Rock Island, July 20, 1834, Henry Chouteau Papers, Missouri Historical Society, St. Louis, Missouri.

55. T.F. Smith to Henry Chouteau, Rock Island, October 4, 1834, Henry Chouteau Collection, Missouri Historical Society, St. Louis, Missouri.

56. T.F. Smith to Henry Chouteau, Rock Island, May 28, 1835, Henry Chouteau Collection, Missouri Historical Society, St. Louis, Missouri.

57. Receipt, sale of slave, negro man aged 21, Samuel H. Lyon of Lafayette County, Missouri, to Henry Chouteau of St. Louis, Chouteau Collections, Missouri Historical Society, St. Louis, Missouri.

58. ADS Henry Papin, Deed and note of promise, October 13, 1855, Chouteau Collections, Missouri Historical Society, St. Louis, Missouri.

59. Siddali, *Missouri's War*, 38–39.

60. A.L.S. J.E. Barrow to P. Chouteau, Jr. & Co., September 14, 1849, St. Joseph, P. Choutea-Maffitt Collection, Missouri Historical Society, St. Louis, Missouri.

61. D.S. Peter D. Papin, deed conveying three slaves to Joseph Papin by Peter Papin, February 22, 1849; transfer of two of the slaves to B.M. Lynch, March 16, 1849, Chouteau-Papin Collection, Missouri Historical Society, St. Louis, Missouri; Vander-Velde, *Mrs. Dred Scott*, 179–181, 285, 377 n.21–23.

62. *Missouri Republican*, St. Louis, Wednesday morning, August 15, 1838, Vol. XV, No. 1620, p.1.

63. *Isaiah Todd & Armstrong Hart vs. John Young*, Bill to foreclose mortgage of two negro boys, in Chancery, No. 235, November Term 1826, St. Louis, Missouri.

64. *Ibid.*

65. *Ibid.*

66. *Ibid.*

67. *Ibid.*

68. Agreement, Exhibits A No. 1, B No. 2, and D No. 4, No. 256, St. Louis Circuit Court, filed November 24, 1828, A. Gamble, clerk.

69. *Laura, Woman of Color vs. Henry B. Belt*, suit for freedom, St. Louis Circuit Court, April Term, 1852.

70. *Laura v. Belt*, St. Louis Circuit Court, petition of Joel C. Richmond, attorney for the plaintiff, February 24, 1852.

71. *Ibid.*

72. *Ibid.*

73. Answer of Edward Curtis, *Laura, a Woman of Color, Plff, Against Henry B. Belt, Defendant*, March, 1852, St. Louis Circuit Court.

74. Answer of James Christy, *Laura of Color, Plaintiff Against Henry B. Belt, Defendant*.

75. *Peggy Perryman vs. Joseph Philibert, Suit for Freedom*, St. Louis Circuit Court, No. 255, November, 1848.

76. W. Sherman Savage, "Slavery in the West," *In* Monroe Lee Billington and Roger D. Hardaway, *African Americans on the Western Frontier* (Boulder: University Press of Colorado, 1998), 16–17.

77. Jeremy Neely, *The Border Between Them: Violence and Reconciliation on the Kansas-Missouri Line* (Columbia: University of Missouri Press, 2007), 3, 33.

78. *Ibid.*, 34.

79. *Ibid.*, 37, 76, 150–152, 156.

80. *Ibid.*, 92–93, 156.

81. *Ibid.*, 48–49.

82. Johnson, 167; Berlin, *Making of African America*, 114.

83. E. Edward Farrison, "Phylon Profile, Xvi: William Wells Brown," *Phylon (1940–1956)* 9, no. 1 (1st Quarter 1940–1956), 13–23.

84. Slave Inventory of A. Leonard, Slavery Papers, Missouri Historical Society, St. Louis, Missouri.

85. *Missouri Saturday News*, Saturday Morning, August 4, 1838, Number 31, Volume I.

86. Letter, February 15, 1858, Slavery, Missouri Historical Society, St. Louis, Missouri.

Chapter 6

1. St. Louis Circuit Court, State of Missouri, August 24, 1840, Preston et al. v. George W. Coons, administrator, Milton Duty, Injunction, Deposition of Thomas P. Follis.

2. *Ibid.*

3. *David Adams to James Adams for Mr. Toney, Filed for Record*, November 24,

1835, Missouri Historical Society, St. Louis, Missouri.

4. *Ibid.*

5. St. Louis Circuit Court State of Missouri, August 24, 1840, *Preston Et Als. v. George W. Coons*, administrator, Milton Duty, Injunction, Deposition of James Adams.

6. Bonnie E. Laughlin, "'Endangering the Peace of Society': Abolitionist Agitation and Mob Reaction in St. Louis and Alton, 1836–1838," *Missouri Historical Review* 95, no. 1 (2000), 3; Order of Sale of Slaves, September 18, 1841, St. Louis Circuit Court; *Preston, Braxton, Et Als. vs. Geo. W. Coons, Et Als.*, *Deposition of Braxton*, May 13, 1843, St. Louis Circuit Court; *Preston v. Coons*, Supplemental Bill, May 22, 1845, St. Louis Circuit Court.

7. St. Louis Circuit Court, State of Missouri, November 11, 1841, *Preston Et Als. v. George W. Coons*, administrator, Milton Duty, Injunction, Deposition of James v. Prathins (last name not clear).

8. St. Louis Circuit Court, State of Missouri, October 9, 1841, petition for freedom; petition, May 29, 1844; May 21, 1845, *Preston Et Als. v. George W. Coons Et Als.*, Supplemental Bill.

9. Dale Edwyna Smith, *The Slaves of Liberty: Freedom in Amite County, Mississippi, 1820–1868* (New York: Garland, 1999), chapter 2, The Color of Law, 22–27.

10. State of Mississippi, City of Vicksburg in Warren County, November 26, 1838, Last Will and Testament of Milton Duty; St. Louis Circuit Court, November 1854, #11, Proceeding on Probate of the Will of Milton Duty.

11. *Stephen Smith v. David Shipman*, Injunction, No. 285, Chancery Court, November, 1829, St. Louis, Missouri.

12. Inventory of Property belonging to the Estate of Milton Duty, decreased, St. Louis, 10 August 1838.

13. *Ibid.*

14. State of Mississippi, Warren County, Vicksburg, Last Will and Testament of Milton Duty, October 26, 1836, recorded State of Missouri, St. Louis Circuit Court, June 22, 1839.

15. Louis S. Gerteis, *Civil War St. Louis* (Lawrence: University Press of Kansas, 2001), 38; Bonnie E. Laughlin, "Endanger-

ing the Peace of Society," *Missouri Historical Review* 95, no. 1 (2000), 11, 20.

16. James Neal Primm, *Lion in the Valley: St. Louis, Missouri, 1764–1980* (Missouri Historical Society Press, 1998, third ed.), 23; Louis S. Gerteis, *Civil War St. Louis* (Lawrence: University Press of Kansas, 2001), 22, 40; Lea VanderVelde, "Mrs. Dred Scott," *The Yale Law Journal* 106, no. 4 (January 1997), 1061, 1083 n.216, 1084–1085; Primm, Lion of the Valley, 179–180.

17. *The St. Louis Directory for the Years 1836–7: Containing the Names of the Inhabitants, Their Occupations, Numbers of Their Places of Business and Dwellings; with a Sketch of the City of St. Louis,* Printed by C. Keemle, 1836, 17. See also, *St. Louis Directory for the Years 1838–39*; *Green's Saint Louis Directory (No. 1) for 1845,* Saint Louis: Published by James Green, 1844; *Free Men and Women of Color in St. Louis, 1821–1860,* Compiled from City Directories of the United States Through 1860, Rare Books and Special Collections, St. Louis Public Library, 1997; *Missouri Republican,* August 15, 1838, Vol. XV, No. 1620 3; Leonard P. Curry, *The Free Black in Urban America, 1800–1850: The Shadow the Dream* (Chicago: University of Chicago Press, 1981), 181, 184, 186; Primm, Lion of the Valley, 179–180; Elinor Mondale Gersman, "The Development of Public Education for Blacks in Nineteenth Century St. Louis, Missouri," *The Journal of Negro Education* 41, no. 1 (Winter 1972), 35–47, 35.

18. *State v. William Cornelias, Man of Color,* keeping disorderly house, October 1824; Jeffrey S. Adler, "Streetwalkers, Degraded Outcasts, and Good-For-Nothing Huzzies: Women and the Dangerous Class in Antebellum St. Louis," *Journal of Social History* 25, no. 4 (1992), 737–755, 742.

19. Cases where slaves claimed to be free based on residence in free western territories include *John Singleton, a Free Man of Color, vs. Alexander Scott, Robert Lewis,* November 1827, No. 23; *Molly Rector, a Free Woman of Color, vs. John Bivens,* November 1827, No. 26; *Mahala v. Martin Mitchell,* November 1832, No. 6; *James Wilkinson v. Aaron Young,* July 1833, No. 102; and dozens more.

The Criminal Index Record documents charges of "Enticing Slaves" out of state and "Enticing Slaves to Escape" through the late 1850's. No less than Mary Meachum, wife of the Reverend John Berry Meachum, was charged with "Enticing Slaves Out of State" in 1853. (Criminal Index Book 8, St. Louis Circuit Court).

20. VanderVelde, "Mrs. Dred Scott," 1047–1049, 155n.87. As Professor Vander-Velde notes, this is perhaps most famously set forth in the materials proffered in the case of Dred and Harriet Scott, both of whom spent time, presumably as slaves, at Fort Snelling near present-day St. Paul, Minnesota, and as a territory where slavery was illegal, which the Scotts asserted as a core issue in their claim to freedom.

21. *Free Men and Women of Color in St. Louis, 1821–1860*, compiled from city directories of the U.S. through 1860, Rare Books and Special Collections, St. Louis Public Library, St. Louis, Missouri; Primm, *Lion of the Valley*, 179–180; Curry, *The Free Black in Urban America, 1800–1850: The Shadow of the Dream* (Chicago: University of Chicago Press, 1981), 186; Greene, Kremer, Holland, *Missouri's Black Heritage*, 67, 69; *Laura, Woman of Color, vs. Henry B. Belt*, St. Louis Circuit Court, February 1852; *Mary, a Free Woman of Colour [Sic], Plaintiff, Against Launcelot H. Calvert, Defendant*, St. Louis Circuit Court, April 1851; *Saint Louis Daily Union*, August 17, 1846, Vol. 1, No. 1, p. 3, ad of John R. White; Missouri Historical Society, Slavery Collection, four transfers/deeds of slaves to John R. White, 1841; *Missouri Republican*, Monday, July 10, 1837, p.2; *Republican*, Thurs., July 1837).

22. *Preston, Braxton, Et Als. v. George W. Coons, Administrator of Milton Duty, Deceased*, Answer of George W. Coons, 1841, November Term, St. Louis Circuit Court, Office of the Circuit Clerk, City of St. Louis, Missouri.

23. *Ibid.*; *Preston, Braxton and Others v. G. W. Coons, Adm. of Milton Duty and Others*, Depositions for plaintiffs, Deposition of Hugh Gallagher, November 15, 1841, November Term 1841, St. Louis Circuit Court, Office of the Circuit Clerk, City of St. Louis, Missouri.

24. Answer of George Coons, November Term, 1841.

25. Deposition of James Adams, December 2, 1841.

26. Deposition of Samuel Farnandis, July 9, 1840.

27. Deposition of Thomas Follis, August 24, 1840.

28. Deposition of Hugh Gallagher, November 15, 1841.

29. *Missouri Republican*, Wednesday Morning, August 15, 1838, Vol. XV, No. 1620, p. 3; Vandervelde, *Mrs. Dred Scott*, 223, 393 n.42.

30. St. Louis Circuit Court, Office of the Circuit Clerk, City of St. Louis, Missouri, Chancery Court, November 1840, #594, *Shelton v. Walton*.

31. St. Louis Circuit Court, Office of the Circuit Clerk, City of St. Louis, Missouri, November 9, 1840.

32. Thomas C. Buchanan, "Rascals on the Antebellum Mississippi: African-American Steamboat Workers and the St. Louis Hanging of 1841," *Journal of Social History* 34.4 (Summer 2001), 797.

33. *Ibid.*

34. *Ibid.*

35. *Ibid.*; Frazier, *Sentences*, 33–34.

36. St. Louis Circuit Court, Office of the Circuit Clerk, City of St. Louis, Missouri, Petition to Probate Court, September 7, 1841; Order of Sale of Slaves, September 18, 1841.

37. The attorney Ferdinand Risque defended more slaves suing for freedom than any other attorney, however, his relationship with slaves and with people of color was as "complicated" and confusing as any in the antebellum era. In the case of *Patrick H. Scott and Sarah B. Scott Against William Bailey, Ferdinand Risque, Eliza M. Kennerly and John F. Darby, Defendants*, No. 63, 1853, October Term, St. Louis Land Court, Risque was brought before the bar regarding his role in a land deal which also concerned Risque's reputed ownership of a black slave man named "Dick." (As we shall see, John F. Darby became an "Administrator" for the estate of Milton Duty.) No less than the free black minister John Berry Meachum owned slaves and was sued by them in St. Louis courts. The case of *Scott v. Bailey, Ferdinand Risque Et Als.* is discussed in detail in Chapter 9, Standing Ground: Free People of Color and the Land Court.

38. *Preston, Braxton and Mary and Others vs. Geo. W. Coons, Adr. of Milton Duty, Decd., David Coons, Et Als.,* No. 871, 1843, November Term, St. Louis Circuit Court, attachment attesting by Charles G. Ramsey, publisher, that the above advertisement appeared in his newspaper, the *St. Louis New Era,* for eight weeks from August 18, 1843 through October of that year; Frazier, *Runaway and Freed Missouri Slaves,* 64–65.

39. *Preston, Braxton, Et Als. vs. Geo. W. Coons, Et Als.,* Deposition of Braxton, May 13, 1843.

40. *Ibid.* Missouri statute also required owners who manumitted slaves to provide for their support. VanderVelde, "Mrs. Dred Scott," 1066–67, 1067n.141, n.143.

41. *Ibid.*

42. *Ibid.*

43. Donald F. Dosch, *The Old Courthouse: Americans Build a Forum on the Frontier* (Jefferson National Expansion Historical Association, Inc., 1979); Missouri Historical Society, Prospectus of "The African, an Anti-Abolition Monthly," Saint Louis, Missouri, September 16, 1843.

44. *Preston v. Coons,* Deposition of Egbert Sessions, November 21, 1843.

45. *Preston v. Coons,* Separate Answer of Henry Chouteau, 1841, November Term, St. Louis Circuit Court.

46. *Preston v. Coons,* The Answer of George W. Coons, May 5, 1843.

47. *Ibid.*

48. *Preston v. Coons,* Supplemental Bill, May 22, 1845, St. Louis Circuit Court.

49. *Ibid.*

50. *Ibid.*

51. *Ibid.*

52. *Harry Duty, of Color v. John F. Darby, Admin.,* No. 17, 1850, April Term, St. Louis Circuit Court; *Ellen Duty v. John F. Darby, Admin.,* No. 18, 1850, April Term, St. Louis Circuit Court; *Nelly Duty v. John F. Darby, Admin.,* No. 19, 1850, April Term, St. Louis Circuit Court; *Jordan Duty v. John F. Darby, Adm.,* No. 20, 1850, April Term, St. Louis Circuit Court; *Preston Duty v. John F. Darby, Adm.,* No. 21, 1850, April Term, St. Louis Circuit Court; *Lucinda Duty v. John F. Darby, Adm.,* No. 22, 1850, April Term, St. Louis Circuit Court; *Caroline Duty v. John F. Darby, Adm.,* No. 23, 1850, April Term, St. Louis Circuit Court; *Mary Duty v. John F. Darby, Adm.,* No. 24, 1850, April Term, St. Louis Circuit Court.

53. *In the Matter of Harry, Preston and Jordan, Persons of Color to Prove the Last Will and Testament of Milton Duty,* 1854, March Term, The Probate Court of St. Louis County; *Milton Duty, December,* Proceeding on Probate of will and appeal, No. 11, 1854, November term, Saint Louis Circuit Court.

54. Manumission, Taylor Blow, March 31, 1854, Slave Papers, Missouri Historical Society, St. Louis, Missouri.

Chapter 7

1. Letter, August 7, 1855, Slavery Papers, Missouri Historical Society, St. Louis, Missouri.

2. *Missouri Republican,* September 27, 1831, Vol. X, No. 497, page 2; October 4, 1831, Vol. X, No. 498, page 3.

3. Deyle, *Carry Me Back,* 248.

4. *Ibid.,* 257.

5. Washington, "African American History and the Frontier Thesis," 241.

6. Buchanan, *Black Life on the Mississippi,* 106.

7. *Missouri Gazette,* February 8, 1810, Vol. II, No. 81, p. 3.

8. Letter, August 7, 1855, Slavery Papers, Missouri Historical Society, St. Louis, Missouri.

9. *Missouri Republican,* Thursday, July 18(?), 1837.

10. *State vs. William Flake, Indictment for Stealing a Negro Man Slave,* April 1821.

11. *Order for the Body of the Within Named Man Committed to Jail,* May 21, 1821.

12. *Deposition of William Smith,* MY 12, 1821.

13. Deposition of William Farmer, May 12, 1821.

14. Twenty-five dollar reward posted for return of runaway slave, Sam (rough draft), Lucas Collection, 12-29-1815, Missouri Historical Society, St. Louis, Missouri.

15. Twenty-five dollar reward posted, Lucas Collection, 12-29-1815.

16. Twenty-five dollar reward posted, Lucas Collection, 12-29-1815.

17. *Missouri Republican,* July 4, 1839, Vol. XV, No. 1877.

18. Buchanan, *Black Life on the Mississippi,* 107.

19. *Ibid.,* 110–111.

20. *Ibid.,* 114.

21. *Walker D. Shumate to Philip and Others,* Manumission, April 29, 1856, Missouri Historical Society, St. Louis, Missouri.

22. Letter of R. C. Nicholas, Richmond, to G. W. Goode, Esq., St. Louis, July 29, 1846, George W. Goode Papers, Missouri Historical Society, St. Louis, Missouri.

23. Letter for R. Dexter Tiffany, Worcester, to John Darby, St. Louis, February 20, 1852, Darby Papers, Missouri Historical Society, St. Louis, Missouri.

24. *U.S. v. Bazile Bissounet,* Indictment, assault and battery, St. Louis Circuit Court, November, 1816; notice to jailor, January 31, 1818, Thomas Riddick, Justice of the Peace, St. Louis Circuit Court.

25. *Ibid.*

26. Index Book 12, Case No. 166 (charge: inciting slaves to insurrection, p.390; Case No. 19 (charge: indictment for murder), St. Louis Criminal Court, September 1863; record missing.

27. Record Book 12, St. Louis Criminal Court.

28. Jack, *The St. Louis African American Community and the Exodusters,* 43–45.

29. *Ibid.,* 45–46.

Chapter 8

1. Hodes, *Beyond the Frontier,* 485.

2. James Neal Primm, *Lion of the Valley: St. Louis, Missouri, 1764–1980* (Missouri Historical Society Press, 1981, 1990, 1998), chapter 1; Charles E. Peterson, *Colonial St. Louis: Building a Creole Capital* (Tucson: Patrice Press, 1993); Hodes, *Beyond the Frontier,* 485.

3. Peterson, *Colonial St. Louis,* 3.

4. *Ibid.,* 11, 44; Primm, *Lion of the Valley,* 15–16.

5. Peterson, *Colonial St. Louis,* 26, 28–30; Primm, *Lion of the Valley,* 15–16.

6. Brent Underwood, "Chouteau's Pond," *Gateway Heritage* 22, no. 1 (Summer 2001), 6.

7. *Ibid.*

8. Peterson, *Colonial St. Louis,* 8, 123, 11, 12–13; Dosch, *The Old Courthouse,* 73–74.

9. Dosch, *The Old Courthouse,* 74–75; Gerteis, *Civil War St. Louis,* 29–30; Primm, *Lion of the Valley,* 146, 180.

10. Samuel A. Floyd, Jr., "A Black Composer in Nineteenth-Century St. Louis," *19th Century Music* 4, no. 2 (Autumn 1980), 123.

11. Floyd, "A Black Composer," 123.

12. *Ibid.,* 124.

13. *Free Men and Women of Color in St. Louis, 1821–1860,* compiled by Thomas A. Pearson, Rare Books and Special Collections, St. Louis Public Library (1997); Primm, *Lion of the Valley,* 180.

14. Primm, *Lion of the Valley,* 83, 97–98.

15. *Missouri Gazette,* Wednesday, September 7, 1808, Vol. 1, No. 9.

16. *Ibid.*

17. *Missouri Republican,* Vol. X, No. 472, April 12, 1831, 5.

18. Primm, *Lion of the Valley,* 175–177.

19. Dosch, *The Old Courthouse,* 102; *Missouri Republican,* Vol. X, No. 501, October 25, 1831, 5.

20. Foley, 90–91; Primm, 180; Shirley Christian, *Before Lewis and Clark: The Story of the Chouteaus, the French Dynasty That Ruled America's Frontier* (New York: Farrar, Straus & Giroux, 2004), 68, 208–211.

21. Primm, *Lion of the Valley,* 317.

22. *Ibid.,* 317.

23. *Thomas M. Knox v. Elizabeth Dickinson, a Free Woman of Color and Victoire Ruell,* Case File No. 112, 1845, November Term; *Laura (Louisa Lewis) Versus Henry Hart, Administrator,* Case File No. 12, 1860, February Term.

24. Judith A. Gilbert, "Esther and Her Sisters: Freedom Women of Color as Property Owners in Colonial St. Louis, 1765–1803," in LeeAnn Whites, Mary C. Neth, and Gary R. Kremer, eds., *Women in Missouri History: In Search of Power and Influence* (Columbia: University of Missouri Press, 2004), 32.

25. *Ibid.*

26. For scholarly analysis, see Julie Winch, ed., *The Colored Aristocracy of St. Louis by Cyprian Clamorgan* (Columbia: University of Missouri Press, 1999); for

the original journal, see Cyprian Clamorgan, *The Colored Aristocracy of St. Louis* (1858), Missouri Historical Society, St. L. 301.45 C511; Primm, *Lion of the Valley*, 58.

27. Primm, *Lion of the Valley*, 58, 60.

28. *Ibid.*, 73, 77, 110.

29. *Ester, a Free Mulatto v. William C. Carr*, No. 295, November term, 1830.

30. *Ibid.*

31. *Ibid.*

32. *Ibid.*

33. *Ibid.*

34. *George Speers and Teresa, His Wife v. Peter Chouteau*, No. 684, St. Louis Circuit Court of Chancery, November Term, 1841.

35. *Ester, a Free Mulatto Woman vs. William C. Carr*, Subpoena, No. 295, Saint Louis Circuit Court, November Term, 1830.

36. Summonses to Charles DeWard, Robert Simpson, and Rachel Camp (a colored woman living lower end of town), August 13, 1838.

37. *George Speers and Teresa, His Wife, Free Mulattos vs. Peter Chouteau*, No. 684, 1841, November Term, Chancery, St. Louis Circuit Court.

38. *George Speers and Thérèse Speers, His Wife, Edward Speers and Joseph Scavener v. Thomas P. Batcher and Agatha, His Wife, Plea*, 1837, February, St. Louis Circuit Court.

39. *Ibid.*

40. *Ibid.*

41. *Ibid.*

42. *Fanny Jackson v. Randolph Taylor*, Case 626, March Term 1857, St. Louis Land Court.

43. *Ibid.*

44. *Ibid.*

45. *Ibid.*

46. *Ibid.*

47. *Ibid.*

48. *Ibid.*

49. *Ibid., Agreement Between Taylor and Dust.*

50. *Fanny Jackson, a Free Woman of Color v. Randolph Taylor, a Free Man of Color*, No. 626, March Term 1857, Land Court.

51. *Ibid.*

52. *Fanny Jackson, Deed, Will*, March 1857, Land Court.

53. *Fanny Jackson, Deed*, February, 1854, Land Court.

54. *Ibid.*

55. *Fanny Jackson, Agreement Between Randolph Taylor and Levi Dust*, July 24, 1855, St. Louis Circuit Court.

56. *Land Court—Its Organization, Jurisdiction, &C.*, §2.

57. *Squire Brown, Man of Color v. William C. Anderson*, Case File No. 119, 1841, July Term.

58. *Ibid.*; *Squire Brown v. Charles Anderson*, Case File No. 232, 1843, April Term, St. Louis Circuit Court.

59. Landon Y. Jones, *William Clark and the Shaping of the West* (New York: Hill and Wang, 2004), 164, 250, 303; Thomas C. Buchanan, *Black Life on the Mississippi: Slaves, Free Blacks, and the Western Steamboat World* (Chapel Hill: University of North Carolina Press, 2004); *Squire Brown v. Charles Anderson and Israel Morris*, No. 328, 1843, November Term.

60. *Squire Brown v. Isaac Breckenridge*, Case File No. 35, 1862, March Term; *Joseph T. Brown v. Squire Brown and George W. Berkeley*, Case File No. 49, 1862, March Term.

61. *Squire Brown Against Isaac Breckenridge*, Petition in Ejectment.

62. *Brown Against Breckenridge*, Motion.

63. *Ibid.*

64. *Brown Against Breckenridge*, Affidavit of R. v. Voorhis.

65. *Ibid.*

66. *Squire Brown Against Isaac Breckenridge*, Affidavit of Isaac Breckenridge, defendant.

67. *Squire Brown Against Isaac Breckenridge*, Affidavit of Charles A. Smith, Affidavit of Isaac Breckenridge, Affidavit of Robert Voorhis.

68. *Joseph T. Brown vs. Squire Brown and George W. Berkeley*, Petition to Foreclose Mortgage, No. 49, 1862, March Term, St. Louis Land Court.

69. *Ibid.*

70. *Ibid.*

Chapter 9

1. Frazier, *Sentences*, 41.

2. Samuel A. Floyd, Jr., "A Black Com-

poser in Nineteenth-Century St. Louis," *19th-Century Music* 4, no. 2 (Autumn 1980), 124.

3. *Ibid.*, 125.

4. ALS Blackledge to Edwards, Chouteau Collection, Missouri Historical Society, St. Louis.

5. Floyd, 125.

6. Sheridan, "From Slavery," 161; Faust, *This Republic of Suffering*, 44; Ira Berlin, Barbara J. Fields, Steven F. Miller, Joseph P. Reidy, and Leslie S. Rowland, eds., *Free at Last: A Documentary History of Slavery, Freedom, and the Civil War* (New York: The New Press, 1992), 333.

7. Berlin et al., *Free at Last*, 17–18.

8. *Ibid.*

9. Siddali, *Missouri's War*, 210; Berlin, et al., *Free at Last*, 350.

10. Berlin, et al., *Free at Last*, 6–7.

11. Siddali, *Missouri's War*, 210–211.

12. Declarations of Emancipation (Alice M., Lucinda, and Winnie Walker), slaves of Washington County, Mississippi, District of St. Louis, Office of Superintendent of Contrabands, October 26, 1863, Slaves and Slavery (also see Civil War Collection), Missouri Historical Society, St. Louis, Missouri.

13. Sheridan, "From Slavery," 164.

14. *Ibid.*, 163–164; Michael Fellman, *Inside War: The Guerilla Conflict in Missouri During the American Civil War* (New York: Oxford University Press, 1989), 66.

15. Chandra Manning, *What This Cruel War Was Over* (New York: Vintage, 2007), 46.

16. Berlin, et al., *Free at Last*, 113–115.

17. *Ibid.*

18. Sheridan, "From Slavery," 162, 164; Fellman, *Inside War*, 66.

19. Sheridan, "From Slavery," 173.

20. *Ibid.*, 159–160, 162–164.

21. *Ibid.*, 157.

22. *Ibid.*, 165.

23. *Ibid.*, 165.

24. Vernon L. Volpe, "The Frémonts and Emancipation in Missouri," *Historian* 56, no. 2 (1994), 340–341; Manning, *Cruel War*, 46; Fellman, *Inside War*, 66.

25. Volpe, "The Frémonts and Emancipation," 350.

26. *Ibid.*, 339, 341–344. Volpe suggests, rather, that although a Southerner by birth, Frémont was a Republican and former candidate for President, who held anti-slavery convictions (345). But politics aside, Frémont on more than one occasion employed free blacks in his exploratory campaigns (346). See also Manning, *Cruel War*, 46–47; Berlin, et al., *Free at Last*, 46.

27. Letter, Anne E. Mason, complaining of Jim Lane's troops taking their Negroes, horses, mules, etc., Jackson County, Missouri, December 10, 1861, Roll 1484, Documents, Office Provost Marshal, Linn County, Brookfield, Missouri, March 19, 1863; Missouri Archives, Jefferson City, MO.

28. Volpe, "The Frémonts and Emancipation," 348.

29. Louis S. Gerteis, *Civil War St. Louis* (Lawrence: University Press of Kansas, 2001), 1.

30. Ira Berlin, *The Making of African America: The Four Great Migrations* (New York: Viking Penguin, 2010), 104.

31. John Blassingame, ed., *Slave Testimony: Two Centuries of Letters, Speeches, Interviews, and Autobiographies* (Baton Rouge: Louisiana State University Press, 1977), 563.

32. Roll 1191, Documents, Office Provost Marshal, Linn County, Brookfield, Missouri, March 19, 1863; Missouri Archives, Jefferson City, Missouri.

33. Letter from William Sauper, December 31, 1862, Missouri Historical Society, St. Louis, Missouri.

34. Jeremy Neely, *The Border Between Them* (Columbia: University of Missouri Press, 2007), 105–106.

35. Gerteis, *Civil War St. Louis*, 219, 224, 273–74.

36. Winthrop D. Jordan, *Tumult and Silence at Second Creek: An Inquiry into a Civil War Slave Conspiracy* (Baton Rouge: Louisiana State University Press, 1993).

37. Frazier, *Sentences*, 41.

38. *Ibid.*, 51–52.

39. Siddali, *Missouri's War*, 211–212.

40. *Ibid.*

41. Volunteer Enlistment Papers (Declaration of Recruit, Consent in Case of Minor, Slavery Papers, Missouri Historical Society, St. Louis, Missouri.

42. Berlin, et al., *Free at Last*, 353–354.

43. *Ibid.*, 345.

44. *Ibid.*, 359.
45. *Ibid.*, 362–363.
46. *Ibid.*, 364–365.
47. Faust, *This Republic of Suffering*, 44–47.
48. Manning, *Cruel War*, 127, 271 n.75.
49. Faust, *This Republic of Suffering*.
50. *Ibid.*, at 45.
51. Manning, *Cruel War*, 160.
52. *Ibid.*
53. Berlin, et al., *Free at Last*, 359–360, 363–365.
54. *Ibid.*, 359–360.
55. *Ibid.*, at 360.
56. *Ibid.*, at 360–361.
57. Fellman, *Inside War*, 211.
58. Berlin, et al., *Free at Last*, 362.
59. *Ibid.*, 362.
60. Fellman, *Inside War*, 213.
61. Berlin, et al., *Free at Last*, 366.
62. *Ibid.*
63. *Ibid.*
64. *Ibid.*, 366–367.
65. Manning, *Cruel War*, 160–161.
66. Faust, *This Republic of Suffering*, 70, 215.
67. *Ibid.*, 226–228.
68. *Ibid.*, at 227.
69. Manning, *Cruel War*, 160.
70. *Ibid.*; Berlin, et al., *Free at Last*, 361–362.
71. Blassingame, *Slave Testimony*, 119.
72. Fellman, *Inside War*, 66–67.
73. Berlin, et al., *Free at Last*, 464.
74. *Ibid.*
75. *Ibid.*, at 355, 383–384.
76. *Ibid.*, 356–358.
77. *Ibid.*, 480–481.
78. *Ibid.*, 481–482.
79. Bryan M. Jack, *The St. Louis African American Community and the Exodusters* (Columbia: University of Missouri Press, 2007), 32–33.
80. Gerteis, 224–225, 286–287.
81. Billington and Hardaway, *African Americans on the Western Frontier*, 182.
82. Petition of Lavina P. Jurden regarding Sarah King, filed February 25, 1865; Register of Inmates Received, State Penitentiary, Missouri State Archives, Vol. B 1841–1865, Page 347 A&B, Reel S213.
83. Elinor Mondale Gersman, "The Development of Public Education for Blacks in Nineteenth Century St. Louis, Missouri," 36.
84. Letter, St. Louis, August 4, 1864, African Americans, Missouri Historical Society, St. Louis, Missouri.
85. Blassingame, *Slave Testimony*, 584–589.
86. Letter, January 15, 1865, Slavery Papers, Missouri Historical Society, St. Louis, Missouri.
87. Manning, *Cruel War*, 189; Berlin, et al., *Free at Last*, xxxiii, 369, 382–383.
88. Siddali, *Missouri's War*, 225–226.
89. Fellman, *Inside War*, 213.
90. *Ibid.*, 70.
91. *Ibid.*, 71.
92. Adam Arenson, *The Great Heart of the Republic: St. Louis and the Cultural Civil War* (Cambridge: Harvard University Press, 2011), 156–157.

Epilogue

1. Paul Finkelman, *Dred Scott v. Sandford: A Brief History with Documents* (Boston: Bedford/St. Martin's, 1997), 227.

Works Cited

Primary Sources

Unpublished

Bonds for Dred Scott and Harriet Scott
Deeds of emancipation/manumission
Form for licensing of free negroes
Records of slave births
St. Louis Circuit Court, Office of the Circuit Clerk, City of St. Louis, Missouri, Case Files Correspondence

Published

NEWSPAPERS

Louisiana Gazette
Missouri Gazette
Missouri Republican

DIRECTORIES

Clamorgan, Cyprian. *The Colored Aristocracy of St. Louis.* Columbia: University of Missouri Press, 1999.

Green's Saint Louis Directory (No. 1) for 1845. Saint Louis: Published by James Green, 1844.

The St. Louis Directory for the Years 1836–37: Containing the Names of the Inhabitants, Their Occupations, Numbers of Their Places of Business and Dwellings; with a Sketch of the City of St. Louis. Printed by C. Keemle, 1836.

The St. Louis Directory for the Years 1838–39. St. Louis: Printed by C. Keemle, No. 22, Olive near Main St., 1838.

Secondary Sources

Directory

Free Men and Women of Color in St. Louis, 1821–1860. Compiled from City Directories of the United States Through 1860, Rare Books and Special Collections, St. Louis Public Library, 1997.

Articles and Books

Adler, Jeffrey S. "Streetwalkers, Degraded Outcasts, and Good-for-Nothing Huzzies: Women and the Dangerous Class in Antebellum St. Louis." *Journal of Social History* 25, no. 4 (992).

Andrews, William L. *To Tell a Free Story: The First Century of Afro-American Autobiography, 1760–1865.* Urbana: University of Illinois Press, 1988.

Arenson, Adam. *The Great Heart of the Republic: St. Louis and the Cultural Civil War.* Cambridge: Harvard University Press, 2011.

Bancroft, Frederic. *Slave-Trading in the Old South.* New York: Unger Press, 1959.

Banner, Stuart. *Legal Systems in Conflict: Property and Sovereignty in Missouri, 1750–1860.* University of Oklahoma Press, 2000.

Barbour, Barton H. *Fort Union and the Upper Missouri Fur Trade.* Norman: University of Oklahoma Press, 2001.

Baumgarten, Nikola. "Education and Democracy in Frontier St. Louis: The Society of the Sacred Heart." *History of Ed-*

ucation Quarterly 34, no. 2 (Summer 1994), 171–192.

Bellamy, Donnie D. "The Education of Blacks in Missouri Prior to 1861." Journal of Negro History 59, no. 2 (Apr. 1974), 143–157.

Berlin, Ira. The Making of African American: The Four Great Migrations. New York: Viking Penguin, 2010.

____. Slaves Without Masters: The Free Negro in the Antebellum South. New York: Oxford University Press, 1981.

Berlin, Ira, Barbara J. Fields, Steven F. Miller, Joseph P. Reidy, and Leslie S. Rowland, eds. Free At Last: A Documentary History of Slavery, Freedom, and the Civil War. New York: The New Press, 1992.

Berlin, Ira, Thavolia Glymph, Steven F. Miller, Joseph P. Reidy, Leslie S. Rowland, and Julie Seville, eds. Freedom: A Documentary History of Emancipation, 1861–1867. Cambridge: Cambridge University Press, 1990.

Billington, Monroe Lee, and Roger D. Hardaway, eds. African Americans on the Western Frontier. Boulder: University Press of Colorado, 1998.

Billon, Frederic L. Annals of St. Louis in Its Territorial Days from 1804 to 1821, Being a Continuation of the Author's Previous Work the Annals of the French and Spanish Period. St. Louis: Printed for the author, 1888.

Boman, Dennis K. "The Dred Scott Case Reconsidered: The Legal and Political Context in Missouri." American Journal of Legal History 44, no. 4 (Oct. 2000), 405–428.

Brown, William Wells. "Narrative of William Wells Brown." Puttin' on Ole Massa, ed. Gilbert Osofsky. New York: Harper, 1969.

Buchanan, Thomas C. Black Life on the Mississippi: Slaves, Free Blacks, and the Western Steamboat World. Chapel Hill: University of North Carolina Press, 2004.

____. "Rascals on the Antebellum Mississippi: African American Steamboat Workers and the St. Louis Hanging of 1841." Journal of Social History 34, no. 4 (Summer 2001).

Bynum, Victoria. Unruly Women: The Politics of Social and Sexual Control in the Old South. Chapel Hill: University of North Carolina Press, 1992.

Catterall, Helen Tunnicliff. "Some Antecedents of the Dred Scott Case." American Historical Review 30, No. 1 (Oct., 1924), 56–71.

____, ed. Judicial Cases Concerning American Slavery and the Negro. Washington, D.C.: Carnegie Institution of Washington, 1926.

Chan, Sucheng, Douglas Henry Daniels, Mario T. Garcia and Terry P. Wilson, eds. Peoples of Color in the American West. Lexington, MA: D.C. Heath, 1994.

Chouteau, Col. Auguste. Narrative of the Settlement of St. Louis. St. Louis: George Knapp & Co., Book and Job Printers, 1858.

Christensen, Lawrence O., William E. Foley, Gary R. Kremer and Kenneth Winn, eds. Dictionary of Missouri Biography. Columbia: University of Missouri Press, 1999.

Cleary, Patricia. The World, the Flesh, and the Devil: A History of Colonial St. Louis. Columbia: University of Missouri Press, 2011.

Cornelius, Janet Duitsman. When I Can Read My Title Clear: Literacy, Slavery, and Religion in the Antebellum South. Columbia: University of South Carolina Press, 1991.

Curry, Leonard P. The Free Black in Urban America, 1800–1850: The Shadow of the Dream. Chicago: University of Chicago Press, 1981.

Delany, Lucy A. From the Darkness Cometh the Light, or Struggles for Freedom. St. Louis, n.d.

Dosch, Donald F. The Old Courthouse: Americans Build a Forum on the Frontier. Jefferson National Expansion Historical Association, Inc., 1979.

Dunne, Gerald T. The Missouri Supreme Court: From Dred Scott to Nancy Cruzan. Columbia: University of Missouri Press, 1993.

Durst, Dennis L. "The Reverend John Berry Meachum (1789–1854) of St. Louis: Prophet and Entrepreneurial Black Educator in Historiographical Perspective." The North Star: A Journal of African American Religious History 7, no. 2 (Spring 2004).

Ekberg, Carl J. *Stealing Indian Women: Native Slavery in the Illinois Country.* Urbana: University of Illinois Press, 2007.

Ekberg, Carl J., and Sharon K. Person. *St. Louis Rising: The French Regime of Louis St. Ange de Bellerive.* Urbana: University of Illinois Press, 2015.

Farrison, W. Edward. "Phylon Profile XVI: William Wells Brown." *Phylon* 9, no. 1 (1st Quarter 1940–1956), 13–23.

Faust, Drew Gilpin. *Mothers of Invention: Women of the Slaveholding South in the American Civil War.* New York: Vintage, 1997.

____. *This Republic of Suffering: Death and the American Civil War.* New York: Vintage, 2008.

Fausz, J. Frederick. *Founding St. Louis: First City of the New West.* Charleston: The History Press, 2011.

Fehrenbacher, Don E. *The Dred Scott Case: Its Significance in American Law and Politics.* New York: Oxford University Press, 1978.

Fellman, Michael. *Inside War: The Guerilla Conflict in Missouri During the American Civil War.* New York: Oxford University Press, 1989.

Fischer, David Hackett, and James C. Kelly. *Bound Away: Virginia and the Westward Movement.* Charlottesville: University of Virginia Press, 2000.

Floyd, Samuel A., Jr. "A Black Composer in Nineteenth-Century St. Louis." *19th-Century Music* 4, no. 2 (Autumn 1980), 121–133.

Foley, William E. "Slave Freedom Suits Before Dred Scott: The Case of Marie Jean Scypion's Descendants." *Missouri Historical Review* LXXIX (October 1984–July 1985).

Foley, William E., and C. David Rice. *The First Chouteaus: River Barons of Early St. Louis.* Urbana: University of Illinois Press, 1983.

Forbes, Robert Pierce. *The Missouri Compromise and Its Aftermath: Slavery and the Meaning of America.* Chapel Hill: University of North Carolina Press, 2007.

Fox-Genovese, Elizabeth. *Within the Plantation Household: Black and White Women of the Old South.* Chapel Hill: University of North Carolina Press, 1988.

Frazier, Harriet C. *Death Sentences in Missouri, 1803–2005: A History and Comprehensive Registry of Legal Executions, Pardons, and Commutations.* Jefferson, NC: McFarland, 2006.

____. *Runaway and Freed Missouri Slaves and Those Who Helped Them, 1763–1865.* Jefferson, NC: McFarland, 2004.

____. *Slavery and Crime in Missouri, 1773–1865.* Jefferson, NC: McFarland, 2001.

Gersman, Elinor Mondale. "The Development of Public Education for Blacks in Nineteenth Century St. Louis, Missouri." *Journal of Negro Education* 41, no. 1 (Winter 1972), 35–47.

Gerteis, Louis S. *Civil War St. Louis.* Lawrence: University Press of Kansas, 2001.

Gitlin, Jay. *The Bourgeois Frontier: French Towns, French Traders and American Expansion.* New Haven: Yale University Press, 2010.

Gordon-Reed, Annette, ed. *Race on Trial: Law and Justice in American History.* Oxford: Oxford University Press, 2002.

Greene, Lorenzo J., Gary R. Kremer, Antonio F. Holland. *Missouri's Black Heritage.* Columbia: University of Missouri Press, 1980, revised 1993.

Gross, Ariela J. "Litigating Whiteness: Trials of Racial Determination in the Nineteenth-Century South." *Yale Law Journal* 108 (1998), 107–188.

Hall, Gwendolyn Midlo. *Africans in Colonial Louisiana: The Development of Afro-Creole Culture in the Eighteenth Century.* Baton Rouge: Louisiana State University Press, 1992.

Hammond, John Craig. *Slavery, Freedom, and Expansion in the Early American West.* Charlottesville: University of Virginia Press, 2007.

Hodes, Frederick A. *Beyond the Frontier: A History of St. Louis to 1821.* Tucson: Patrice Press, 2004.

____. *Rising on the River: St. Louis 1822 to 1850, Explosive Growth from Town to City.* Tooele, UT: Patrice Press, 2009.

Hunter, Tera. *To Joy My Freedom: Southern Black Women's Lives and Labors after the Civil War.* Cambridge: Harvard University Press, 1997.

Hurley, Andrew, ed. *Common Fields: An Environmental History of St. Louis.* St. Louis: Missouri Historical Society Press, 1997.

Jack, Bryan M. *The St. Louis African American Community and the Exodusters.* Columbia: University of Missouri Press, 2007.

Jensen, Richard E., ed. "Last Years of the Missouri Fur Company: The Correspondence of Angus William McDonald." *The Museum of the Fur Trade Quarterly* 37, no. 2 (2001), 2–21.

Johnson, Walter. *Soul by Soul: Life Inside the Antebellum Slave Market.* Cambridge: Harvard University Press, 1999.

Jones, Landon Y. *William Clark and the Shaping of the West.* New York: Hill and Wang, 2004.

Kaufman, Kenneth C. *Dred Scott's Advocate: A Biography of Roswell M. Field.* Columbia: University of Missouri Press, 1996.

Keckley, Elizabeth. *Behind the Scenes: Thirty Years a Slave and Four Years in the White House.* New York: Arno and New York Times, 1968.

Kerr, Derek N. *Petty Felony, Slave Defiance, and Frontier Villainy: Crime and Criminal Justice in Spanish Louisiana, 1770–1803.* New York: Garland, 1993.

King, Wilma. *Stolen Childhood: Slave Youth in Nineteenth-Century America.* Bloomington: Indiana University Press, 1995.

Kolchin, Peter. *American Slavery, 1619–1877.* New York: Hill and Wang, 1993.

Laughlin, Bonnie E. "'Endangering the Peace of Society': Abolitionist Agitation and Mob Reaction in St. Louis and Alton, 1836–1838." *Missouri Historical Review* 95, no. 1 (2000), 1–22.

Litwack, Leon. *Been in the Storm So Long: The Aftermath of Slavery.* New York: Vintage, 1980.

Malone, Ann Patton. *Sweet Chariot: Slave Family and Household Structure in Nineteenth-Century Louisiana.* Chapel Hill: University of North Carolina Press, 1992.

Manning, Chandra. *What This Cruel War Was Over: Soldiers, Slavery, and the Civil War.* New York: Vintage, 2007.

McCandless, Perry. *A History of Missouri, Vol. II, 1820–1860.* Columbia: University of Missouri Press, 1972.

McLaurin, Melton A. *Celia, A Slave.* New York: Avon Books, 1991.

Miller, Randall M. "Black Catholics in the Slave South: Some Needs and Opportunities for Study." *Records of the American Catholic Historical Society of Philadelphia* 86, no. 1 (1975), 93–106.

Milner, Clyde A., II, Carol A. O'Connor, and Martha A. Sandweiss, eds. *The Oxford History of the American West.* New York: Oxford University Press, 1994.

Mintz, Sidney, and Richard Price. *The Birth of African-American Culture.* Boston: Beacon Press, 1992.

Morris, Thomas D. *Southern Slavery and the Law, 1619–1860.* Chapel Hill: University of North Carolina Press, 1996.

Morton, Patricia, ed. *Discovering the Women in Slavery: Emancipating Perspectives on the American Past.* Athens: University of Georgia Press, 1996.

Nasatir, A.P., ed. *Before Lewis and Clark: Documents Illustrating the History of the Missouri, 1785–1804, Volume I.* 1952. Lincoln: University of Nebraska Press, 1990.

Neely, Jeremy. *The Border Between Them: Violence and Reconciliation on the Kansas-Missouri Line.* Columbia: University of Missouri Press, 2007.

Oglesby, Richard Edward. *Manuel Lisa and the Opening of the Missouri Fur Trade.* Norman: University of Oklahoma Press, 1963, 1984.

Pease, Jane H., and William H. Pease. *They Who Would Be Free: Blacks Search for Freedom, 1830–1861.* New York: Atheneum, 1974.

Peterson, Charles E., FAIA. *Colonial St. Louis: Building A Creole Capital.* Tucson: Patrice Press, 1993.

Pirtle, Carol. *Escape Betwixt Two Suns: A True Tale of the Underground Railroad in Illinois.* Carbondale: Southern Illinois University Press, 2000.

Poole, Stafford, and Douglas J. Slawson. *Church and Slave in Perry County, Missouri, 1818–1865.* Lewiston, NY: Edwin Mellen Press, 1986.

Primm, James Neal. *Lion of the Valley: St. Louis, Missouri, 1764–1980.* 1981, 1990. Missouri Historical Society Press, 1998.

Rawick, George P., ed. *The American Slave: A Composite Biography.* Westport, CT: Greenwood, 1972.

Sandweiss, Lee Ann, ed. *Seeking St. Louis: Voices from a River City, 1670–2000.*

St. Louis: Missouri Historical Society Press, 2000.

Saxton, Martha. *Being Good: Women's Moral Values in Early America.* New York: Hill and Wang, 2003.

Schafer, Judith Kelleher. *Slavery, the Civil Law, and the Supreme Court of Louisiana.* Baton Rouge: Louisiana State University Press, 1994.

Schweninger, Loren, "Prosperous Blacks in the South, 1790–1880." *American Historical Review* 95, no. 1 (Feb. 1990), 31–56.

Sheridan, Richard. "From Slavery in Missouri to Freedom in Kansas: The Influx of Black Fugitives and Contrabands into Kansas, 1854–1865." Rita Napier, ed., *Kansas and the West: New Perspectives.* Lawrence: University Press of Kansas, 2003.

Shick, Tom W. *Behold the Promised Land: A History of the Afro-American Settler Society in Nineteenth-Century Liberia.* Baltimore: Johns Hopkins University Press, 1980.

Siddali, Silvana R. *Missouri's War: The Civil War in Documents.* Athens: Ohio University Press, 2009.

Slaughter, Thomas P. *Exploring Lewis and Clark: Reflections on Men and Wilderness.* New York: Vintage, 2003.

Smith, Dale Edwyna. "Dred Scott." The Dictionary of World Biography, Volumes V and VI, The Nineteenth Century. Salem Press, 1999.

____. *The Slaves of Liberty: Freedom in Amite County, Mississippi, 1820–1868.* New York: Garland, 1999.

Sterling, Dorothy, ed. *We Are Your Sisters: Black Women in the Nineteenth Century.* New York: W. W. Norton, 1984.

Stevenson, Brenda. *Life in Black and White: Family and Community in the Slave South.* New York: Oxford University Press, 1996.

Still, William. *The Underground Rail Road.* Philadelphia: Porter and Coats, 1872.

Stowe, Steven M. *Intimacy and Power in the Old South: Ritual in the Lives of the Planters.* Baltimore: Johns Hopkins University Press, 1987.

Sunder, John E. *The Fur Trade on the Upper Missouri, 1840–1865.* Norman: University of Oklahoma Press, 1965.

Tadman, Michael. *Speculators and Slaves: Masters, Traders, and Slaves in the Old South.* Madison: University of Wisconsin Press, 1989.

Tushnet, Mark V. *The American Law of Slavery, 1810–1860: Considerations of Humanity and Interest.* Princeton: Princeton University Press, 1981.

Underwood, Brent. "Chouteau's Pond." *Gateway Heritage* 22, no. 1 (Summer 2001, 4–15.

VanderVelde, Lea. *Mrs. Dred Scott: A Life on Slavery's Frontier.* New York: Oxford University Press, 2009.

VanderVelde, Lea, and Sandhya Subramanian. "Mrs. Dred Scott." *Yale Law Journal* 106, no.4 (January 1997), 1033–1122.

Volpe, Vernon L. "The Frémonts and Emancipation in Missouri." *Historian* 56, no. 2 (1994), 339–354.

Waal, Carla, and Barbara Oliver Korner, eds. *Hardship and Hope: Missouri Women Writing About Their Lives.* Columbia: University of Missouri Press, 1997.

Wade, Richard C. *Slavery in the Cities: The South, 1820–1860.* New York: Oxford University Press, 1964.

____. *The Urban Frontier: Pioneer Life in Early Pittsburgh, Cincinnati, Lexington, Louisville, and St. Louis.* 1959. Chicago: University of Chicago Press, 1968.

Wagner, Allen E. *Good Order and Safety: A History of the St. Louis Metropolitan Police Department, 1861–1906.* Missouri History Museum, 2008.

Washington, Margaret. "African American History and the Frontier Thesis." *Journal of the Early Republic* 13, no. 2 (Summer 1993), 230–241.

White, Deborah Gray. *Ar'n't I a Woman? Female Slaves in the Plantation South.* New York: W.W. Norton, 1985.

Whites, LeeAnn, Mary C. Neth, and Gary R. Kremer, eds. *Women in Missouri History: In Search of Power and Influence.* Columbia: University of Missouri Press, 2004.

Wiethoff, William E. *A Peculiar Humanism: The Judicial Advocacy of Slavery in High Courts of the Old South, 1820–1850.* Athens: University of Georgia, 1996.

Williamson, Joel. *New People: Miscegenation and Mulattoes in the United States.* New York: Free Press, 1980.

Wilson, Carl. *Freedom at Risk: The Kidnapping of Free Blacks in America, 1780–1865.* Lexington: University Press of Kentucky, 1994.

Wilson, Elinor. *Jim Beckwourth: Black Mountain Man and War Chief of the Crows.* Norman: University of Oklahoma Press, 1972.

Winch, Julie, ed. *The Colored Aristocracy of St. Louis by Cyprian Clamorgan.* Columbia: University of Missouri Press, 1999.

Wong, Edlie L. *Neither Fugitive nor Free: Atlantic Slavery, Freedom Suits, and the Legal Culture of Travel.* New York: New York University Press, 2009

Woodson, Carter G. *Free Negro Owners of Slaves in the United States in 1830.* 1924. Westport, CT: Negro Universities Press, 1968.

Index

201